SUPERMARRIAGE

SUPERMARRIAGE:
Overcoming the Predictable Crises of Married Life

Harvey L. Ruben, M.D.

BANTAM BOOKS
TORONTO • NEW YORK • LONDON • SYDNEY • AUCKLAND

SUPERMARRIAGE
A Bantam Book / June 1986

*The examples discussed in this book are all true; however,
the names and certain identifying characteristics have been
changed to protect the privacy of the individuals discussed.*

Library of Congress Cataloging-in-Publication Data

Ruben, Harvey L.
  Supermarriage : overcoming the predictable crises of
married life.

  1. Marriage.   2. Interpersonal relations.   3. Life
cycle, Human.   I. Title.
HQ734.R795   1986   306.8'1   85-48236
ISBN 0-553-05121-0

Published simultaneously in the United States and Canada

PRINTED IN THE UNITED STATES OF AMERICA

FG   0   9   8   7   6   5   4   3   2   1

To Diane, my lover, collaborator and partner, to my sons Adam, Justin and Marc, to our families and close friends, all of whom have been part of the passages of our marriage, and to my patients and Talknet callers through whose lives I have been able to develop the insights I share with you in this book.

ACKNOWLEDGMENTS

With gratitude and sincere appreciation I acknowledge the insight, support and help of my wife Diane, Tom Cowan, Linda Cunningham of Bantam Books, Richard and Arthur Pine, my agents, and Marilyn Green, my secretary.

CONTENTS

PART I

HOW A MARRIAGE WORKS

1.

Introduction

It was a beautiful, crisp fall day. As we sat there holding hands, the sun shone brightly through leaves just tinged with autumn color. I was sitting only a few feet from Gail and Arthur, watching them intently as they peered into each other's eyes while the minister spoke to them about their marriage vows. Diane, my wife of twenty years, grasped my hand tightly. I knew what she was thinking about: *our* wedding day, *our* vows, the many things that happened to us through the past twenty years. I thought about Gail and Arthur, what had happened in their first marriages, whether they would be able to avoid making the same mistakes the second time around, whether they would now be able to find lasting happiness with each other. And, like Diane's, my thoughts turned to our marriage.

I remembered our early years, how we got to know each other, how we grew into our roles as husband and wife. I thought of some of the problems we had had getting to know each other's families and adjusting to different ways of doing things. I remembered how angry my brother Richard had been when he found out that Diane had been pregnant for three months and we hadn't told him. We were superstitious and didn't want to tell anybody but our parents. He was very hurt. It took Diane and me a long time as a couple to work out our joint relationships with all our brothers and sisters.

I remembered back to the difficulties we had after the birth of Justin, our second son. Since we didn't have very good insurance coverage, I wanted to save money by getting Diane and the baby home as soon as possible. So I whisked her from the hospital the day after Justin was born. Unfortunately, hordes of relatives from both sides of the family descended upon us immediately. Diane was suffering from severe headaches caused by the anesthesia, and at the same time she was trying to be a good hostess, serving coffee and cake to relatives. What should have been a very happy and exciting time for us as a couple became chaos. It took us several months to regain our equilibrium from those first stress-filled weeks that I inadvertently had caused.

I recalled also how the stressful circumstances surrounding Justin's arrival caused us some sexual difficulties. Being out of the hospital too soon, suffering from headaches, undergoing the stress of having a new baby, and helping our three-year-old Adam adjust to his new brother, coupled with the hubbub of curious relatives, were overwhelming for Diane. Although I tried to help, her chronic fatigue lasted for several months. Naturally, in the face of such stress anyone's sexual appetite will wane, and hers did. I tried to be understanding, but it was hard for me to accept that for the first time in our relationship, we were out of phase sexually. It took a number of months of work and understanding until we finally achieved a new pattern of making love that we both enjoyed.

Financial pressures caused us problems too. After getting her master's degree, Diane taught high-school English, but decided in the fifth year of our marriage that she wanted to study law. I was in the army at the time and started doing part-time private practice in order to pay for law school, which, along with the new baby, put financial pressures on us that we had not dealt with during the first five years. However, the real money crunch came after Marc, our third son, was born. Diane had been working as an attorney for about eight years and, in spite of her part-time status, had become a partner in her firm. Then she had to put in increasing amounts of time and was no longer able to come home by three o'clock every afternoon. Unfortunately, she was still being paid on a part-time scale. We debated for several months whether or not she should become employed full-time and what effect this would have on the children. Because we were feeling the financial demands of a growing family, we decided in favor of her working full-time. So we had to adjust our roles as parents. She worked into the late afternoon, and I made myself available to be with the older boys each day when they came home from school, to help them organize their activities, even to drive carpools for various events.

I also recollected another financial dilemma I accidentally got us into. Once, feeling overly optimistic, I convinced Diane that—based on what I projected our joint income would be—we could do some refurnishing, take a nice family vacation, and buy a new car—all in one year. But the recession caused a decrease in both her legal practice and my psychiatric practice. So we felt a far greater economic pinch than we had anticipated. Looking back, I realize I should have heeded her warning and not have spent all that money. During the next year, we readjusted our financial lives, took a more cautious approach, and got back on our feet.

Finally, I contemplated how we had changed individually. I remembered how Diane, who is five years younger than I, started to win our arguments just as she had learned in law school to "perform" successfully in the courtroom. And then my thoughts drifted off to the awful time she became severely ill with an acute stomach virus while we were on vacation with the boys in British Columbia. She was hospitalized for over a week before we could even come home, and then it took several months for her to recover fully. Again, our relationship was severely strained, and we had to make important adjustments in the way we divided responsibilities at home and with the boys.

And I remembered how wonderfully Diane shored me up with her love and support as I grappled with my own mid-life issues, reassessing some of the goals I had failed to achieve and reordering my priorities based on a new realization of what now seemed important to me as I headed into my forties.

So there we sat, the two of us, basking in the warm fall sun, holding on to each other tightly, as we always had through the good times and the bad, through all the joys and sorrows of the preceding twenty years. And as I heard the minister pronouncing Gail and Arthur man and wife, I found myself praying that our next twenty years would be as fulfilling, as gratifying, and as glorious as the first twenty had been.

2

The Passages of Marriage

Marriage to Diane has been the single most important influence in my adult life. It has brought me happiness and satisfaction I could not imagine achieving with anyone else, or even on my own. It's as though everything prior to being twenty-three and meeting her was aimed at preparing me for that relationship which has changed the entire course of my life. Had I not been with her over these years, I don't believe I would have become the person I am today or have achieved the happiness I have. I know she feels the same way about the roles we play in each other's lives. Our lives would never have been as wonderful if we hadn't had each other. And yet our relationship—still heady, vibrant, and full of excitement—has not been without pain and turmoil. We've had our problems like everyone else. But by resolving these problems, I believe we have developed a truly "super marriage," just as some of our close friends and family have also done. We are not alone. But we are in a minority. I don't believe that most marriages qualify as super marriages. Most couples are not able to make such positive statements about their relationships. They have not experienced the same degree of gratification and fulfillment from working out their problems together. For them, marriage is not the single greatest source of happiness in their lives. I am firmly convinced, however, that most marriages *could* provide the same kind of joy and satisfaction

7

that Diane and I have known, if the couple is able to cooperate and work together in facing all the difficult issues that arise in five very important areas of married life:

family and friends
career and finances
sexual fulfillment
parenting (if we choose to have children)
illness and change

Every married couple will confront stressful issues in these five areas. Some of them will become critical turning points in the course of the marriage. Life gets unsettled. The marriage seems unstable. We know some action must be taken. But what? At this point it is crucial to resolve the issue together, strengthen the marriage, and grow as a couple into higher levels of understanding, devotion, and love for each other.

If we are unable to resolve a particular problem, it will continue to plague us, ultimately undermining the strength of our relationship, making it harder for us to move forward successfully and grapple with the next issue that arises. Then things can begin to snowball. Small problems lead to larger problems, which lead to even bigger problems, and finally our marriage and our lives are out of control.

Of course, not all these issues are of the same magnitude for each of us. A major issue for one couple may be of little consequence for another. What's important, however, is not the magnitude of a given issue, but whether the couple resolves it successfully. For instance, a decision for a wife to go to work or for a couple to have another child may be made quite easily by some people while others agonize over this for months. One husband may have horrendous problems with his mother-in-law, while for another it's just a matter of deciding how often they are going to get together socially. Some issues are minor aggravations, others become severe marital problems. Some even reach crisis proportion. Regardless of the size or nature of the issue, the underlying principle remains the same: each issue creates a turning point in the relationship, a passage through which the relationship can grow stronger and mature. If a particular passage is not negotiated successfully, the marriage will take a turn for the worse. Thus, the way in which you negotiate marital passages will determine the course of your marriage, the quality of your lives together, and whether you end up with a super marriage or with a disaster.

In her best-selling book, *Passages*, Gail Sheehy popularized the concept of predictable turning points in adult life, which she called "passages." Because of her book, many people now use the term "passages" for transitions in life related to personal growth and development. They usually accompany what behavioral scientists term "the predictable crises of adult life." In short, men and women go through passages at rather predictable times in their life cycles— roughly corresponding to the decades of their lives—and these become the major turning points that set their lives in new directions. The concept of passages in our lives is important because it allows us to predict when we are most likely to experience turmoil, worry, and doubt about the progress of our lives and in so doing be better prepared to deal with them. Sheehy preferred the word "passage" rather than "crisis" because many of these turning points are not experienced as severe problems by every man and woman. But with or without the emotional upheaval, they are still transitions to increased levels of emotional maturity.

Since the turmoil experienced in resolving any marital issue can vary in intensity from couple to couple, and since not every issue becomes a severe problem or crisis, I, too, prefer to use the term "passage" to mean the predictable transitions between the stable periods of a marriage, just as Sheehy uses it for the transitions between periods in one's own life. Even though not every couple will go through every marital passage we will look at, no marriage can progress without transitions of one sort or another. Marriage, like life, is on the move, advancing from one stable period to another. Because of this, marital passages of one kind or another are inevitable, even though no one can predict which specific issues will become marital passages *for you.*

Passages are truly challenges. Each one gives us the opportunity to deepen our love as we help each other along the course of our marriage. In doing so, we grow stronger in our relationship and more sure of ourselves; as we come through each passage, our marriage grows and thrives. To the extent that we don't take advantage of these opportunities or are unable to resolve each issue success- fully, we slowly chip away at the foundation of our marriage.

Our ability to negotiate a particular issue successfully and have it become a positive passage in our marriage depends upon a number of factors: our basic personalities, what our past experience has been, how much we trust each other, how committed we are to making our marriage work, and how strong our love for each other is. In spite of all the personal differences and variations in each marriage, we are all enough alike that certain patterns emerge. Hence, you can help each other through your own marital passages by understanding the possible issues that can arise in the five important areas of married life and by learning how others have worked successfully with these problems and turned them into opportunities for mutual growth. Then you can apply the same techniques to your situation and revitalize your own marriage.

3.

Marriage: Playing for Keeps

Marriage is an amazing and wonderful institution. A fulfilling and satisfying marriage can be the most critical element in achieving happiness throughout your life. Marriage is something that most of us will experience at least once during our lifetime. Currently, ninety-six percent of all Americans who are old enough to get married will be married at some point in their lives. A "good marriage" can be one of life's greatest joys and a source of great strength and support. In fact, it can be the single most important factor that makes life worthwhile.

Unfortunately, this is not the case for many people. Although we like to *get* married, as the statistics show, many of us are not able to *stay* married. The divorce rate is currently running at fifty percent. If you are just getting married this year, the statistics are even more dismal. Seventy-five percent of those marrying this year will see their marriages end in divorce. What's more, if you are both under the age of twenty-one or you've dropped out of high school to get married, the divorce rate will be even greater—eighty percent. Yet we continue to get married at a very rapid rate. Even divorced people remarry quickly. Four-fifths of all people who become divorced remarry within five years, and most of those, within three years of the divorce. However, over half of those remarriages will end in divorce once

11

again! Thus, it appears that although we *want* to be married, many of us have a hard time understanding what to *do* to make marriage work.

During the last eighteen years of my psychiatric practice, I have come to know hundreds of couples whose marriages have ranged from the disastrous to the fantastic. The ones with disastrous marriages often came to me for couple's therapy. The ones with fantastic marriages may have come to me with other kinds of problems or may have been couples I knew socially. Also, during the last three and a half years, I have been hosting the NBC Radio Network show, "Talknet," every Saturday and Sunday from eleven p.m. to two o'clock in the morning eastern standard time. "Talknet" is heard on over 250 stations around the country by four to five million people; and with our eight toll-free lines, I speak with about thirty callers on every show. In addition, I have been receiving about ten thousand cards and letters a year, many of them with lengthy descriptions of people's life circumstances, asking me for advice. As a result, I've come to know thousands of marriages, as I am regularly exposed to numerous issues and questions concerning marriage every week.

From this wealth of material it has become clear to me that only about ten percent of all marriages are what I could call super marriages. Since fifty percent end in divorce, the remaining forty percent fall somewhere in the range between "mediocre" and "pretty good." What I hope you receive from reading this book are the knowledge, insight, and practical methods to move your own marriage from the "disastrous" or "mediocre," even from the "pretty good," into the ten percent of super marriages. After all, this is what most of us strive for; and I firmly believe that more of us could achieve this goal if we simply knew how exceptionally good marriages really work.

4.

A Happy Marriage and a Healthy Family

Ideally, we hope that every passage in marriage leads to the same goal, namely, a super marriage based on equality, mature intimacy, trust, communication, and romance. To illustrate such a marriage, let's consider the case of a mythical, perfect couple, "Bonnie and Steve."

When Bonnie and Steve fell in love, they had a strong drive to pair up and spend as much time together as possible. Each had a restless drive for a fulfilling relationship. Even before they decided to get married, they knew that being together was the greatest source of happiness for both of them. Nothing else seemed to matter. They wanted it to last and be permanent, so they tied the knot. They had an idealized picture of marital happiness based on the experience of being together while they dated. The question for them and for all of us is: How closely can we approximate that concept of happiness? How can we preserve it and nourish it through times of trouble?

The couples who find successful answers to these questions are the couples who have marriages based on equality. Fortunately, more and more people are meeting each other, falling in love, and getting married as equals than was true in the past, when marriages were arranged for social, economic, or political reasons. While there are still inequalities in jobs, salaries, and other aspects of society, many people

marrying today do so with the intention of being true partners and mates, sharing the responsibilities and privileges
of married life as equally as possible. Although we are each
individuals with personal needs and goals, we marry with
the intention that marriage will satisfy these goals. But we
understand that the goals are reciprocal, that it is in giving
that we receive, in loving that we are loved. Happy couples
such as Bonnie and Steve realize that to be understood they
must make efforts to understand, and that to be comforted
they must provide comfort. They recognize that their spouse's
needs are on par with their own, and to achieve a happy
marriage both partners must meet and accept each other as
equals.

In addition, happy marriages are founded upon what I
call mature intimacy, that is, a heightened degree of self-
knowledge and the ability to evaluate marital problems patiently and wisely. Many people who marry in their late
twenties or early thirties already have achieved a reasonable
level of mature intimacy because they have behind them ten
or more years of falling in love, evaluating their relationships, and abandoning them when necessary. They know
what they need in a relationship, what to expect, what they
can compromise, what they can't live without. Bonnie and
Steve went into marriage with this kind of emotional maturity; it allowed them to create a stable marriage. After a
number of years in the marriage, they were able to evaluate
their own performance from the vantage point of this sea-
soned self-knowledge. They had the experience and skills to
assess patiently their marital difficulties without fear of destroying their relationship. As a couple, Bonnie and Steve
grew in maturity and realized that they were playing for
keeps and not just playing around. As they matured, they
became a sensitive, less defensive, less self-protective couple.
Each one knew how to listen to the other's needs.

Trust is another key ingredient in a happy marriage.
Without it, literally nothing works. Getting through all the
issues and problems of marriage requires unswerving trust
in each other. We must be able to count on our mates to act
in our best interests. Fortunately, Bonnie and Steve had this
type of trust. Regardless of the level of misunderstanding
or misperception that occurred in a particular argument or

difference of opinion, each one knew that the other one would not knowingly or willingly do the other harm. Thus, trust was the bedrock for the care, concern, and commitment in their marriage.

Another essential ingredient of the happy marriage is the joy of being able to communicate effectively with one's spouse. How often we spend time during the day in conversations with others who never seem to understand the fears, worries, desires, even joys that we want to express. How satisfying it is to be united in the evening with one who understands and appreciates, who knows from what depths of our souls we speak. How important it is to share those depths with someone who loves us. Communication is the magic wand that can transform an average relationship into a wondrous and grand marriage. Bonnie and Steve had developed that skill through the years. It was a skill that they, as all of us, had to master. It did not come easily. Human beings are curious and paradoxical creatures. More than any other life form, men and women have the marvelous talent for communicating with one another; yet how often that talent lies dormant or is wasted on frivolous conversation concerning shallow topics that never touch them deeply. It is rarely easy to communicate, and some couples need help to learn this delicate art.

In order to communicate a thought, idea, or feeling to another person, there must be a sender, a receiver, and an effective way to transmit or express that message with the minimum of distortion. It helps when both people are lying in the same bed, or looking up at the same moonlit sky, or sitting in front of a fire, or even whispering over the phone to one another. Communication, as Bonnie and Steve learned, is an act of intimacy, and couples whose marriages are grounded in true intimacy usually find it easier to communicate.

So Bonnie and Steven experienced equality, mature intimacy, trust, and communication; this was all possible because they loved each other deeply. In fact, love is what marriage is all about! If you don't want love or romance, you should not be married! After all, the partnership on which a marriage is based is different from that of roommates. It is based upon a love available only to those who bond themselves together—emotionally, intellectually, and physically—for the rest of their lives. In a happy marriage, romance should not die out after a few years of living together. Far from it! It should grow, mature, develop, and enrich the partners' lives. By romance I mean that constellation of urges that are affectionate, erotic, physical, and emotional. It's true they may vary in intensity, sometimes stronger, sometimes weaker, but they are invariably present. Even when Bonnie or Steve were angry with one another, romance was still present. Although they did not experience it in the midst of a heated argument, romance returned, frequently as a way of ending the argument, when the blowup had subsided. The old fervor for each other came back, and they began to express their feelings of love for one another. Through their own personal, private rituals of touching, kissing, and endearments that only the two of them shared, the anger subsided. Making up is, was, and always will be the best part of any argument!

When I work with couples, I help them relearn those basic activities that nourish love and romance: how to share time together; how to express thoughts of love and devotion to each other; how to go for a walk, take a ride, go window shopping, skip out on a short trip; or even how to rendezvous in a local motel for a night! It's strange how all these techniques, which come naturally to young lovers, can be forgotten by people who live together and tend to take each other for granted. Familiarity doesn't breed contempt; it breeds forgetfulness. What most people must do to strengthen their marriages is to begin remembering how to be friends, how to play together, how to love each other in ways that rekindle the romance they knew when they were newly in love.

From the happy, super marriage that Bonnie and Steve experienced, we see the development of the stable, healthy family. Since the majority of marriages in this country will produce children, we see that at the basic core of every healthy family is the happily married couple. The relationship you share with your spouse will spill over onto your children. So your children develop their personalities based on living with you over the years, acquiring your insights, sharing your values, and, in fact, living like you. If you as parents believe each other to be special and unique, and communicate this to your children, they will grow up realizing that they, too, are special and have a one-of-a-kind relationship with each person in the family. They will develop their own personal sense of self-esteem and ultimately become healthy, well-adjusted adults.

The healthy family both fosters autonomy on the part of its members and encourages initiative. Children learn how to stand on their own feet and reach out to seek their own interests. They don't feel guilty about this, but rather share a sense of pride for having contributed to the life of the family. Since family members have learned to be appropriately intimate with each other, they also learn how to express their feelings and emotions to each other.

Furthermore, the healthy family has a shared belief system, a sense of values and ethical behavior that acts as a cohesive force during times of disagreement and disputes. In some families the belief system involves active participation in religion. In others, it simply rests on the strong will and integrity of the parents. The value system that is accepted by all members of the family provides a sense of commonality that helps the children through the usually difficult teenage years. The children learn to respect their parents' moral strengths and their faith in human dignity that inspired them to love each other and provide a happy and healthy home life for everyone. And finally, the children learn that their parents' faith is what pulled them through the most trying marital passages and cemented the marriage bond through the stormy periods of their life together. When children from solid families like this are ready to begin their own lives as married adults, they go into marriage with a healthy attitude that can sustain them through their own marital passages.

5.

The Periods of Marriage

To understand the concept of passages as critical turning points in a marriage, it is useful to think of a typical marriage as being made up of three periods. The "Early Years," which cover approximately the first ten years of marriage, include the initial "Acquaintance Phase," followed by a "Settling-In Phase." During the Acquaintance Phase, a couple is literally getting to know each other as husband and wife. They establish living arrangements, finish school or begin careers, perhaps plan their first child. During the Settling-In Phase, they continue to pursue their careers, make decisions about having children, and refine the roles each of them must play in their relationship. Traditionally, people entered this stage of marriage in their early twenties. In recent times, however, people have been postponing marriage until rather late into their twenties or even into their thirties, since more people are going to college and more women are beginning careers outside the home.

The second period of marriage is the "Middle Years," which extends from roughly the tenth to the thirtieth year of married life. There are two variations in this period. If you have children, this is the "Child-full Phase," which makes up the major part of the Middle Years and ends in the "Us-Again Phase," when the children have grown and left home. In the Child-full Phase, the parents concentrate

18

on developing and rearing a family and setting new goals for the future as they learn the ever-shifting demands of being parents. They must also resolve conflicts that arise between them, in order to stabilize their marriage for the future. After the children are grown and gone, a couple enters the Us-Again Phase. They rediscover and rebuild their relationship, set new priorities, and learn to enjoy a renewed intimacy without the children at home. If a couple has chosen not to have children, their childless Middle Years are dedicated to careers, community activities, and social obligations, all of which become opportunities for the couple to explore the nature of life together and learn how each becomes the focal point for the other's happiness and well-being.

Then comes the final period beginning with the thirtieth year, the "Mature Years"—the years of growing old together, of retirement plans, of being grandparents, of living alone with each other as you once did when you were first married. This is a time when you can recall the Early Years of your marriage, when you were young and just starting out, when there were just the two of you against the world. Now it's just the two of you against the world again; but my, how the world has changed!

These marital periods and phases are typical, but not universal. They may not reflect exactly your own marriage. For example, you might be in your second marriage, which began in your late thirties. Or, you might be settling down with your first mate at age forty-five. So keep in mind that even though we will consider the passages of marriage in terms of Early, Middle, and Mature years, you will still have to apply the issues, the case studies, and the advice to your own life situation. Obviously the young married woman who is twenty-one will not experience the passages of the Early Years in exactly the same way as a newly married woman of thirty-four. So, too, a retired couple who has never had children will not confront the grandchildren issues during their Mature Years. Nevertheless, the techniques that successful couples use for whatever issue or problem they must negotiate can serve as worthwhile models for you in your own passages. Moreover, if you don't successfully resolve an issue into a positive passage during an early phase of your marriage, it is likely to return to disrupt your relationship during a later phase.

6.

Three Primary Tools
for Successful Passages

Negotiation rather than compromise: Compromise is good. We've all been taught to compromise, to give in, to not be stubborn. The problem with compromise, however, is that it's just that—giving in. When we give in, we rarely feel satisfied. We may feel noble. We may feel that we've played fair, we've been reasonable and good, but we rarely feel satisfied. We feel that the solution was not the best solution and that it was somehow the *other person's* solution. Through the years of marriage, there are rarely perfect compromises. Usually what happens is that one spouse gives in on one occasion and then the other gives in later on. Over time it looks as if the couple is relating well; but repeated compromise, based on taking turns and giving in, is frustrating. Somebody always feels like a loser.

Negotiation, on the other hand, is more creative; and when done correctly, neither partner should feel cheated. In negotiating, two people work to come up with an alternative solution to those they have already proposed. I look at your way, you look at my way, and then we come up with a new way that suits us both. And that becomes *our* way. It is a more dynamic and creative process that should produce a more fulfilling solution. Negotiating is an interactive process that brings the married couple together in a nonconfrontational setting. It demands the best creative efforts of

20

each. It can adapt to all the changing issues that may threaten a marriage. Most of all, it encourages a team approach by which a couple can express their love and regard for each other. It de-emphasizes the competitive, argumentative tone that characterizes so many problem solving endeavors. You may never have been taught to negotiate. It may be a new strategy for you. But if you and your spouse love each other and want to have a super marriage, then employing the next two tools will help you learn to negotiate.

The sixty-forty solution: As human beings we are basically imperfect. We try to reach beyond our grasp and usually fail. If you set "fifty-fifty" as your goal ("I'll go half way, if you'll go half way"), you'll most likely fall short of it, even with the most sincere intentions. Then your combined efforts for strengthening your relationship will be much less than one hundred percent. In the "sixty-forty" relationship, each of you is willing to be a little more selfless than selfish. You each promise the other that you will try to give sixty percent and expect only forty percent in return. In other words, each of you is trying to please the other, while the other is trying to do exactly the same thing for you. In this way, the one hundred percent commitment level of the truly super marriage is more attainable. The "sixty-forty" solution means putting your partner's needs above your own a great deal of the time. It means thinking ahead to what he or she needs—wants, desires, or expects—and then delivering. The "sixty-forty" solution guarantees success because as you try to please your spouse, you don't have to worry about your own needs being fulfilled. He or she is there doing the same for you. The "sixty-forty" ploy may sound too mechanical, but it really works. And I've seen it help couples achieve success in negotiating the most difficult passages.

The "I love you, but" formula: Sometimes repeating a little formula helps negotiate a reasonable resolution when you're trying to work out a problem. It can go something like this: "You know I love you, but I don't always understand you or agree with you. Sometimes I don't see things your way, and I need help to understand all that is bothering you. I want to feel what you feel, so that I can know what you need. I want to be there when you need me. Also, I don't always see what I did to make you get angry with me. If you help me understand things like that, then I can be more careful about your feelings and your needs in the future." A formula like this will couch your discussion in terms of love and trust for each other and the sincere desire to understand each other. There are many messages in every conversation, but the one that should prevail in any touchy dialogue regarding hurt feelings and misunderstanding is: "In spite of our problem communicating with each other, I still love you." This, too, may sound rather contrived, and you surely don't have to recite the whole formula every time you sit down to have a discussion with your spouse. But some abbreviated version that you yourself develop, which your spouse understands, and which your spouse will also use, will do a great deal to help facilitate your negotiating difficult passages.

7.

A Word about Remarriage

This book is about marriage, not divorce. If you are currently in the process of divorce, I recommend you read one of the books on how to divorce successfully. If you are already divorced and are contemplating remarriage, or you have just recently remarried, here are a few words of advice.

If you are "on the rebound," as the saying goes, and you fall in love with someone, be aware that remarriage on the rebound is a dangerous course to pursue. Having just come through the disastrous psychological trip of divorce, you're probably hurt, upset, in need of love and support, and vulnerable! You're looking for someone who understands and cares for you. Marrying hastily seems to be a quick way to relieve some of your pain. But marriages on the rebound have a very high failure rate. It seems that when the first serious crisis comes along, it becomes a passage through which the newly married couple fail to navigate. My advice is that people should not remarry for at least two years. If you fall in love soon after a divorce, date each other and be together as much as you want; but don't get married. Give yourself time to recover from the psychological shock of divorce before jumping "heart first" into another relationship without using your head. "Heart-first" marriages the second time around usually don't last a year.

Secondly, don't make the same mistakes the second time around. Freud called it the "repetition compulsion." Simply put, this means we are creatures of habit, both good

23

ones and bad ones. Even though we vow to break the bad ones forever, we don't. Some blind impulse lures us into the same situations we've known before without considering how much pain or pleasure they will cause us. I see this every day in my patients and in my "Talknet" callers. The child of an alcoholic marries an alcoholic. The daughter of an abusive father marries a man who turns out to be a wife beater. What's going on? Why do we replay unfortunate situations over and over again?

It seems we have an unconscious need to repeat earlier life experiences because they had a major impact on our psychological development. As much as we hated the alcoholic or abusive parent, we had a need to love them; and we wanted to change them, to make them whole, to heal them. Perhaps then they would love us more. Failing to do that, we felt somehow responsible. We somehow believed that we deserved the abusive treatment. Hence, part of the repetition compulsion is our unconscious need to correct those earlier circumstances, to change that other person, to make him or her the way we always wished he or she would be.

If you are coming out of a marriage in which your best efforts to "heal" your spouse failed, you have a sense that *you* failed. You may unconsciously want another chance with someone else. The result is a strong tendency to marry a carbon copy of your former spouse. And statistics show that you'll likely fail again, and then your marriage will fail.

Regardless of the quality of your first marriage—the things you loved about it, the things you hated—you were partially responsible for its demise. You must realize the part you played so that you can avoid repeating the same mistakes. The way to prevent the repetition factor from influencing your next marriage is to acquire as much understanding about yourself—your emotional growth, your childhood experiences, how you treat people near and dear to you, and how you react to interpersonal problems. Some people are able to do this by themselves, others may need psychotherapy to help them. But the principle is the same— you must do it if you are to remarry successfully. Self-knowledge and learning from your past mistakes will greatly help you negotiate the passages of your next marriage.

8.

The Blended Family

Finally, if in remarrying, one or both of you have children, then you will have a unique passage that first marriages never have: that of blending your respective families together so they function as a healthy family unit. Even though you and your new spouse are thrilled about the new life you are carving out for yourselves and your children, the children may be less than thrilled. They may be terrified, angry, confused. Until you create a successful blended family, you'll be living under rather unstable circumstances that need to be resolved.

Blended families usually have divided loyalties because children, as a rule, maintain a relationship with and some positive feelings for the absent parent. Also, the children may have trouble adjusting to each other and may not even get along well with their new step-brother or -sister. The way your children adjust to and accept their new half-siblings is totally dependent on how you, as a couple, deal with the situation. During the Acquaintance Phase, the children are going to feel competitive with one another and be uneasy about how to treat you and your new spouse. It's important that you never play favorites. Even though only one of you is the natural parent for each child, together you must work as a team and deal consistently, honestly, and directly with each of them.

There is a three-fold strategy for blending two families successfully. First, the children should perceive your commitment to building the new family as a place of love, support, caring, and comfort. They should sense that something wonderful is occurring and that they are part of it. Second, unlike in their former families, your children must see that you and your spouse are willing to communicate openly, honestly, and fully with each other, that you trust each other, and that neither one of you is going to do anything intentionally to hurt the other. Similarly, they must be encouraged to be open and honest, to say what they like and dislike about the family to you. They should do this privately if it would hurt someone else's feelings; but by no means should they keep things bottled up. Making the new family work will depend on clear, direct communication. Third, children must see you negotiate with each other to resolve issues in your relationship. They must learn quickly that in this new blended family, they are not going to be the losers in unfair or one-sided compromises, but rather that everyone will work together to resolve differences and come up with new solutions that meet all your needs.

If your children see you and your spouse working together in a creative and mature manner, establishing your new family with a sense of excitement and joy, it will eventually rub off. They'll realize that you are all "in this together" and that the new family is going to make everyone's life richer and more rewarding.

9.

How to Read this Book

If you are having problems in your own marriage, I suggest you read this book together if possible. Try getting away for a weekend to a place where the two of you can be alone and uninterrupted by the daily commotion of children, work, and other commitments. The honeymoon atmosphere of a weekend away creates a wonderful background for getting a fresh perspective on the passages of your marriage. You need peace and quiet for truly mutual exploration. If you can't do that, try to set aside an hour several nights a week that will be your time alone together. Do this after the kids are in bed. Take the phone off the hook, and use this time to begin talking and communicating with each other—sharing your thoughts and feelings about what you read here.

You are going to meet some extraordinary and ordinary couples in the case studies that follow. Each couple is a compilation of true cases that I have dealt with either in my practice or in my work on "Talknet." The names, places, and externals have been changed when necessary to protect confidentiality. But these are real people just like you, struggling with the same predictable issues of married life, some of which will sooner or later be counted among the passages of your own marriage. Some of these couples have needed couple's therapy; others have resolved issues successfully on their own.

As you reflect on these cases together, think about the

emotional strengths and weaknesses of your own marriage. Imagine how you would have handled a particular issue. Try to recognize areas where you would have had difficulty dealing with a problem, and realize that this is an area where you and your spouse have some work to do. Remember that you must be open and honest with each other and nonjudgmental about what the other says. This process should allow you to learn things about yourselves that you were previously unaware of. Accept what you learn, and receive critical comments as constructive attempts to straighten out your situation. Remember that everything you learn about your marriage has the potential to heal your relationship, if you will use it appropriately.

If your marriage is undergoing some vague, undetermined restlessness, and you're not sure what the "real issues" are, you'll probably want to read this book cover to cover. Don't omit the sections on the Middle or Mature years just because you haven't arrived there yet. Some of your discontent may be an unconscious fear of what's lying ahead. Similarly, don't omit the sections on the earlier phases that you've already passed through. You may discover the roots of your current problem by learning how you failed to handle earlier passages in your marriage. Early unresolved issues must be cleared up if you hope to move forward in your relationship.

If you know exactly what the issues are in the current phase of your marriage, you can turn to those sections and read them first. Read the entire section for all the issues in your particular marital period; then read elsewhere in the book. As you will see, marriage really is a tapestry interwoven with many textures, colors, and patterns. What may appear to be a mid-life crisis can also have a component of sexual boredom. A financial problem might be compounded by children or aging parents. Most of all, don't feel defeated if you decide that you need couple's therapy in order to straighten out your marriage. I've included a section in the conclusion describing couple's therapy and how to obtain it.

My purposes in writing this book are several. The obvious one, of course, is to provide a guidebook to help couples understand and strengthen their own marriages by themselves. But it's possible that by reading the book together, you realize that you need more help than you can obtain from a book. Don't give up. This book is also intended to serve as a beacon to you that more intensive help is necessary. Accept the fact that your marriage may be stalled in a troublesome phase that you don't have the ability to negotiate. You may need outside direction. Even the strongest people occasionally need a friend to pull them through. If this is your situation, by all means seek couple's therapy. You can contact either your local family service agency, a community mental health center, or the department of psychiatry in a nearby hospital or medical school and ask for a referral to a good couple's therapist.

Another reason I had for writing this book is to compliment the truly outstanding marriages, the super marriages, where devoted and loving couples are weathering the vicissitudes of married life together. If you are one of those couples, and you're reading more out of curiosity than necessity, you will find case examples of couples like yourselves who have pulled through marital crises by sticking together, sharing the burdens, and totally supporting each other. I congratulate you. You're the people who make my work rewarding. You are living examples of my own personal vision that two human beings can pledge themselves to each other "for better or for worse"—and make it better.

PART II

THE EARLY YEARS

10.

Introduction

We are ready to look at the issues that can unsettle the peace and harmony of the Early Years and create the typical passages for a newly married couple. Remember, even though a particular issue may be a minor one for you, it must be resolved successfully. *Every* issue that destabilizes your marriage becomes a passage, that is, a critical turning point for your relationship, even though it may not seem so at the time. It is critical because by resolving it together you restabilize your relationship for the immediate future. By helping each other through the rocky periods of marriage, your relationship will grow and mature, and you'll be prepared to meet the next issue successfully. If you don't resolve each problem as it arises, it doesn't mean that your marriage will end tomorrow; but a series of negative passages is likely to lead to distrust, defensiveness, dissension, and upset feelings that weaken your love for each other and diminish your ability to work together on later problems. Over a period of time, a series of negative passages will undermine your marriage.

During the first three-to-five years of married life you are in the Acquaintance Phase, getting to know each other as a married couple; and during the second three-to-five years, you are in the Settling-In Phase, when you solidify and strengthen your marriage for the coming years. The particular issues that confront you during these crucial first six-to-ten years become your marital passages. Which ones arise for you depend on your own individual life circumstances, your past histories, how long you've already known each other, whether you are in your twenties as most newly married couples are, or whether you're older, whether this is your first marriage, or whether you've been married before. Even prior experiences with your family, your temperament, and your personality will play a part in determining which issues become passages in your own unique relationship.

Power, Boundaries, and Intimacy

Every passage requires you to adjust to changing circumstances. Healthy couples adjust whenever necessary by renegotiating these three important components of every relationship: power, boundaries, and intimacy.

Power relates to your decision-making process. Who's in charge? And of what? Who makes decisions in what areas? How are responsibilities handled? At various times in your life the focus of power and authority may shift and be divided differently between you, but the critical issue is that you recognize this and *negotiate* each adjustment as the need arises.

Intimacy means not just sexual intimacy, but rather how close the two of you are emotionally. How much of your own personal worries, fears, joys, and surprises do you share with each other? How reliable is your partner when you're under personal stress? Do you go through things together and communicate your feelings to each other clearly and honestly? Do you feel that being too close to your mate emotionally stifles your own individuality?

Boundaries refer to who is included and who is excluded from your relationship, and to what extent. Boundary issues arise at many different levels. They exist between you and your spouse, between you and your children, between the family unit and your parents and siblings; and they exist between each one of these particular units and the rest of the world. At various times throughout the course of your marriage, you will have to decide whom you will allow in and whom you will keep out, how much intrusion you will accept, and how much outside involvement you yourselves will have. You will have to consider whether friends and social acquaintances impinge upon your time together, whether parents and siblings are monopolizing your time, whether your spouse or your children have outside activities that disrupt the flow of family life.

If you are having difficulty getting along with each other and you seem stuck in a passage that is going nowhere, you should consider whether the crux of the problem involves one or more of these three critical issues. In the case studies we're going to look at, you'll see how other couples came to terms with these situations and redefined them so that they satisfied the changing needs of their own lives.

Other factors, too, can shed light on marital problems, and we should consider these before we delve into the passages of the Early Years.

Similarities and Differences

The chemistry of love seems to be built on the principle that "likes attract." This is one of the reasons why we often fall in love with people who are physically similar to ourselves. We walk into a crowded room and are immediately drawn to people who in some way reflect our own perceptions of ourselves, especially if we feel good about ourselves and have had reasonably healthy and fortunate experiences with our families earlier in life. The chemistry works. We feel more comfortable with a person of similar socio-economic background, with similar values, maybe even with the same religion and level of education—someone whose approach to life is basically like our own. On the other hand, if we had painful or negative experiences with our families as we were growing up, we may be attracted to somebody who is just the opposite of ourselves and our families in a number of ways. But for the vast majority, falling in love means meeting your soul mate, someone who understands you because you share so many things. And the more the better, because even in the best of marriages, there are always areas in which the couple has to make adjustments.

Yet variety is the spice of life, and differences are important. It would be terribly boring if we married clones of ourselves. In fact, most of us possess faults and shortcomings that need to be changed, and the influence of a loving husband or wife will often help us smooth out our rough edges. This, too, is an important principle in the chemistry of love—recognizing and sharing compatible and complementary differences.

Not only do healthy differences compensate for deficiencies in our personalities, but they also liven up the relationship. There is no question in my mind that the chemistry between Diane and me creates a whole greater than the sum of the parts. We complement each other's personalities and fulfill our own needs in ways we never could have done alone. I bring certain organizational skills and a sometimes unwieldy compulsiveness to our marriage, while Diane contributes certain sensitivities to people and insights into social situations.

While it is important that there be both basic similarities and compatible differences, it is also important that there not be *many* conflicting differences, and that they not be too severe to resolve. Recognize early in your relationship where these differences are, and try to come to terms with them. For example, you may have differing emotional styles. One of you may keep things bottled up inside, while the other lets everything come gushing out. One of you may tend to become emotional and fly off the handle, while the other one may be very controlled and emotionally unexpressive. The point is to acknowledge conflicting differences and work out a modus vivendi. Otherwise, they will hinder your ability to deal with your marital passages together.

Marital Expectations

During the Acquaintance Phase of our Early Years, we should realistically assess our marital expectations. While we were dating and learning about each other, we also started tuning into each other's expectations—what we each hoped to find or derive from the marriage. These hopes covered a wide range of topics—from lifestyle, to children, to careers, to relating with each other's families. We were thrilled and excited when we found ourselves fitting together; but because of our enthusiasm, it is likely that some differences in expectations were dismissed as being of little importance. In fact, it is likely that we were not even aware of a number of unconscious expectations that may have been programmed into us from earlier life experiences.

It is easy to be aware of our conscious expectations, because we think about them and discuss them with each other. Our unconscious expectations pose a greater problem because we are unaware of them. We can be alerted to their existence, however, when we continually find our spouses failing to act or behave as we had hoped they would. When this happens, let your disappointment be a warning signal to sit down and start discussing with your mate how he or she is letting you down as far as you're concerned. It is through this kind of dialogue—and you will see examples of it as we go along—that we become aware of our own unconscious expectations and learn how to assess their validity.

Each of us went into marriage believing that the love and devotion of a good mate would satisfy all our needs. Most of us may not admit this; but from my experience in working with couples, I usually find it to be true. Many people describe this feeling of falling in love as being "whole" for the first time in their lives. The problem is that in the Acquaintance Phase after the honeymoon is over, you realize that your spouse is only human, that he or she has similar frailties, misperceptions, emotional shortcomings, and weaknesses, and that you both have unrealistic expectations that are not likely to be met. By discussing this with each other and determining where each of you finds the other falling short, you can get in touch with your own unconscious expectations. Then, as you reveal these to each other mutually and slowly over a period of time, you can start to negotiate the differences and build a more realistic base for your relationship. If you don't do this, it is likely that you will have more difficulty dealing with important passages in your Early Years.

Unconscious Expectations? Like What?

Here, in capsule summaries, are some of the more common unconscious expectations that can unsettle your Early Years. You'll see these in more detail when we consider the case studies that follow.

Physical and emotional energy levels: Different people have different biological and psychological rhythms that determine how they respond or react physically and emotionally to various situations. If you and your spouse are out of phase, you may continually fail to meet each other's needs simply because you haven't the energy to be there when the other needs you.

Sexual energy: It is usually hard for couples still getting acquainted in the Early Years to discuss sexual expectations. It is important to understand and accept the fact that each person is unique when it comes to sex. We must respect each other's sexual needs and energy levels if we want a solid foundation for marriage.

Role playing: Very often the roles we watched our parents play over the years determine our expectations regarding our own marital roles. These preconceived notions are often deeply entrenched in our unconscious, whether we consider ourselves "liberated" from our parents or not. There is obviously no single way to determine roles in a relationship; but once you find that you're at odds with each other in what you expect, it's a signal to focus on this area and develop unique roles that suit your personality and expectations of married life.

Intensity of interaction: The way we saw our parents interact will greatly determine how we expect our spouses to behave in terms of spending time together, sharing tasks, relaxing together, and being dependent upon each other. If our expectations in this area differ, they'll need to be resolved early in the marriage.

Emotional needs: We all have emotional needs that were formed in early life. We call this the "emotional baggage" that we bring with us into marriage. If we never learn to articulate these needs, we may find ourselves defensive, hostile, or aggressive at times without understanding why. It might be that emotional expectations of which you are not even aware are causing you to behave irrationally. This is often a sign that you should seek individual counseling.

Low self-esteem: The problem with low self-esteem is that we are either attracted to somebody who has a high sense of self-esteem in the hopes that he or she will shore us up, or we are attracted to somebody with a similarly low sense of self-esteem in the hope that someone with similar weaknesses will understand us and know how to heal us. But it rarely works that way. As a rule, the partners in this kind of "pseudo-therapeutic" alliance are so needy themselves that they cannot adequately meet the other's needs. So if you are beginning to realize that your spouse is not making you whole in the ways you had anticipated, and you view this as a failure on *his* or *her* part, it is another indication that *you* should seek counseling.

Now that we've looked at some of the major psychological components of the Early Years, let's look at the everyday issues that might become critical turning points in your own marriage. As you reflect on all the possible passages during these years and meet the couples whose marriages we are going to use as case studies, remember that it takes *more emotional energy* to live in an unsatisfying and upsetting relationship than it does to be in a happy and fulfilling one. When a couple argues and fights with each other, they expend more emotional energy than they would if they sat down and successfully worked out a solution. And, what is worse, every fight and long-running argument takes its toll. It has not strengthened your relationship. In a super marriage the couple soon realizes that fighting doesn't create a satisfying passage. So watch the couples you are going to meet, and notice how they deal with each passage. Some will fail, others will succeed. Keep in mind, the more rationally and expeditiously an issue is resolved, the better. Then the passages of marriage truly become positive steps forward into deeper understanding and greater happiness with each other.

11.

The Passages of Family and Friends

Shifting Allegiances

When two people marry, chances are they are not at the same psychological and geographical distances from their respective families. When my wife Diane and I married in Chicago, we were both relatively equidistant from our families psychologically: we had each achieved about the same emotional independence from our parents. But geographically? That was another story. My parents lived in Pittsburgh. Diane's lived only two blocks away! For the first two years of our marriage we were within shouting distance of them. Fortunately, neither of us came from a family of shouters! In fact, Diane's mother was so sensitive to the situation that when she saw us walking down the street, she would cross over to the other side and pretend she had not seen us coming. How wonderful if everyone's mother-in-law were so considerate! Of course we told her that she did not have to avoid us for fear of interfering with our new marriage.

In a sense, every newly married couple has to discover ways to get the mother-in-law—and the father-in-law, the brothers and sisters, and even old friends—to cross to the other side of the street. Why? Because new boundaries need

41

to be drawn between the newlyweds and the people who had previously played such important roles in their lives. The old attachments to parents, friends, and siblings need to be redefined so that the married couple can establish a family space that is uniquely and privately their own. They must learn to live in their own way with as little unwanted intrusion from outsiders as possible.

Frequently, one partner's need to retain close ties with parents and siblings differs from the other's. This can cause problems if the amount of involvement in the new marriage is greater than the more independent partner would like. And it may have nothing to do with his or her disliking the in-laws. It's just that the Early Years is the time to establish your own family style, which may or may not reflect the families in which you each grew up. When one partner feels obligated to include family members all the time, the other may soon feel that the in-laws are encroaching on what should be a period of settling down and being together, getting to know each other on a daily basis, and beginning the routines and rituals that will make your new life together unique.

The important goal at this stage is to shift allegiances away from family and friends that once meant so much to you (and will continue to), and focus your interest and time on your new domestic partner. There's nothing disloyal or ungrateful about shifting allegiances at this point in your life. If the allegiances do not shift, you can expect a rather difficult transition in these Early Years.

PAULA AND JIM: UNWANTED ADVICE

In the mid-1970s, I spent several years meeting with a group of community clergy on a monthly basis as part of the Clergy Consultation Program at the Connecticut Mental Health Center. Father Doherty, one of the participants, told me about Paula and Jim.

Jim left his family on the West Coast as soon as possible. Having little use for his parents, who never expressed the interest and love he really needed, he deliberately chose to go to college as far away from Seattle as possible. From then on his contacts with his parents were, as Hobbes might say, "infrequent, painful, and short." Paula, on the other hand, came from a large Italian family and had a close relationship with her parents that she wanted to preserve even after marriage. They had been warm and devoted to her, and she felt a deep sense of gratitude and obligation not to disappear from their lives. In truth, it would have hurt them considerably had she done so.

From the start Paula's mother accompanied the two of them every Saturday morning when they went grocery shopping. Paula had invited her along the first few times when, like for most newlyweds, shopping for items to establish a household involves buying all those odds and ends you hardly ever think about once you've got them: brooms, dust pans, ice cube trays, washcloths, detergents, etc. But Paula's mother wouldn't stop helping them on Saturday mornings, and eventually it got on Jim's nerves. By then Paula didn't want to hurt her mother by telling her they didn't need her assistance. So Jim quit shopping with Paula.

More serious intrusion developed when, after three years of marriage and two good salaries, they bought a small house. Paula's mother decided that now was the time for the first baby, even though Jim and Paula had agreed to postpone children until Jim was earning enough as an architect to handle the mortgage payments on his salary alone. But Paula's mother was insistent, dropping little hints that eventually became outright nagging from Jim's point of view. In their arguments over whether mother was right or not, Jim threatened to leave Paula, who felt caught in the middle between two people she really loved.

When she sought help from Father Doherty, her parish priest, Paula learned that the only way to save her marriage was to find acceptable ways to decrease the intensity of her relationship with her mother. Together, she and Jim would have to establish marital boundaries that would keep mother "on the other side of the street," as it were, until she was invited over. They did manage to set stricter limits on Paula's contact with her mother, much to mother's consternation. However, a much sounder relationship developed eventually as they moved through their Early Years.

*   *   *

In order to solve problems such as Paula and Jim's, it is crucial that the spouse "caught in the middle" between family members and mate recognize that allegiances need to shift. In practical terms this means spending less time with the family, making it clear to the intruding parties that you need more time alone, giving up some family traditions, and realizing that your love and devotion to your old family can still be expressed, but in ways that are not destructive to your marriage.

Losing a Daughter and Gaining . . . a What?

How often the old phrase "losing a daughter and gaining a son" or vice versa comes to mind during the engagement and nuptial period. And how often the in-laws are so slow to accept this. You will always be your parents' child; and during the Acquaintance Phase your spouse is still an outsider to your parents, maybe even perceived as someone who "stole" your love and affection away from them. Even if you married a "knight in shining armor" or "the girl next door," it is understandable that parents will be critical at first and that it will take time for them to see the same sterling qualities that you do in your new mate. Initially, the new son- or daughter-in-law will always pose some threat to the in-laws; and if such was the case in your marriage, the situation has the potential of causing an emotional crisis for you as well. Everyone hopes to marry a person who will be accepted and loved by his or her family.

As you move through this period of helping your parents appreciate your spouse and accept him or her as a son or daughter, a number of issues must be faced. First, how does your spouse behave in relation to your parents? A husband or wife who is courteous, thoughtful, respectful and goes out of the way to be pleasing and charming will make this adjustment much smoother. But a second issue, over which you really don't have much control, is how your parents perceive your spouse. Perhaps they have a blind spot because they made up their minds you were marrying someone who wasn't good enough for you. In order to clear up your parents' misperceptions, you will have to be careful how you act toward each other when you are with them. Part of their perception is based on what they actually see the two of you do, how you behave in front of them, and what you say.

If your parents have negative feelings about your spouse, for instance, those feelings will undoubtedly be reinforced if they see the two of you during stressful times or in the midst of an argument. They will most likely side with you, and if your relationship with your husband or wife is particularly tense, your parents may even encourage you to end your marriage. It is easy for parents to get the notion that you married the wrong person if you constantly complain to your parents whenever you've had a fight with your spouse. Talking only about marital difficulties is bound to give them a distorted picture. You've got to offset their observations with positive information about how well the two of you get along at other times and how much each of you cares for the other. When you do occasionally complain to your parents, make sure they know you are merely ventilating some of your upset feelings and that the incident you're bothered about is not representative of your feelings for your mate.

You both may need to learn how to act as married persons in front of your parents. You're still your parents' "little boy or girl," but you're also someone's "grownup partner." When Diane and I got together with her parents during the first months of our marriage, it seemed she and I would always end up in a minor argument that could have given her parents the impression our relationship was rather tense. Actually, Diane and I got along very well with each other and her parents, and all four of us genuinely liked each other. But what sparked the dissension between Diane and me when we were with them?

When it became evident to us that we always spatted when visiting her parents, we decided to talk it over and look for the source of the trouble. In doing so we became aware that Diane always behaved differently in front of her parents than she did when we were alone or with other people. In subtle ways she reverted back to being their "little girl." She temporarily lost the independence and maturity that I loved about her, and this, in turn, irritated me to the point that I would get impatient with her and start scolding her. It would have been easy for my in-laws to conclude that our marriage was not a very happy one had we not noted the problem in time. And it's a difficult problem for many people to spot and correct. Subtle behavioral changes frequently and naturally occur when we are with our parents with whom we have had to play deferential roles for so many years. We need to retain our adulthood even when facing the people for whom we have been—and always will be—children. And we have to open their eyes to all the good qualities that we, as adults, saw and came to love in our spouses.

To help your parents appreciate and accept your spouse, it is necessary for the two of you to maintain an open and honest exchange of thoughts and feelings. If, inadvertently, you have been taught not to say what is on your mind because you'll regret it, you might keep important issues inside. You might avoid saying what's really bothering you for fear that criticizing your spouse's parents will hurt too much, and he or she will side with them rather than with you. This is a dangerous trap, and one you should attempt to avoid in order to establish a solid base for your marriage during the Early Years.

VINCE AND SHIRLEY: FEELING LIKE A NOBODY

Vince and Shirley were a couple we knew socially. Vince was an only child whose parents doted on him from birth. In their eyes the sun rose and set on Vince and he could do no wrong. As he breezed through school and began a successful career in business, they were all the more convinced that Vince was truly special. Shirley, unfortunately, came from a home with a crude, abusive, alcoholic father, who could not tolerate any expression of love and affection and who chided Shirley and her mother whenever they expressed any negative thoughts or feelings about his drunken behavior. Consequently, Shirley grew up wary about voicing what really was on her mind.

The combination of Vince and Shirley was potentially explosive: a husband unused to criticism or faulting, and a wife with her emotions and opinions bottled up, always letting him have his way. During their Acquaintance Phase, she learned to tell Vince only what he wanted to hear, and this kindled a slow anger in her that would eventually need release.

Unknowingly, Vince's parents became the catalyst for the inevitable eruption. Throughout the five years of their marriage, Vince's mother and father did not really accept Shirley as their daughter. They continually heaped praise on Vince. They ignored Shirley and overlooked whatever part she played in each accomplishment. Even though Shirley planted the garden, it was Vince's garden in their eyes. Shirley had tastefully decorated the house, but Vince received the compliments. Even the two well-behaved and somewhat precocious children were Vince's children, "following in Vince's footsteps." Everything good in their marriage was attributed to Vince's doing, and what finally became too much for Shirley to tolerate was Vince's refusal to share the credit with her. Just as when he was a boy, he continued to accept the compliments and glory in the accomplishments. He did nothing to improve Shirley's relationship with his parents. When Shirley timidly tried to point out to him that he should share the credit with her and help his parents realize her contributions to their family life, he became defensive and argumentative. Ultimately, Shirley had it. She told Vince she wanted a divorce.

It took the issue of divorce to shake Vince into realizing something was seriously wrong with their relationship. In order to save his marriage and the woman he really did love, he finally began to listen to Shirley and to understand how he—by continuing to play the "only child"—had inadvertently allowed his parents to drive a wedge between them. He also came to realize that Shirley could no longer continue in a marriage where she was not only not a "daughter," but a "nobody" who was never appreciated for what she did either by her husband or her in-laws. Over the following year Vince worked hard at allowing Shirley to speak her mind without his feeling threatened by it. He learned to accept criticism. He also went out of his way to educate his parents regarding the indispensable part Shirley played as a wife, mother, and homemaker. As they moved into their Settling-In Phase, their marriage became a strong one based on openness and honesty; and Vince's parents started to accept Shirley as a true daughter-in-law.

The Mother-ectomy

Our poor mothers! They are the brunt of so much sarcasm and venom! But let's face it, sometimes they deserve it! So do our fathers. I suppose mothers get heaped with abuse more often than fathers simply because in our society the mothers have been more intimately involved in raising the children than have the fathers, who often weren't around very much. Perhaps, as more modern fathers assume an equal role in child-rearing, the painful and strained relationship that one can develop with the mother will be balanced by a more equally strained relationship with the father! But all joking aside, many a marriage can use some type of "parent-ectomy." It can be a painful and disturbing operation. If this is one of your marital issues, the "mother-ectomy" or "father-ectomy" requires delicate surgery to separate your spouse from his or her parent.

ELLIE AND TIM: NO ROOM FOR MOTHER

Tim called me on "Talknet" to ask for advice and then wrote me a follow-up letter to tell me how things had worked out. Ellie and Tim grew up in the same Ohio town and had known each other since they were kids. But it wasn't until they went to Ohio State University that they fell in love. Ellie and Tim married and moved to Cincinnati, about three hundred miles away, where Ellie began teaching grade school and Tim began working as a computer salesman. They each had separated physically from their families, and together they created the boundaries within which their marriage could thrive. The boundaries dissolved, however, on the birth of their first child, Marty.

Three hundred miles wasn't far enough! Not for Ellie's mother, who always perceived Ellie as being frail and less competent than her older sisters. She came to help Ellie "during that difficult time after the birth" and ended up staying several months. When she retired to central Ohio, she still expected weekly phone calls on little Marty's progress. Ellie and Tim adjusted to the phone calls and holiday visits—even the audiotapes on child care that she occasionally sent for more explicit instruction on how to raise a baby through the first two years!

On the birth of their second child, Kathy, Ellie's mother became even more intrusive, and as Tim put it, "abusive." Not only did she come and stay for the several months after the birth, but she became critical of the way they were raising Marty, predicting doom for his future if certain childish faults weren't corrected—and soon. Ellie tended to believe her mother a fair amount of the time. As a result, the dissension between Ellie and Tim escalated. This time when her mother went home, she promised (or threatened!) to use her senior-citizen bus pass to visit them in Cincinnati more frequently. And she kept her word.

After Tim spoke to me about his intolerable situation, he told Ellie that she would have to choose between her mother and her husband. Ellie realized that because her mother had always had such little faith in her competence, she felt inadequate and actually needed chances to prove to her mother that she was a successful, competent mother, just as her older sisters were. So separating from her mother was painful, both because it upset her mother and because it deprived Ellie of her exaggerated need to prove herself to her mother after all these years. But to save her marriage, Ellie embarked upon a "mother-ectomy," which ultimately was successful and actually relatively bloodless. Both Tim and Ellie learned to present a united front in their opposition to Ellie's mother's unwanted visits. They also learned to lay down rules concerning the amount of involvement of any sort they could tolerate from Ellie's mother. Ellie's mother was intelligent, and wanted to maintain the relationship

with Ellie and her grandchildren; so when she realized what
was happening, she accepted it.

*   *   *

As in the case of Ellie and Tim, it is extremely important that the married couple present a united front to the
intruding in-law. You must support each other. Meddle-
some in-laws have an uncanny way of snooping out disagreement between a husband and wife. And you can be
sure that if the pesty parents sense support from one of
you, they will use it to get what they want and in the process
cause the two of you to drift even more apart. Your primary allegiance should be to your spouse and your children, not to your parents. Choosing between the people
you love can be painful, but your marriage will not with-
stand the crisis unless you are willing to make some hard
choices. If you can't do it yourselves, a wise marriage counselor or therapist can help you perform the "parent-ectomy"
as bloodlessly as possible. But as in all operations, there will
be discomfort, some pain, and a necessary "recovery period."

Feuding In-Laws

A difficult issue for newly married couples is how to
handle in-laws who don't get along with each other. Battling
in-laws have the ability to drive a wedge into your marriage.
It is paramount, however, that you not take sides, especially
siding with *your* parents against your spouse and his or her
parents. At all costs, you must resist the desire to defend
your parents exclusively. Doing so may drive your mate to
defend his or her parents, further aggravating an already
troublesome situation. The two of you need to sit down and
open up a dialogue between yourselves—being as honest
about your feelings as possible—on this issue. Only when
the two of you unite in support of each other can you
reasonably assess the problem with the two sets of parents.
What to do with them is both simple and difficult.
Simple, because the solution is obvious: you simply cannot
tolerate your parents' behavior since their fighting inevitably puts strain on your marriage. It is difficult because you

and your spouse may not have a lot of leverage in forcing your parents to accept or like each other. Once they have declared a state of hostility between each other, your own best peace-keeping efforts may not be enough. It is even more difficult because, in some ways, it is your battle and yet it is not. It's hard to stay neutral. And as the war goes on, just like in real military combat, there are victories and setbacks on each side. If the feuding continues for long periods, and if you come to believe that your spouse's parents are acting inappropriately, you should tell your partner so. Only a strong relationship based on honest communication and impartial assessment will keep the two of you united in your stand against the in-laws' squabbles. Negotiate with each other to discover the best way for each of you to handle your own parents and to deal with the other's parents. If you do anything less, it is likely to be at the expense of your own marital happiness, which will be the real victim of the feud.

MARNIE AND BILL: LEAVING THEIR PROBLEMS BEHIND

Marnie and Bill came from almost identical families: Catholic, Northern European stock, midwestern, college-educated parents living in the same section of town. Both families even voted Republican. But when it came to personality types, the two sets of parents might as well have been from different solar systems. Bill's parents were loud-talking, boisterous, aggressive people who liked to party, drink, and dance all night, and banter with each other in more-than-slightly off-color jokes. Marnie's folks were quiet, retiring homebodies who valued their privacy and time together and treated each other with an almost Victorian respect. In short, they considered themselves a polite, refined couple whose responsibility in life was not to make waves. When the two couples met during their children's engagement period, Bill's father behaved in a crude and insensitive back-slapping manner that offended Marnie's parents' sense of propriety. They quickly decided that after the wedding they would have as little as possible to do with Bill's family.

Bill's parents, however, thought it their duty to maintain an ongoing relationship with his in-laws and tried repeatedly to socialize with them. When Marnie's parents ignored their overtures and turned down invitation after invitation, Bill's folks felt insulted. The parents' problem soon filtered down to Marnie and Bill, creating tension in their own marriage. Bill could do nothing to change his parents' behavior, which, in the final analysis, was more a matter of style than content. Marnie, on the other hand, was not in a position to force her parents to get involved with Bill's. They did their best never to have the two sets of parents over at the same time on holidays and family celebrations, but this did little to squelch the snide comments each set of parents liked to indulge in regarding the other. Whenever a family affair came up and Bill and Marnie knew they would have to spend time with either set of parents, they would become irritable and eventually begin arguing between themselves. They began to realize that if they didn't take some radical action, their marriage would be in jeopardy.

Fortunately, at that point, fate played into their hands. When Bill was offered a position in a branch of his company in another part of the country, he took it. Marnie and Bill literally left their troubles behind, and saved their marriage.

*   *   *

Not every couple has an easy way out of the feuding in-law syndrome as did Marnie and Bill. If you're caught in similar crossfire, the best advice I can give you is to vow to each other that you will be honest about what you feel is right, promise to try to see the other's point of view, giving the benefit of the doubt, and, most of all, stand united to defend your own marriage against any onslaught from insensitive parents. Let your parents know the trouble they are causing you, and appeal to their better nature to call a truce for *your* sakes if not for theirs.

Sibling Rivalry

One of the personal passages most of us go through while we are children is the arrival of a little brother or sister. An intruder! Someone to vie for our parents' affection. Someone we will love to hate over the years! Most of us, however, get through this sibling rivalry and develop meaningful and rewarding adult relationships with our brothers and sisters. Nevertheless, some of us never quite get over the struggle to be better than our brothers or sisters, to keep up with them if they are older or hold them in their place if they are younger. When sibling rivalry continues into adulthood, it can create a fault line in the geology of marriage.

PETER AND JANE: KEEPING UP WITH THE SIBS

By the Settling-In Phase of their marriage, Peter and Jane were doing fine. They were intentionally childless, both making reasonable salaries, enjoying their work, budgeting their combined incomes carefully so they could save for a down payment on a house. A cheerful, outgoing couple in their late twenties, they seemed to have everything going for them. Nevertheless, they felt some strain in their life together that was causing each to doubt the wisdom of their having married. They just couldn't put their finger on the real source of their discontent.

During the first hour of talking with me in couple's therapy, they discovered the real reason for their doubts—Ellen, Jane's younger sister. It became clear to them that much of their social life and the way they spent their money was in trying to keep one jump ahead of Ellen and her husband Dick. Until they sat down and thought about it, they had never realized how many decisions were being made on their need—actually Jane's need—to compete with Ellen. Looking back, they could see that marital tension began when Ellen and Dick got married. The younger sister attempted to duplicate her older sister's wedding right down to the color of the bride's maids' dresses. From then on the two couples inadvertently got locked into a contest of one-upmanship. If Jane gave a dinner party for the family, within weeks Ellen would give an even bigger bash. When Peter and Jane vacationed on Nantucket, Ellen and Dick had to take a Caribbean cruise. Jane bought a simple ten-speed bicycle. Ellen showed up a week later with a Peugeot racing bike. When the two couples went skiing, Ellen and Dick flaunted the latest, most expensive ski equipment.

In therapy, Peter admitted that the incessant competition really didn't bother him, but it worked Jane into a frazzle. She became irritable and would usually end up fighting with Peter. Peter's main concern was that each time Jane felt the need to keep ahead of her younger sister, it would involve an expense that they could really do without. As Jane slowly began to realize that she had been striving to outdo Ellen almost from the time Ellen was born, she recognized how many of her decisions were influenced by this sibling rivalry, which should have ended years ago. Jane eventually came to see that she did not have to compete every time Ellen "matched" her. Together, Peter and Jane reassessed their priorities as a couple. They decided that doing what *they* wanted to do was more important than competing with Ellen. Jane saw that her efforts to strengthen her relationship with Peter should be the center of her life. She could be pleased with Ellen and Dick's success without feeling threatened.

Once that was put to rest, she and Peter could get on living their own lives. In time, their new attitude toward Ellen and Dick had its effect on the latter's marriage too. Ellen discovered that she didn't have to compete with her older sister, and the rivalry began to subside.

His Friends and Her Friends

The average couple can't do everything together, nor should they try to. Every marriage is a combination of dependence and independence. A husband enjoys bowling; the wife doesn't. The wife plays tennis; the husband finds it boring. One joins a meditation group; the other goes to lectures. Inevitably, we each develop exclusive friendships with the people we meet in our separate activities. Many of our core friendships emerge out of our separate careers. Even a homemaker, whose time is spent at home raising the children, will most likely develop friendships with other mothers in the neighborhood. None of this should be threatening to marriage. In fact, it can be beneficial because it eliminates the pressure of either spouse having to be all things to his or her mate. Unless you married your clone, you will surely have different interests and needs, and your spouse's friends free you from having to share every interest and activity. The boundaries of the healthy marriage allow good friends to move in and out of the couple's personal orbit, becoming a source of support for the times and activities when your husband or wife cannot be there. Good friends, whether they are your personal friends or whether you and your spouse share them, can enrich your marriage.

As with family members, in-laws, and siblings, however, friends can also disrupt marital bliss. In my experience with couples I have treated and known (and even as I reflect on my own marriage), the truly solid marriage is the best immunization from the problems friends can create. If you love each other and consider your spouse to be your best friend, then no outside friend can really threaten your relationship. In most of the ten percent of truly super marriages, the husband and wife are each other's best friends. If you don't consider your spouse to be your best friend at the moment, work to make him or her a better friend. It isn't something you can just wish to happen.

How do you know if there is someone else whom you hold higher than your spouse? Ask yourself the simple question: If I had a choice (all things considered), would I rather do such-and-such with my spouse than with someone else? In other words, if your husband liked to play canasta, would you rather play with him than with others? If your wife enjoyed hunting, would you rather go hunting with her? If your husband enjoyed English literature, would you rather discuss the novel you just read with him rather than someone else?

Complementary differences enrich and balance a marriage. Just because you *can't* share everything doesn't mean that your mate can never be your best friend. Having a favorite tennis partner or luncheon companion is not necessarily an indication that there is something wrong with your marriage. The ideal—and it is just the ideal, not something to become depressed over when it is not met—is to ask: *If* he liked Dickens . . . *If* she liked duck hunting. . . . The point is not that you shouldn't enjoy your times with friends; rather, it is whether you can honestly say that, all things considered, you have more fun with your spouse than with anyone else.

Often we need someone to talk with; and even in ideal marriages, issues come up, worries arise, problems develop, and we need another opinion. Sometimes our mate doesn't know enough about our problem, particularly when it is job related, to be the shoulder to cry on. Sometimes we get into disagreements with each other, and we wonder if the source of our disagreement is gender related, that is, are we not seeing eye to eye because one of us is male and the other female? At times like these, we do need to get an outside opinion. We need a male viewpoint or a female viewpoint to back us up or show us that we are being unreasonable. Then, a good friend is a godsend.

But even in a marriage where the couple are truly each other's best friend, suspicions and jealousies can arise. A solid marriage is the best immunization against these, but they will still occur. The most common situation to breed jealousy is the case where one partner has opposite-sex friends at work.

PRUDENCE AND SIDNEY: COLLEAGUES OR COLLUSION?

Sidney was a professor of English literature I knew at a nearby college, and his wife Prudence had been an English major there. Sidney told me about their situation when he learned I was writing a book on marriage.

Although Prudence had no interest in making literature a career, she enjoyed the academic life, and Sidney always brought home the latest "academic gossip" and shared his professional interests and frustrations with her. Each considered the other his or her best friend, and they were truly a couple who had more fun with each other than with anyone else. But halfway through the fall semester, Prudence noticed changes in Sidney. He was more quiet at night and talked less about what was going on at the university. He seemed moody and secretive.

The first substantial clue that led Prudence to suspect Sidney was having an affair was when a phone call from Marta, a new instructor in the English department, came late at night. It lasted two hours. It was unlike Sidney to spend that much time on the phone. Later Prudence noticed that Sidney changed his office hours so that he came home later and occasionally called to say he couldn't make it for dinner because he was working with a student who "had a problem."

At a faculty party, Prudence met Marta and, as she had suspected, the young professor was a real knockout. She also overheard someone mention that Sidney and Marta were spending an awful lot of time together. Eventually, Prudence knew she had to confront Sidney. She asked him outright one Saturday afternoon if he and Marta were "carrying on." As it turned out, Sidney explained all of Prudence's "charges." Yes, he had been spending time with Marta for several good reasons. Together they were hoping to establish an interdisciplinary program in Renaissance studies. Because of department politics, Sidney couldn't take a strong stand on this because he didn't want to alienate the "purists" among his colleagues, who feared that interdisciplinary programs would destroy the department. Word had it that Sidney was up for election as department chairman in the spring. He was really caught in a bind and needed the advice and support of someone like Marta who was new, not in either "camp" as yet, and who could work toward realizing Sidney's dream of a Renaissance studies program, since she herself had a background in literature and history. In other words, Sidney hoped to groom her to carry on the fight for the program at a time when he needed to keep a lower profile if he hoped to be elected chairman.

When Prudence asked why he hadn't mentioned any of this to her, he said that he just didn't want to bring that worry home to her; and even if he had, there was little she could do except support him emotionally. What Sidney needed was real political support from someone on the faculty.

Prudence and Sidney had a solid marriage and were each other's best friend. The crisis quickly passed.

* * *

Sidney and Prudence's situation is not unique. Many men and women have attractive colleagues with whom they strike professional and personal relationships. It's unavoidable. Unless a couple works together at the same place and the same job, no matter how much they love and understand each other, there will always be areas of concern at work for which one of them needs another ear to listen or another shoulder to cry on. An understanding mate will realize that he or she cannot be your confidant in all things, particularly regarding issues that come up at work.

But could Sidney have prevented the weeks of worry and distress that circumstantial evidence caused poor Prudence? Yes. A solid marriage should have open lines of communication, and with a little forethought, a person can prevent his or her mate from undue worry. The best thing to do if you know you are becoming professionally involved with an attractive colleague of the opposite sex is to warn your mate! Yes, warn him or her. Have a preamble. Tell your spouse that you've been working long hours or very closely with someone who could physically replace the leading man or lady on the most glittery soap opera. But also let your spouse know that you have no sexual interest in your sexy colleague. As I say, in a marriage based on trust and honesty, a simple preamble to that may prevent other pieces of gossip or misleading clues from undermining your mate's trust in you. Another preventive technique is to introduce your mate as soon as possible to the "threatening" colleague. Socialize with him or her in a setting where your spouse is not threatened and the two of them can get to know one another. They may not become good friends, but your spouse will see that the relationship the two of you have is truly professional, as well as friendly, and that as far as you are concerned, any romantic dalliance between you and your colleague is only in the eyes of other colleagues who are envious!

Marital Confidences

In one area, no family member or friend should pass the boundaries you and your mate set: and that is the matter of marital confidences. Disclosing information, problems, secrets, even hopes and dreams that are private and special to the two of you can be the crack that splits open your marriage. The very foundation stone of a healthy marriage is truth and honesty. Once you violate the trust that you have established, the doubt that it could happen again will forever be there. The precedent will have been set: you cannot be trusted *completely*. It is that loss of "completely" that shatters a truly solid and comfortable marriage. The violated partner will become more reticent and less willing to share thoughts and feelings.

Each couple must decide for themselves which matters are truly confidential. Traditionally, married people have withheld from outsiders information about their sex lives, finances, certain matters related to their children, and the misunderstandings and troubles that have arisen between the two of them. In recent years society has become more open in general. We have passed through an era where it was considered "in" to "let it all hang out." Many of us were raised on T-groups, sensitivity training, and TV talk shows, where the rich and famous discuss their most personal matters. We have grown accustomed to hearing the details of other people's private lives. Perhaps you and your spouse are not as close-lipped about the same issues that your grandparents would not have dared to whisper to their closest friends. But however the two of you decide the matter, you should not speak about topics that you know your mate would not want discussed with a third party.

The best thing to do if you ever do slip and let drop some piece of private information is to tell your spouse as soon as possible that you have done so. Let him or her know that you mentioned such-and-such to someone. You'll likely be embarrassed temporarily, but you've prevented your partner from learning about it elsewhere or by having it blown all out of proportion. You can also reassure your spouse that it really was an isolated incident and that you don't make a habit of discussing private information with your friend, or sister, or mother.

I truly believe from the troubled marriages I've seen that no good comes from talking about private matters with people outside the marital boundaries you and your mate have established. Especially problematic is the case of expressing discontent with your sexual life to someone of the opposite sex. Even in the best of relationships between friends or colleagues, to say that you are having sexual problems with your mate opens the door to a growing intimacy and eventually may lead to an extramarital affair. Discussing sexual problems even with a friend of the same sex is a betrayal, but to disclose your sexual frustrations to a person of the opposite sex can be an invitation to infidelity.

ELLIE AND TIM: WHAT ELLIE DIDN'T KNOW

When Ellie and Tim were having trouble with Ellie's mother, who traipsed three hundred miles through rural Ohio to check up on how the two of them were raising her grandchildren, their marriage was tremendously strained, as we have seen. But there were spinoff problems that seemed to have nothing to do with mother's presence.

Because their relationship was strained, Tim began confiding in Karen, an attractive young secretary at the company where he worked. At first he simply "sounded off" to her about how tiring it was to have his mother-in-law around all the time and how he resented her intrusion into matters of childrearing. As the situation grew steadily worse, he mentioned to Karen that mother's presence was disrupting their lovemaking rituals and that they seemed to be making love less and less. It was also becoming less satisfying. Karen, who found Tim a turn-on, interpreted his openness about his sexual frustrations as a come-on, and she began dropping hints that she was "available." When hints grew increasingly less subtle, and the possibility of going to bed with Karen became an obsession with Tim, he knew it was time to do something about it. He didn't tell Ellie about this, but it was actually his talking informally to a close friend about the "Karen problem" that eventually led Tim to call me and to realize that the root of the problem was neither Karen nor his love life with Ellie. Rather, it was the strain of having mother around.

It was Tim who put the bug in Ellie's ear that she needed to figure out how to handle her mother. As we have seen, they resolved the problem with a successful "mother-ectomy." And once mother went home, Tim's fantasies were no longer ruled by Karen. Ellie and Tim soon got back into a pattern of enjoyable love-making.

*   *   *

When Tim sought advice from his friend and from me, he wasn't betraying a marital confidence in the sense that we have been discussing. There will be times in your marriage when the advice of someone "wiser" will be necessary to help you successfully make the passage through an unsettling period. It usually happens in extreme cases such as Ellie and Tim's where you seriously suspect your marriage is at stake. You may have to talk over some of the more personal and delicate details of your marriage. But this is far different from making a habit of "chatting" about confidential issues with your friends.

Should you believe that you can't discuss an issue with your spouse and that you need the advice and support of someone outside your marriage, you must be sure that that person understands that your spouse is never to find out about it. This is not being sneaky or unfaithful to your mate, even though it may sound like some kind of double cross. Strictest confidence is essential to avoid undermining your relationship further. When the problem is resolved and you're back on stable ground, it's best to forget it and never bring it up with the outside person again.

As you can see, I think a situation like this is fraught with potential trouble that could harm your marriage. But being a realist, and being a therapist to whom individuals do come in such emergencies, I know that there are times when it is the only solution. Hopefully, you and your confidant will assume the professional standards of the best therapist and hold your meetings and what you say to each other in strict confidence.

12.

The Passages of Career and Finances

Bread and Bacon

"Bringing home the bacon" was the expression that grew out of earlier times when the traditional American family had one "breadwinner." Winning bread and transporting bacon to the family enclave were always considered the male's responsibility. Today these quaint expressions do not describe the situation for most families. What lies behind the bread and bacon? It's not just a question of money.

Now it involves the issue of lifestyle and career choice. The new wrinkle in the scenario is the woman's career as well. In over half of all two-parent families in America today, the wife and mother will work at least part-time during some stage of the marriage. Furthermore, the combined salaries and types of occupations the couple pursue can dictate much of what will become the lifestyle they and their children enjoy. Throughout your own marriage, whether you, or your spouse, are the primary breadwinner, or whether you are approximately equal, how much money you have and what you spend it on will be recurring issues. Sometimes your job and your financial situation are not the best. Problems arise that disrupt your normal pattern of living. Through these transitional times, questions of money, career, and lifestyle can challenge the stability of your marriage. As you work through these issues, you can strengthen your relationship by creating a series of positive passages for your marriage.

Two Can Live as Cheaply as Two

Budgeting during the Acquaintance Phase of a marriage can sometimes be a worrisome challenge. Not only have the man and woman no experience in sharing one income or combining two, but unexpected costs have an insidious way of eating into the monthly paychecks. No matter what you might have heard in folklore, two cannot live as cheaply as one. It's wiser to assume that two can live as cheaply as two, and if you find out that it's not quite that expensive for two, consider the extra money left over as a reward for having been so economical!

Compounding the challenge is the unpredictable nature of today's economy: taxes, inflation, interest rates, and the aggravating way that even brand new appliances break down and need repairs or replacements. It takes a few years of setting up house and getting settled to work out a comfortable arrangement that meets your financial requirements, when your material needs are paid for and after which there is enough money left over for entertainment and leisure activities.

In your early years together you both must be sensitive to the way you are spending money. What you would *like* to spend it on and what you truly *need* to spend it on may be two different things. It's difficult to grow up in a consumer society without being overloaded with wants and desires that are not really necessary. If you need to cut corners in your expenses, be honest with each other over your needs and wants. New clothes, for instance, are not always needs. Expensive meals are not necessary, although they may be the way you and your mate enjoy relaxing and treating yourselves after a long week of work. Deciding what's a necessity and what's a luxury is a responsibility that falls on both of you. Not deciding can lead to more arguments and worse disasters than trying to decide. It's better for your marriage to express openly how you would like to spend your income, prioritize your needs, and make long-range plans so that you can save for the big expenses that lie down the road. Both budgeting and spending money are expressions of power, and in well-balanced relationships both partners exercise this power jointly.

Behind every discussion of finances is the question of lifestyle. Before you married you probably fantasized a lot about the quality of life that you hoped to live together. There was a lot to dream about then—the kind of home, car, neighborhood, schools for the kids, vacations, social activities. Some of these may have been realistic goals; others, just pipe dreams. But once you're married, you must decide which of them you can hope to achieve within a realistic time frame and commit yourselves to the sacrifices you will have to make for these goals. For example, if you decide that you want three children and you want to send them to private schools, it's not too early to begin some type of financial program for the enormous tuition bills that will face you in a few years. If you hope to live in a semirural environment, away from big cities, you may have to make career changes if your present career goals can't be realized "out in the boondocks." You may have dreams of belonging to an elegant country club that will take not only money but time, while your mate prefers to allocate time and income to more modest organizations. The point behind all these lifestyle issues is that the mix of fantasies, dreams, and realistic goals needs to be sorted out early in your marriage so that you can plan and save for the expenses that the two of you decide are necessary to create the kind of life you jointly choose.

EILEEN AND JIM: ROUGHING IT

Jim liked to quote Thoreau when they were dating, and "life at Walden Pond" seemed to Eileen to be pure bliss. Especially with someone like Jim whose quiet inner strength attracted her the first time they met at a noisy, raucous party at college. During their courtship days, they spent most of the time alone together, strolling through the woods, walking around the lake, dreaming about their life together out West where Jim hoped to find a job in the small Oregon town where he had grown up. When they graduated, they married and headed West.

Problems began almost immediately. The low-paying clerical job that Jim landed with a medium-sized lumber company did not provide the capital they had hoped to have. For Eileen this became a major catastrophe because the only home they could afford a down payment on was an hour out of town. For Jim, the rural retreat was no hardship. On the contrary, it played right into his dreams of living away from the demands of urban life. It was idyllic. He enjoyed wood carving, hiking for hours through the forests, and "roughing it," as he liked to say. Eileen, on the other hand, realized how much she missed friends, parties, movies, and dining out. After the first six months of married life, she felt "walled-in" rather than enjoying the "freedom of Walden Pond."

Her perceptions of Jim changed too. Rather than being quiet and strong, she began to see him as shy, boring, and unaggressive. He seemed to be content to live in the sticks with an unpromising job and trade off affluence and social pleasures for the lonely solitude of nature. Within a year it was clear to her that they had totally different expectations for the kind of married life they would lead. Eventually, they could not discuss their differing points of view without ending up in arguments and confrontations. She accused him of "dragging" her out to the West where he was "married to" his romantic notions of living close to the land. She also told him that she didn't find him in the least romantic anymore. When she raised the issue of her finding work, Jim adamantly refused. Her arguments that they would never be able to have a more comfortable lifestyle on his salary and meager promotional raises fell on deaf ears. For him, the challenge of two people living on one salary and scaling down their material needs was noble. He also felt that Eileen's place was in the home. It became clear to her that one of the reasons he enjoyed their isolated life was

precisely that it was too far away from the kinds of jobs that
Eileen might want to have. He favored a traditional wife
who would be home, care for the house, and raise the
children.

Finally, Eileen decided she had had enough and returned to her parents' home in Chicago. She filed for divorce, and the couple terminated their marriage. Years
later when I met Eileen, she admitted that Jim was really
"quite a guy," but that she had married not realizing just
the kind of guy he was. Unfortunately, he was the type
whose career and financial expectations were too severe for
the kind of lifestyle that Eileen had envisioned for herself in
her younger days.

A Lifestyle to Which You are not Accustomed

For Eileen and Jim it was a double bind: disagreements
on finances *and* quality of life. Had they agreed upon the
rural quality of life, they might have been able to make it
with two incomes that would allow them to own a nicer
home closer to town where they could enjoy a modicum of
social life to please Eileen. Looking back on it, Eileen said
she would probably have been able to adjust to Jim's out-
doors lifestyle if they had not been faced with near poverty
and a drab existence cut off from civilization. It was the
thought of being stuck in that for the rest of her life that
made her panic so quickly.

It's normal for a newly married couple to experience
moments of panic as they look at their lives ahead and
contemplate what will or will not be possible for them either
because of finances or a demanding career or a social position that requires a certain lifestyle that one of the partners
is not willing to live up to. In the next case of Peg and Steve,
we see a woman who thought that the lifestyle they would
share would be prestigious and meaningful, but which in
reality turned into one that required more sacrifices than
she thought she could make without the support of her
husband.

PEG AND STEVE: WHY THE CAGED BIRD SQUAWKS

After seven years of an unsatisfying marriage, three children, and one separation, Peg felt like a caged bird. For her, the church was the cage. When she and Steve planned their life together, she hadn't realized that his desire to enter the clergy would make unbearable demands upon her. They both had been basically solitary individuals, emerging from lonely, unfulfilled teenage years; and they had clung to each other out of insecurity and a feeling of inadequacy. It seemed to both of them that the ministry was the perfect lifestyle where they could be together, support each other, and share common interests. But Peg had no idea how demanding that lifestyle would be for her. She soon learned that "a parson's wife" had her life cut out of a very rigid mold. It was even more rigid when she discovered that Steve was a male chauvinist at heart and had very inflexible ideas of what a parson's wife could and could not do.

Peg had numerous complaints. Because Steve had to move around the country a lot, she ended up living in climates that were not easy on her frail constitution. Also, the minister's salary did not provide the amount of income she had hoped would be theirs for raising three children. Lastly, her own hopes of working part-time were dashed by Steve's belief that a minister's wife should be available twenty-four hours a day for church duties. When Peg finally came to me for therapy, she said that after seven years she realized that the prestige and satisfaction that comes from church work falls only on the clergyman, not on the poor wife. All that fell to her were diapers, meals, laundry, and the subservient role of a minister's wife. She came to resent constant scrutiny of the congregational setting and the church members who were quick to gossip about any slip in decorum.

In couple's therapy I helped Peg and Steve sort out their different expectations. Steve realized that much of what he thought was proper stemmed from the strict tradition he had grown up in, where his mother waited on everyone's every need. All Peg wanted was a little help with the house and with raising the children. Also, her request to work was not really out of line for a minister's wife, since she only wanted to teach part-time in a local grade school.

Steve agreed to Peg's requests, and eventually, he even agreed to letting her have a more prestigious role in church affairs. He began to include her in more church activities on an equal basis rather than just as the minister's wife. Finally, he let Peg use the money she earned from teaching to bring a few frills into their lives and to allow the children to have more enriching experiences.

After a year of negotiating and changing, both Steve and Peg saw their love for each other grow and deepen. Since they were basically altruistic people, they came to appreciate the adjustments and sacrifices they were making to mend their personal problems for the good of the church and their growing family. Whereas before, differences of opinion led to fights and threats of divorce, now they discovered that disagreeing was often the first step in creativity. And the result? A more creative and meaningful lifestyle for both of them as they moved into their Middle Years.

Children: A Budgetary Line Item

It sounds cold and calculating, but it's true: children should be considered part of the budget. Even in your Early Years you need to consider the economic impact children will have on your financial resources. No matter when they arrive, they will require each of you to make financial sacrifices. It may mean fewer expensive nights out, getting by with last year's clothing fashions, postponing a new car or home. In financially hard-pressed families, it may even entail changing your eating habits by learning how to prepare and enjoy cheaper meals. Always the question of finances ends up becoming a question of lifestyle, and the need to earmark money for feeding and raising children may cut into the lifestyle that you thought would be yours. Having children is a very expensive proposition, but well worth it. Sure, there will be times as the bills roll in when you'll wonder if you made the right choice. I've had those doubts myself, now and then, when I've considered how my three sons impinged upon the boundaries of my marriage; but when I've compared the assets with the liabilities, I've always appreciated how much richer our lives are with three growing boys around the house.

Whenever you have children, it must be an affirmative decision. Nothing halfhearted. Having children is a serious passage for any marriage. It is not like buying a new car or a house. You can get out of those commitments by selling them off. Children are here to stay. You and your mate need to make the decision to be parents as fully cognizant as possible of how a child (or another child) will affect your lifestyles, your careers, your financial situation. When you make the initial commitment, it should be based on your current financial resources, not later ones. It's not a good idea to have children on expectations that you will someday be affluent enough to afford them. That's like spending next year's Christmas bonus in July! Of course, barring no nationwide disruptions in the economy, you can predicate your decision on the realistic assumption that as you advance in your career, you'll indeed be making more money ten years from when you decide to have a child. But keep your expectations within the realm of economic realities.

Another word of advice from someone who is unabashedly a lover of children: if possible, have a pair of children, not just one. From my experience in dealing with both children and adults who have no brothers or sisters, I can tell you that it's a much harder burden being an only child. Think of the responsibility! Growing up is far more enjoyable if you can share that responsibility with a brother or sister. Admittedly, a pair of kids is a more expensive proposition; but for family coherence over the years, the extra child is well worth the sacrifices you'll need to make when they are youngsters.

So how do you plan for them? Decide when you can afford to have a baby, what forseeable changes you are willing to accept, what sacrifices you will make, and when the best time will be in terms of your own education and career. Remember, school and a job become the financial base on which to raise a family. In addition to the financial base, you and your partner must have a sound emotional base. If your Early Years are troublesome, having a child won't make the troubles go away. A baby is not Mighty Mouse, coming to save the marriage. In all likelihood, the little mouse will aggravate your personal problems. So first get your own life in order, smooth out whatever interpersonal problems the two of you are having before your first child. Believe me, having a child is a difficult passage for a marriage already steeped in problems. And the problems will linger only to create anxieties for your children later on. So hold off having children until you get your act together, even if it means postponing them into your Middle Years. It's better to have children born into a financially and emotionally stable environment at a later time than to rush them into a household short of both money and love.

Cutting Financial Purse Strings

In today's economy it is hard for children, especially of middle- and upper middle-class families, to become financially independent simply by graduating from college and beginning a job. Being accustomed to a certain standard of living and often having tuition loans to pay off, middle-class couples often ease the passage of setting up house by continuing to receive support from one or both sets of parents. Sometimes the tuition money itself is the financial purse string. Sometimes it is the down payment on a house or a car; sometimes, money to finance the birth of the first child. Although it has become less common than a generation ago, some married couples continue to live with one set of parents for a time until they accumulate enough savings for a home or land a job that pays well enough to cover the rent no an apartment.

You know that parents believe they have the right—and duty!—to meddle in your marriage. Even when you've drawn your marital boundaries tightly, they find ways to intrude. Unfortunately, giving you money or letting you live in their home merely reinforces the notion in their minds that they have the right to interfere in your married life. If the supporting parents have a basically healthy relationship themselves, and your own dealings with them have been grounded in mutual love and respect, you probably won't suffer too much unwanted advice and mismanagement. Basically stable parents know that young couples want to make their own mistakes and learn from their own experiences, without having to live up to unrequested standards and suggestions. On the other hand, if your own parents have been using you for the attention or love that they failed to receive from their spouses, they may continue to be overly involved in your life in ways that will become problematic for both you and your spouse.

It's best to cut the financial purse strings as soon as possible. As long as they have an "investment" in your life, they will feel called upon to protect that investment by sharing the wisdom they have acquired over the years. Even the best intentioned parents will find it next to impossible not to exercise some type of control over the money—and love—they put into your marriage.

PAUL AND MARION: TOO MANY FAMILIES UNDER ONE ROOF

Until circumstances changed for the better, Paul and Marion felt their marriage would be swamped by the amount of parental input into their lives. But until then, they had little choice if they were to survive financially.

The two had started dating while in high school, and after two years, Marion became pregnant. Because of their religious convictions and the fact that they lived in a small western town where everyone knew everyone, abortion was not an option. They felt very much in love, so they chose to marry. Paul was a freshman in the local state college and was working part-time to pay for tuition. There was no way that they would be able to live independently if he hoped to continue his studies. So they moved in with Paul's parents, who were affluent and owned a large, rambling house where the couple could live comfortably. When little Sarah was born, Paul's parents made remarkable efforts to stay in their own end of the house and give the new mother, father, and baby as much space as they needed. They were acutely aware of not wanting to be overly involved in the young couple's affairs.

When she was able, Marion got a part-time job to help meet expenses, and Paul's mother baby-sat while Marion was at work. After several months of this arrangement, Marion felt that she was shortchanging herself by not going to college, so she enrolled in a couple of night classes. Paul's parents did not object, since Paul was happy to care for Sarah on the evenings Marion went to school. Everyone seemed content. Everyone, except Marion's parents! They still thought of her as their "little girl," since she was the youngest of three daughters and the only one who was "rushed into marriage." They had never accepted the fact that the couple was making the best of a troublesome situation. They always harbored suspicions that their daughter was not happy, especially living with her in-laws. Now that she was trying to be a mother, a student, and a part-time worker, they were convinced that they should express their true feelings. They began by dropping by unannounced more frequently, offering advice on how to raise Sarah, and prying into the role that Paul's parents "really" played in the couple's lives.

For the next year and a half, life became tense for everyone involved. The two sets of parents began to vie with each other for influence in their children's marriage, and Paul and Marion's relationship was strained under the brunt of so much parental interference. The only sane solution was to move out and prove to both families that they were able to stand on their own financial feet. They saved enough money to pay the rent on a modest apartment about thirty miles away, closer to college and Paul's job. They moved out six months before Paul graduated and set up housekeeping on their own. After Paul graduated, he began an executive training program with a large company; Marion began to go to school full-time. They both managed to pay for some childcare so that neither grandmother had to feel obligated to babysit. Within a year their relationship had stabilized. They also proved to themselves that they were indeed adults and responsible parents—something that was never clear to them while living in Paul's boyhood home and listening to Marion's mother deliver a constant monologue on how to be parents. In short, when the flood waters of parental intrusion became too swift, they had to bail out to avoid drowning.

*   *   *

In our society, making money and knowing how to manage it is a rite of passage that marks the transition from adolescence to adulthood. So is getting married. Unfortunately, the two don't always coincide. If you find that you're going through two personal passages somewhat out of sync with each other, keep in mind that it's as much society's fault as your own. Don't be alarmed if you find it difficult. There's nothing wrong with you. It's difficult for most young couples. You can make it an easier passage by keeping a balanced attitude and dealing with the economic situation as realistically as possible. Keep in mind the major crises that are likely to strike: discovering that two cannot live as cheaply as one, realizing that the type of lifestyle the two of you had dreamed about may not be within your financial grasp for some years, and (the big one) accepting the sacrifices and adjustments necessary for having a baby. If you need to rely on your parents during this period, do so, understanding that you will feel dependent and less "grownup" until you cut those financial ties. But keep your perspective clear: You *are* an adult, and someday you will be financially independent.

13.

The Passages of Sexual Fulfillment

There's an old saying that if you put a penny in a jar every time you make love the first year of your marriage and take one out each time you make love in later years, you'll never empty the jar. I don't know any couple who actually tested this theory, but my hope would be that they either did not have enough pennies or enough jars. In the first year of a truly healthy marriage, there should be a lot of lovemaking. After all, these are the weeks and months of really getting to know each other in many ways, not the least of which is sexually. In fact, your sexual relationship during your Acquaintance and Settling-In Phases is a very accurate reflection of other aspects of your relationship. Love dominates your every thought and deed in these years, and even though love is expressed in many different ways, nowhere is it more intense and more exciting than in your sexual relations.

And yet, of all earth's creatures, how fumbling and clumsy human beings can be when it comes to sex! The Irving Berlin song, "Doin' What Comes Naturally," should never have been written for men and women. Birds and bees maybe, but not people like you and me! The fact is that making love does not come naturally. It is a learned activity, and every culture has rites to instruct its young people on the tricks, techniques, and taboos of procreation.

Sadly, our culture, in spite of its obsession with efficiency, does not provide very effective initiation into the methods and mysteries of sex. And I use those two words purposely. Methods can be learned and mastered given time, experience, and a willing partner. But no matter how good you get at it, there will always be some mysterious dimension to sex, an unknown, unpredictable aspect that will never be completely understood. Possibly because sex involves another human being who will always be to some extent totally "other," and possibly because sex is our feeble attempt to annihilate that "otherness" and become one with the beloved, sex always leaves us feeling satisfied and yet unsatisfied, complete and yet incomplete, fulfilled and yet unfulfilled. In short, there is always more mystery to unravel and more truth to discover about the one we love.

Even if you are sexually knowledgeable and experienced when you marry, you still need to adjust to the realities of day-to-day living, which can cast a different light on sex and romance. Significant stress is part and parcel of learning to live together, and stress cannot help but influence your sexual needs, desires, and performance. If a couple is not experienced sexually with each other, they must then learn the methods and mysteries of pleasing each other—what the other likes and doesn't like, what one may find embarrassing or morally repulsive, what unique gestures, moves, and words the other desires and returns. Even timing and setting can be crucial. Should you make love in the morning or at night? Lights on, lights dimmed, lights off? Only in the bedroom, never on the couch? Totally nude? With or without music? Is the TV a distraction? And what about closing the curtain so the neighbors can't watch? The list could go on and on.

With time, you'll both learn what the other expects, including the delightful surprises your lover doesn't expect! But it takes time. "Fitting together" sexually is a process, not a snap. And as a significant passage of marriage, it's a learning process that may involve as much "unlearning" as new learning. We all bring a lot of myths and misconceptions about sex into every relationship, and it's not our fault. Our society bombards us with misinformation. What we must learn—as all those who styled themselves "swingers" in the seventies and hopped from bed to bed can attest—is that each individual is unique. Indeed, each act of sex is unique! You can't simply assume that what you learned in bed with one person will be enjoyed by another. Nor that just because your lover went wild over something last night, you'll be able to achieve the same heights of ecstasy tonight. Individual differences must be respected, and the first step toward sexual fulfillment is to discover and respect those differences.

The Sexual Cornerstone

Your sexual relationship is one of the cornerstones of your marriage. Excellent marriages that survive, mature, and deepen over the years are built upon a solid cornerstone of sexual expression. If one or the other partner finds sex dull, boring, or not worth the bother, it is exceedingly difficult to sustain a lasting marriage. The sexual relationship usually mirrors the total relationship. When married people are undergoing severe psychological stress or anxiety due to financial worries, children, career problems, or family tensions, that stress will be reflected in their lovemaking. At times you may go for days or weeks without having sexual intercourse. Or, you may make love perfunctorily because you assume it's your duty, but you'll find it very unsatisfying. Sometimes physical illness or fatigue will prevent you from engaging in your favorite rites and rituals. In times like this, a couple must discover other physically gratifying ways to express their love. As an indicator of the stresses and strains of a marriage, and as a cornerstone on which the marriage is built, sexual expression is a key responsibility. Your goal in the Early Years, as well as throughout your married life, is to be able to "read" that indicator accurately and shore up the sexual foundations of your relationship whenever necessary.

Because staying intimate with each other is so important "for the good times" as well as "the bad times," you must understand the sexual pressures that can occur during each period of your marriage and consider how they impinge upon other issues. One of the most important safeguards for any relationship is to pinpoint the core problem in each difficult passage from one stable period of your life to another. In your sexual relationship, it is too easy to assume that "sex is the problem" when, in fact, it is only reflecting other worries and tensions. The better you become at understanding how your sex life is interwoven with other areas of your personal and psychological development (and that of your spouse, of course), the better you'll be at predicting and avoiding areas of potential difficulty. The couples we'll look at in this section may have situations similar to your own; and yet, no matter how familiar these situations sound, remember that your marriage and your sex life are unique. Use the case studies not as templates for solving your own sexual problems, but as slices of life with which to compare your own life. Remember, not everyone gets the same slice.

Shotgun Weddings

It sounds like something out of Dogpatch, primitive as moonshine and backwoods stills. Pappy grabs the rifle from behind the door and marches his pregnant daughter and her rapscallion beau up to the preacher for a quickie marriage ceremony. But it still happens—without the gun, without pappy, and without the rustic romance. Even today in urban environments where birth-control information is readily available, many young couples begin the Early Years of their married life under the gunpoint (so to speak) of an unwanted pregnancy. Because of changing morals and a growing sexual freedom in our society, a greater number of late adolescents and young adults are finding themselves in the predicament of choosing between abortion and marriage; and though abortion is more generally acceptable than it used to be, many couples opt for marriage.

MARIANNE AND TONY: PARENTS TOO SOON

Tony was in charge of freshman orientation when he met Marianne, a young, scared freshman from Dubuque. Only a year older, Tony was her sophomore counselor; and although he was in charge of twelve students, it was love at first sight. A torrid love affair resulted, rushed into without either of them considering some form of contraception; and three months later, Marianne was pregnant. They considered abortion, but both had religious prohibitions against it. And although their parents were shocked and upset, Tony and Marianne decided to marry.

Marianne moved into Tony's apartment and was able to finish her first year of college before little Andrea was born. The following year Tony enrolled as a part-time student so that he could work in a clothing store. Marianne stayed at home to care for the baby. Both of them found the adjustment to being married and being parents difficult because, in their hearts, they really wanted to be students and lovers. And it was studying and making love that suffered. In the second semester Marianne started attending classes two evenings a week; Tony worked the evenings Marianne was home. They were too tired to have sex very often.

Marianne adjusted better to this than Tony, since she had not had sex before meeting him and had a lower sexual appetite than her husband. Tony, on the other hand, had a stronger sex drive, which intensified in the third year of marriage when he was made assistant manager at the store. The enhanced sense of his own ability and an increased paycheck made him feel better, and this carried over into his relationship with Marianne. Still, having sex only once a week was all they could manage.

In his senior year, Tony became sexually involved with a girl in one of his classes. They met regularly at lunch time. At first he felt guilty over it, and Marianne suspected something was up when he started acting differently toward her at home. But the result was that he made fewer sexual demands upon her, which pleased her; so she let it pass. But after graduation, Tony slipped into his second extramarital affair and ended up wondering if it had not been a mistake to marry Marianne in the first place. He did not know what to do about it because he did not see divorce as an option.

As he grew steadily more distant from Marianne, they argued more. One night in the midst of a heated debate over raising Andrea, he confessed to her that he had been seeing other women. Marianne was shocked. She threw him out of the house for a few days. When she calmed down, she suggested they seek professional help rather than lose their marriage; but Tony refused. He wasn't crazy, he told her, and they didn't need help. They'd work it out themselves.

Marianne wrote to me at "Talknet" for advice. After considering the information she sent me, it seemed obvious that one of their problems was that they had not successfully adjusted to each other sexually because they had never had time to get to know each other as people, as individuals who could be lovers without playing roles as husband/wife and father/mother. They had married under great pressure. The transition from being late adolescents into young adults with family responsibilities went too fast, depriving them of time needed to get to know each other sexually and learn how to reconcile their differing sexual needs.

Second, Marianne had come from a rigid and oppressed background, which had programmed her to be aloof and restrained sexually. She had a strong sense of what was right and acceptable sexual activity, and it was inevitable that she would have had an adjustment problem with Tony even under the best of circumstances. Tony apparently was a more relaxed, experimental, easygoing type. He told Marianne that his two affairs were purely physical attractions, that he still loved her and little Andrea, and that he didn't want to break up their family. Yet he remained totally opposed to getting professional help, which was my recommendation.

A year later I heard from Marianne again. She had been unable to trust Tony after learning of his escapades. They fought a great deal during the ensuing year. Every time he came home from work late, she was sure that he was out "fooling around." Toward the end of the year she threw him out again, and he moved in with his girl friend. Marianne wrote to tell me that she had filed for divorce.

Beauty and the Beast

The psychological wisdom hidden in the famous fairy tale about beauty and the beast is that only when beauty can love the beast as he is—ugly, hideous, animallike—does her love free him from the state of "beasthood" and reveal him to be the handsome lover he really is. Traditionally, the story has been interpreted as the need on the part of young girls to overcome their supposedly natural repulsion toward sex and to love the male who is a slave to his animal nature. In sexist terms, the girl wants candlelight, roses, and tenderness; the boy wants "a quick lay." But let's not be sexist. The truth of the matter is that many young women and men harbor sneaking suspicions that sex is either dirty, sinful, immoral, or, in varying degrees, disgusting. And yet nothing could be further from the truth!

In listening to couples relate their sexual fears and anxieties, I frequently hear variations on this fabled tale from both women and men. What's going on? How is it that something as glorious and enjoyable as sex can appear somehow "beastly"? The answer is quite simple. First, many young people grow up hearing that sex is somehow "wrong" or part of our so-called lower nature; and second, there will always be some sexual activity that will be disgusting to some people. Think about it for a moment. Most likely you know of some sexual act you would never dare dream of performing. It's perfectly normal not to be ready and eager for every conceivable sexual experience. Even if they were all socially and morally acceptable, we wouldn't have the time or energy for all of them because there is such a vast panorama of sexual expression. It reminds me of a t-shirt I saw on a young woman recently. It read: "So many men . . . so little time."

But, seriously, overcoming the normal fears and worries about sex is a very difficult transition for many newly married couples, especially if they are relatively inexperienced sexually. Let's take a look at an extreme example of this, the case of Paul and Sandra, who, surprisingly, shared their marital bed for three years and remained virgins.

PAUL AND SANDRA: UNDYING VIRGINITY

Sandra and Paul were a clear example of the principle of likes attracting. When they met in college, they were temperamentally and socially carbon copies of each other: shy, reserved, studious, on the fringe of group activities. Each had been an only child. What's more, each had come from a family background that had fostered negative feelings about sexuality and the human body.

When Paul was fifteen, his father caught him leafing through a pornographic magazine. He was soundly lectured about the "filth" of sex and severely punished. His father, a senior editor with the local newspaper, was a stern perfectionist who inculcated a sense of "deadlines and accuracy" into everything Paul did. The boy learned early that he was to do everything right and make no mistakes. The incident with the dirty book made him feel he had failed miserably and disappointed his father, whom he genuinely admired and worshipped.

Sandra's mother was pregnant with her when she got married. As the little girl grew up, her mother took every chance she could to impress upon her that sex can "get you into trouble," that it was an uncontrollable desire on the part of men, and, as in her own case, could "ruin your life." Consequently, Sandra grew up with a strong need for male emotional support to counteract the distorted image her mother created for her. But at the same time, she harbored an overwhelming fear that giving herself emotionally or sexually to a man would be disastrous.

In college they found each other. They dated until they graduated, but understandably neither wanted the relationship to turn physical. Both were comfortable in the platonic, but warm respect and love each had for the other. On their honeymoon night, Sandra became weak and nauseous, blam-

ing it on all the food and drink at the reception. The rest of
their honeymoon she had "stomach flu." So neither pressed
for sexual intercourse.

When they returned, Paul immediately began a job as
cub reporter, which required that he work nights. Sandra
taught kindergarten. For the first several months of their
marriage, they successfully managed to avoid having intercourse. The fact that neither of them was interested in sex
was very convenient. It made the passage of getting to know
each other seem smooth. For three years, they shared the
same bed and never consummated their love physically.

The more Paul got involved in his work, the more
Sandra began to perceive him as cold and uncaring. She
wanted more meaningful demonstrations of his love, which
he interpreted as covert sexual demands. Each time Sandra
got physical with him, it triggered his adolescent emotional
block that sex was somehow involved with losing his parents' love. He couldn't do it. Eventually, they saw a lawyer
to seek an annulment. He convinced them that they should
seek therapy first, before ending a three-year relationship
that, in spite of its peculiarities and hidden fears, meant a
lot to each of them. So they came to see me.

In therapy, I started Paul and Sandra on a series of
exercises to learn the Sensate Focus technique. This is a
nonthreatening method of overcoming one's psychological
fear of sex. Through guided instructions, they learned about
their individual sexual responses in a gradual, nondemand-
ing way. Each explored the other's body gently and sensi-
tively, noticing physical and sexual responses, without any
pressure to consummate the procedure with sexual intercourse. To normal, healthy individuals with average sexual
response, this method may seem peculiar, like revving up
the motor of a car without any intention of driving away.
But for people who are anxious *about* (rather than anxious
for) sexual intercourse, the Sensate Focus technique may last
as long as several months. It did for Sandra and Paul, but
eventually, in their own good time, their desire for consum-
mation quickened, and . . . well, as Irving Berlin would say,
they were ready for "doin' what comes naturally." They
successfully consummated their relationship, and after al-

most four years of marriage, were ready to confront the
other issues of their Settling-In Phase with enhanced skills,
sensitivity, and understanding of each other.

Sex and Romance

Love is blinding, especially in its early stages. The couple in love can see nothing but each other. It's wonderful.
S'marvelous. But the rude disillusionment that hits most
couples after they marry is that the blinding, glamorous
fervor of falling in love can fade. Sometimes quickly. Sex
play that was once so erotic, affectionate, and passionate
becomes routine. It's easy to fall in love, but it takes effort
to *stay* in love. Too many couples take the easy way out and
sink into drab sex roles that do little to stimulate the intimacy that made courtship so thrilling. Often, the roles we
assume are the identical ones our parents played and which
we have consciously or unconsciously anticipated as our
own.

While attempting to maintain the romance that charged
you both with boundless energy before you were married,
you must be realistic about the demands of daily life together and how those demands may dampen your ardor.
The intensity and frequency of making love is a case in
point. Some young couples think that if they don't continue
making love on a daily basis, they are not fulfilling their
marital obligations or that their partners will grow restless
and stray. Some newlyweds retain the "gotta score" mental-
ity and think they must make the jar bulge with pennies!
The man begins to doubt his virility if he doesn't make love
every day, and the woman may feel it's her wifely duty to be
"available" at all times. With either of these attitudes, sex
becomes mechanical because no one can be sexually respon-
sive at all times on a continuing basis.

I've had men complain to me that their wives turned
into nymphomaniacs after they married, developing such
voracious sexual appetites that they were getting worn out.
Later, in talking to the wives, I learned that they mistakenly
believed that men prefer sexually aggressive women and

that if they didn't initiate sex early and often, they would lose their men to more insatiable women. The sad thing is that neither sex partner really enjoys such a relationship. If sex doesn't come spontaneously and smoothly most of the time, the bond of intimacy between the couple weakens.

Many couples have unrealistic expectations about orgasm. Since men never feel satisfied unless they experience orgasm, they assume the same is true of women. But no matter how often we men are told that it just "ain't so," it's hard for us to accept. Whether we admit it or not, we unconsciously measure our prowess as lovers by our being able to make our women climax, and unless we can provide a rollicking orgasm every time we make love, we begin to doubt our sexual abilities. In truth, many women enjoy sex and find it satisfying without being aroused to orgasm every time. Men who refuse to accept this can become so focused on the female orgasm as the "goal" of sex that it detracts from their own pleasure. Similarly, when this becomes a spoken issue between husband and wife, it then puts pressure on the wife to "perform" each time. Feeling like she's being observed and rated whenever she makes love usually makes it all the more difficult for her to relax and enjoy sex with or without the long-awaited climax.

MARY AND TOM: PASSION BY NATURAL MEANS ONLY

As a teenage girl and even as a young woman, Mary devoured magazines and books about sex. Her natural curiosity, however, led her into much misinformation about human sexuality, particularly the female orgasm. Without any sexual experience, she married Tom believing that the vaginal orgasm should be achieved easily and by "natural" means. For her this meant simply through vaginal intercourse without any use of mechanical devices or manual stimulation, which her reading of the more prurient books and magazines convinced her was disgusting. She was in a double bind: she wanted frequent sex, but on her terms; and she was repeatedly disappointed and frustrated when she was unable to achieve orgasm.

Furthermore, her excessive demands on Tom for making love became a real turnoff for him. He began to feel inadequate and to doubt his own sexual prowess because he could not arouse her to orgasm simply by intercourse. It became a degrading experience for him, and he started to fear having sex because he knew he was expected to "perform" and would inevitably fail. Eventually, he refused to make love with Mary except on rare occasions, which turned out to be about once or twice a month. Neither was having much fun in bed.

Because their sexual relationship had deteriorated so severely, Mary considered the possibility of an affair with Randy, one of her co-workers, who had let it be known to her that he was "willing" and hinted through crude remarks that he was quite the "stud." This greatly appealed to her fantasies of "wild, uncontrollable passion," which she had read so much about, and her need to have a climax by purely "natural" methods. Certainly she knew that the state her relationship was in with Tom would never produce the passion she so much desired. But Mary was great for double binds. Because of religious prohibitions, she couldn't bring herself to have an extramarital affair.

Finally the only solution seemed to be marriage counseling. Together they went to see their minister, who later consulted with me professionally about the case. With him they shared their desires, fears, and expectations about sex. Mary realized that her unreasonable demands were creating a psychological block for Tom, and that unless she relented and changed her notions of what was "natural" and "unnatural," she ran the risk that Tom would never feel comfortable and spontaneous enough with her to develop a mutually satisfying sexual life. Even after several months of talking openly and frankly about their sexual needs, Mary still was unable to begin experimenting with different sexual techniques. She was too hung up on their being somehow "unnatural." Unfortunately, they failed to follow my recommendation for professional couple's therapy, and a year later they got a divorce.

Sexual Hang-ups

As we have seen, there is a long continuum of sexual hang-ups, from virgin marriages that go unconsummated for years to misinformation about the frequency and intensity of sexual activity. And in between the abstainers and the overindulgers lies a wide range of sexual problems. Frequently, young couples misinterpret their difficulties in physical terms, expecting a physical cause for their frustrations. Rarely is such the case. The physical manifestation is usually covering up an emotional difficulty or psychological block. In the Early Years, sexual activity usually runs into minor and temporary problems, which can return in the Middle Years as full-blown sexual dysfunction, such as frigidity, impotence, and premature ejaculation. For most young couples, the minor manifestations of these problems are simply the "rough spots" of getting sexually acquainted with each other, the rough spots in what is usually a rather pleasant passage of marriage.

But sex is such a controversial issue (and always has been) that it's normal for us to enter marriage with somewhat skewed notions about sexuality. After all, there's so much misinformation floating around and so many impossibly romantic images of the "perfect lover" displayed in the media, that for any of us to escape these distorted perceptions would indeed be a miracle. I suspect that even if you were raised in total isolation from other human beings, you would still grow up with some outrageous sexual fantasy.

The main point about overcoming sexual hang-ups in the Early Years is to remember that some minor difficulties are quite common among married couples. Chances are you entered adulthood with at least a few simplistic or moralistic attitudes about sex that need to be discarded in the real give and take of conjugal lovemaking. Keep in mind that as human beings we are creative and inventive. The circumstances, frequency, and style of making love are open to much innovation. As mates who've sworn to be true to each other for life—or as long as your love shall last—it is your responsibility to be creative, to make it last for life.

The solution to many early problems (and preventing

these from becoming major crises later) is direct confrontation of the issue. Get it out in the open with your partner. There's a tendency to ignore a sexual problem, thinking that it's just yours and that you'll get over it. Sex is a two-way street. Most likely, if you're feeling frustrated, fearful, or guilty over some issue, so is your spouse. Mutual sexual satisfaction is the goal, and it truly must be mutual. It does more harm than good to hide problems or fake enthusiasm. You shouldn't feign enjoyment, happiness, or an orgasm if it really isn't there. Be open, honest, and willing to experiment.

Fidelity

If you were sexually active before you met your spouse, there came a point at which your love for him or her became exclusive. You wrote the "Dear John" letters or their equivalents and called off other relationships. Falling deeply in love with someone, by its very nature, calls forth the deepest human feelings in us, and one of those is fidelity. We are "believers" by nature, and in love we want to believe that we are loved exclusively, for ourselves alone. In short, we are monogamous people.

Much debate has raged over the last two decades about the exclusive nature of sexual relationships. We've experimented with "free and easy, no questions asked" sex; we've had multiple and simultaneous liaisons; we've glorified the "swinging single" and glamorized the uncommitted lifestyle. We've had sequential divorce, communal families, and a host of mix-and-match sexual activities that would have made our stodgy ancestors green with envy—or so we thought.

But it is my firm conviction that a truly good marriage is unalterably a monogamous relationship. Why? If you have developed a complete physical, emotional, and intellectual attachment to another person who feels the same about you, there is simply too much at stake to risk the loss of that person's love. Love must be based on faith and trust, and to jeopardize that faith and trust is to run the risk of losing your partner's love. At times you might rationalize yourself into a position where an affair on the side seems appropriate. We are good rationalizers: "My spouse doesn't understand me. I'm bored. I need to know I'm still sexually attractive to others. I need a change. I can't resist. I'm depressed. My spouse will never know about it. I need to know I can still satisfy someone else," and on and on. But does satisfying any of these urges really justify risking the love and devotion of your own mate? Can any of these passing needs equal the long-range need of having a healthy and intimate relationship to last your whole life through?

In the Early Years you may suddenly wake up one day and notice you have unexplained longings to go to bed with someone new or different. Or you may have entered your marriage with the inherited notion from one of your parents that extramarital flings are common and to be expected. Often the children of unfaithful parents follow in their footsteps, considering infidelity to be the norm. But in either case, whether you half consciously plan to be unfaithful, or whether "lusting after someone else in your heart" pops out of the blue, consider very seriously what you stand to lose: a sexually exclusive relationship that is one-of-a-kind in all the world because it has grown out of a love that will never happen again, a love that is pure and unique to the two of you.

KAREN AND DAVE: LIKE FATHER, LIKE SON

Dave was programmed to follow in his father's footsteps. As a teenager he came to accept what his father's lifestyle implied, namely, men have "wild oats to sow," the supply of which doesn't diminish with matrimony. He believed that, like his father who had outside affairs, he had inherited a "wild nature," and so he was prone to seeing extramarital affairs as natural. He married figuring that sooner or later he would stray. Having been considered a mother's boy most of his life, he may have unconsciously hoped that by adopting his father's behavior toward other women, he could prove to himself that he had, indeed, cut the apron strings that bound him to his mother.

When Karen's suspiciousness over any attention Dave showed other women began to nag at him, he decided that on a business trip he would go "all the way." He reasoned that if he was going to suffer accusations from her anyway, it might as well be for something tangible. His beliefs and attitudes allowed him to have the one-night stand without emotional or psychological hang-ups. He didn't feel at all guilty, not even when Karen spotted the proverbial lipstick on his handkerchief and confronted him with it. He did feel bad that Karen's hysterical response almost ruined their relationship and his one-night's indiscretion might have ruined their marriage.

When they came into therapy with me, they had a lot to work through. Eventually Dave recognized the weak excuse about the "animal drive" he couldn't control for what it really was: a convenient rationalization, but an understandable one based on his upbringing by a father who flaunted his loose ways with other women. In time, he learned that the sex drive could be controlled and channeled within the bounds of the marriage bed. For her part, Karen realized that she would have to accept the fact of infidelity, but that if their marriage was to survive, she would have to move beyond it. Together they came to understand and appreciate each other more fully, and they helped each other become more mature and committed partners.

*   *   *

Sex can be a difficult issue for a young couple to talk about, but not talking about it can create even greater difficulties. If you've picked up any insight from the couples we've considered, it should be that there are many varieties of sexual predicaments. Yours—no matter what it is—needs open discussion with your partner, and possibly a therapist if you hope to resolve it. The passages of sexual fulfillment may not be easy for you, but with love, understanding, and patience, you can progress through them successfully to strengthen and deepen your marriage.

14.

The Passages of Parenting

One of the great passages of marriage is the arrival of the first child. Whatever your lifestyle was like before the child arrived, it is bound to undergo transition in the first few days and weeks after the baby is born. The first child is the *great divide* in marriage. If you have had your first baby, you know how steep that *divide* can be. If you have not had your first child yet, ask your friends who have, or observe for yourselves how their lives have changed. Suddenly there is little time for bridge, weekend golf, or spontaneous sex. Time and money are now allocated with greater concern. Old routines are altered. There is less time to spend with your friends and former families.

Ideally a couple should have two or three years to work through their Acquaintance Phase passages. Becoming husband and wife and getting to know each other on a daily basis is a major adjustment. Becoming father and mother is another distinct and separate adjustment. When the two are made within the same year, the relationship between the married couple is unduly strained. If the couple is particularly young, in their early twenties, they might also be making the transition from living at home to moving out and living with someone new. The old family ties are loosened, and the family members you used to rely on are no longer around.

In the best of all possible worlds, therefore, a newly married couple should have time to assume the roles of wife and husband without the added complication of assuming parenthood. Changing roles requires time and patience to learn the ropes. No couple moves from being friends and lovers into being husband and wife without a certain amount of stress and worry. Learning to live with each other "full-time" means discovering the habits and routines with which each feels comfortable and secure. Only then, after two or three years, can you more easily make the transition from being husband and wife to that of being father and mother.

Even in marriages involving older couples, the Acquaintance Phase is crucial. It doesn't matter whether you're twenty-eight, thirty-five, or forty-four, learning how to live with another human being with whom you hope to establish a lifelong relationship requires a few years' grace period. Rushing into parenthood is like skating on thin ice. You hope there is some support beneath you, namely, a sound marital bond, but such a bond, like ice, takes time to form.

A clear example of why this grace period is so crucial can be seen in what happens to many men when they become fathers: they become jealous. The woman who had been the new father's lover and constant companion now has less time to spend with him: less time, less energy, less concentration. Even making love can become an exercise in strategy to find the right time without an unexpected interruption. Whether the new baby is a boy or a girl, it becomes a rival, another suitor, a threat to the comfortable relationship the father had developed with his bride. The truth is that she is no longer just a bride or a wife: she is a mother.

Even if you are in your second marriage, with children from your first—the yours and mine situation—you will still need a grace period to get to know each other. And in addition, it will take time for the two sets of children to become acquainted with each other. Even if the kids are not all living with you, they deserve a chance to adjust to their new siblings on neutral ground where both sets of children are treated as equals. If they must compete with a new kid—who is not "yours" or "mine," but "ours"—resentment over the new marriage can grow as the older children try to maintain their birthrights in the face of an unwanted threat. It's hard enough for children to accept their new parent and new siblings without having to deal with the additional rivalry that a small baby can create.

Unexpected pregnancies can occur any time in a marriage, but in the Early Years, they are frequently due to plain ignorance. I've known couples who decided not to worry about birth control until after the wedding, went on their honeymoon, and came home pregnant. Nothing could be more disastrous for the first few months of a new marriage, especially between young people. We saw in the case of Marianne and Tony, who had to get married, how the presence of a baby drastically impinged on their ability to learn how to be husband and wife to each other. All the problems we've talked about are greatly increased when the new baby was not wanted or expected at that time.

Looking Ahead

Every passage of marriage is easier when there is open communication between the wife and husband. Becoming parents is one of those events that demands early and frequent dialogue. The basic issues are: How will the baby change the marriage? How will our roles be altered? What changes in our daily lives are we willing to make? What sacrifices are we prepared to accept in order to have a child? Too often couples rush into parenthood without a clear idea of how each partner feels about the dozens of changes that the new baby will require. The more realistic you are about what will happen and how each of you will react, the better off you'll be to meet the challenges and crises that lie ahead.

For example, if the wife works, what will happen to her job or career? Will she quit for good and be willing to devote her life to being a mother? Will she want to return to work? After how long? Part-time or full-time? Who will care for the baby during the day? How involved will the father be? Will he be expected to take time off from work or hobbies to care for the baby? Will one of the grandparents be involved in day care? What luxuries or, possibly, necessities are the two of you willing to give up should the baby prove to be more expensive than you anticipated? How will you make it clear to the grandparents what their roles will be? How will you keep them from intruding and causing the havoc that we looked at in the section on family and friends?

These and similar questions should be talked over at length before the baby arrives. In general, the better prepared you are for any unexpected occurrences, the better you will be able to handle this passage as a team and fortify your marriage. As in all things, you should be in agreement on the issue of boundaries, presenting a united front to grandparents, friends, and acquaintances about the changes you will make in your lives now that you are parents, and the extent to which outsiders can enter the family orb.

One of the major power issues that should be settled as much as possible before the baby comes is the manner in which you will divide up the various responsibilities of caring for the baby. Experience has shown that the more intimately involved the father is in the mundane aspects of child care, the better the relationship between father and child will be. Feeding, changing diapers, watching while the baby sleeps, being there when the baby wakes up crying—all these duties that were traditionally the mother's responsibilities are now being shared by fathers, and a healthier father-child relationship results. Not only does such concern on the part of the father free the mother from having to shoulder the sole burden of caring for a newborn baby, but the extra energy she experiences usually carries over into the husband-wife relationship and improves the couple's intimacy.

MAGGIE AND CLIFF: SEPARATE ACCOUNTS, SEPARATE PRIORITIES

Maggie, one of my "Talknet" listeners, called to tell me how she had resolved her situation. From everything she had ever said about having children to her husband Cliff, he assumed that she looked forward to being a mother. And she did. But what she never hinted to Cliff was that she also wanted to continue being a private secretary for the corporation in which she had worked for the past five years. In all their long talks (of which they had many), both before they married and before Megan arrived, the subject of whether Maggie would go back to work never came up. Maggie just assumed that Cliff knew she would want to, and Cliff just assumed that being a mother was her life's ambition. Shortly after Megan was born, Maggie began making comments about how they would arrange for day care when she went back to work part-time. Cliff secretly hoped that as Maggie grew attached to Megan, she would change her mind.

But in six months, Maggie was ready to return to work. When they scouted around for day-care services, the question of financing bred an argument. Because Maggie commanded a good salary, the couple had kept separate accounts. Cliff, an account executive with a major advertising agency, did not need his wife's income, and Maggie was happy to have it at her own disposal. Actually, she couldn't understand why Cliff objected to paying for a sitter when they were financially so well-off. Finally Cliff agreed to Maggie's going back to work only if *she* paid for the sitter. Maggie thought Cliff was being petty about the whole matter, but decided it was easier to give in, even though she thought it foolish of him.

They hired an elderly woman from a home day-care service, and Maggie paid her. After four months, however, Maggie realized that her salary was not stretching as far as it used to; the sitter's fee ate into a large part of it. Maggie asked Cliff to share in the expense, and he did so grudgingly. Because he resented the fact that his wife had returned to work—he felt she was not living up to her duties as a mother—Cliff began to express his resentment by budgeting too severely. They stopped going to the theater as often as they liked. He convinced Maggie that they should replan their summer vacation to Brazil. Realizing what Cliff was up to, Maggie began to burn inside. She seemed trapped in a hopeless situation. She didn't want to be a full-time mother, she didn't want to pay for the sitter entirely out of her own income, and yet, she didn't want to sacrifice needlessly the activities they both enjoyed and looked forward to.

However, she didn't want to raise the issue and reopen the old argument.

Finally, a solution occurred like a miracle. Cliff's parents moved out of town. Maggie and Cliff had decided earlier that they would not play favorites with the grandparents or create situations where one or the other set of grandparents would feel left out. With only Maggie's parents in town, she felt it wouldn't alienate Cliff's parents if her mother sat in with Megan on the days that she worked. Cliff thought that was reasonable, and so they dispensed with the professional sitter altogether.

And as Maggie had suspected, Cliff reworked his budget figures and decided they could go to Brazil after all.

*   *   *

Although Maggie and Cliff had their problems, they did have one thing going for them: solid boundaries. They were always in agreement about what to tell their families and to what extent to let their families intrude in their marriage. Whatever you decide about having babies or not having babies, you will have to inform your parents and siblings and offer some sort of explanation. As concerned relatives who love you, they will expect to know "what's going on." Of course, you don't have to give them all the reasons, but you do owe them some kind of explanation they can accept.

Birth Control You Can Live and Love With

By now there is irrefutable evidence that a brown sock over the bedpost, making love at the foot of the bed, and withdrawal don't work. The evidence consists of the hundreds of babies born with these types of birth control! Folk methods aside, too many people are still confused, misinformed, or ignorant about safe, reliable methods of birth control. Your first duty is to become as well-informed as possible about the options, and then discuss quite frankly what you each feel about them. If you want to have a satisfying sexual relationship and a sure method of contraception, you need to agree upon the type of birth control you will use. When one partner feels guilty, unnatural, or uncomfortable using a particular method, it is bound to harm the overall relationship and render lovemaking unfulfilling.

An attitude that ignites many arguments between husbands and wives is the notion that "It's *your* problem, not mine!" A major crisis can erupt during a discussion of simple methods of contraception or surgery for either partner. You should never foist the problem off on your mate. It is not hers or his alone. It is both of yours. And together you need to consider and talk through the various options. Choosing a method of birth control must be a joint decision with a joint resolution by both of you to be faithful to the method you select. Also you must share any changing needs or difficulties that arise in using it. It is never fair to harbor the attitude that your mate should be solely responsible for limiting the number of children that will be born to both of you. Just as both partners shoulder the responsibilities after the child is born, so must you share the responsibility of planning for that birth.

STEWART AND RHODA: IT'S OUR PROBLEM

Together Stewart and Rhoda decided to postpone children for a number of years after their marriage so that Rhoda could finish graduate school and launch a career as a nutritionist. Stewart's own career goals coincided well with his wife's, since he felt he would have very little free time during the first few years of medical practice. Coming from strict religious backgrounds, they decided to postpone sexual relations until after they were married; so Rhoda didn't begin using the pill until two months before the wedding (to ensure that she was on cycle before their much-awaited honeymoon).

Shortly after they returned and settled down together, Rhoda began experiencing some side effects from the pill. She gained ten pounds and became exceptionally moody. Concern over her self-image would have been enough to make her moody, but the pill worked as a catalyst causing even more severe mood shifts than she was used to. The situation produced considerable tension in their relationship to the point that Stewart wondered what happened to "the girl that he married." Rhoda didn't seem to be the same person, and Stewart began to doubt the wisdom of their having married in the first place.

Rhoda's gynecologist, who consulted with me on the case, advised her to discontinue the pill. So the decision of what to use in place of it raised an issue neither Rhoda nor Stewart had thought about, both assuming that oral contraceptives would work for them. Rhoda didn't want to use an IUD because of reports from several of her female friends about the discomfort and inflammation they caused. She considered a diaphragm too "premeditated" and feared it would destroy the spontaneity of their lovemaking. Her preference was to use the rhythm method because she had extremely regular menstrual cycles and to "make do" with condoms during the fertile days of the month. Stewart, on the other hand, had his mind made up. To him, IUDs were the most reasonable method next to the pill, and in the midst of a prickly argument over it, he accused her of shirking her responsibility. "It's your problem, anyway," he threw at her.

When they reached this impasse, Rhoda returned to her gynecologist who impressed upon her the need to reach a mutually agreed upon decision and suggested he talk with both of them. Over several meetings they aired their feelings and came to understand their individual hangups about various methods of birth control. Stewart came to realize that he had as much responsibility for this as did Rhoda, and they decided to experiment with several methods to see which they could live with. Thus an issue which had turned into a crisis for them and disrupted their life was resolved successfully. It became a positive passage into a deeper understanding and love for each other, which in turn helped move them through their Early Years with greater ease.

Labor Pains: The Division of Labor

Biologically, giving birth is a woman's responsibility, nature giving her the key role. And historically, cultural attitudes have isolated the father from the entire experience of delivery, so that we have come to accept the familiar image of the new father pacing the floor of the waiting room while mother brings a new child into the world in the delivery room. Hence, millions of fathers have literally waited while a most momentous marital passage occurred just a few rooms away! Happily, we are breaking out of those stereotyped roles, and more fathers demand an active part in the delivery process. Recent experience has shown that when both mother and father participate, everyone profits: the husband, the wife, the newborn babe.

Not every expectant father, however, eagerly looks forward to this new responsibility.

TROY AND NANCY: IRRATIONAL FEARS

Troy and Nancy were married four years before they had their first baby. Even before the marriage, Troy had expressed hopes that he would be able to accompany Nancy into the delivery room and assist her during the birth. But in the intervening years, Troy's attitude changed. His own queasiness over hospitals and pain weakened his decision to be with his wife; and three months into the pregnancy, the wife of a member of his bowling team died in childbirth. One evening Troy announced to Nancy that he had "reservations" about being with her, although he didn't spell out his reasons.

Nancy grew depressed in the days following Troy's announcement. She had been looking forward to having a child with Troy's support and help. All her girl friends were having babies using natural childbirth. Their stories about how wonderful the experience was with their husbands present made Nancy feel that all her dreams about becoming a mother would be ruined. She even began fantasizing about Troy not taking an interest in the baby after it was born. She ultimately wondered how much she could trust Troy's commitment even to their marriage. Furthermore, by nature Nancy was insecure and overly dependent upon Troy. As the delivery date grew closer, she panicked.

Nancy spoke to my obstetrician colleague about her fear of delivering the baby alone, without Troy there to help her. She also indicated that the tension created by their divergent needs was causing arguments over other issues related to the baby, such as finances, the involvement of in-laws, even what to name the baby. I advised her doctor to ask Troy to join Nancy during her next few visits, probe with them the roots of their individual fears, and explore ways to get them out of their predicament. This helped Troy to realize that his fear of Nancy dying in childbirth was unrealistic, that very few women with Nancy's good health had serious complications. The fact that her pregnancy was perfectly normal also helped to quell his fears. Furthermore, he came to realize that if Nancy did indeed have a complicated delivery, it would probably be due to the emotional state she was in having to go through it alone. Without him at her side, it could very well be difficult because of her lack of confidence in herself and her reliance upon Troy to give her moral support.

After several visits, Troy understood the situation much better. Nancy, too, learned that Troy's refusal to be with her was due to his own fears and misconceptions, rather than to anything concerning his love for her or his commitment to being married and having a child. So resolving this crisis together became a successful passage that helped prepare them for the birth of little Belinda.

Troy and Nancy used the Lamaze method of natural delivery, which gives the father an important role. It is an excellent experience for young couples. The training that both mother and father receive can deepen intimacy during the gestation period, when the mother might withdraw into her own needs and concerns, and the father might feel shut out from an event that should be one of the most important in his life. While attending classes, the couple has time together to think about their child, talk over fears and worries, and make plans for the new member of their family.

When my wife Diane and I had our children, we used the Lamaze method. It was wonderful. Even though I was trained as a physician and knew the technical aspects of pregnancy and childbirth, and had even delivered babies in medical school, it was a new experience for me to share this passage in our lives. Of course, natural childbirth is not for every woman, but if, as a couple, you choose it, it gives you both the opportunity of being as intimately involved as possible.

I also recommend having the baby in a hospital that has "rooming-in" facilities. These are rooms where the mother and newborn babe can stay together until they leave the hospital. In traditional hospitals, where a woman has only certain "visiting hours" with her baby, the mother and child leave the hospital as strangers. The additional time the two share together while "rooming-in" creates a strong bond between them starting during the first hours of the infant's life. Also the father, the siblings, and other family and friends can see mother and baby together in a more natural situation.

*   *   *

So as the Settling-In Phase of your marriage comes to a close, it is likely that you will have gone through the marvelous passage of becoming parents. You may have actually crossed it two or three times by then! Hopefully you will have established routines that keep the family running smoothly and will have grown accustomed to your role as parents. Marriage itself can be a marvelous way of life; and nowhere do you experience the joy and wonder of it more intensely than when bringing new children into the world, so they too can share the joys of your life.

15.

The Passages of Illness and Change

Many people go into marriage with the unspoken assumption that their spouses will remain forever the young, carefree, dynamic, exuberant people they were when they fell in love with each other for the first time. Only to the young man on Keats's Grecian Urn can we say, "Bold Lover . . . She cannot fade . . . Forever wilt thou love, and she be fair." Real living people, not etched in marble, are not "forever panting, forever young." No, we age, grow older and saggier, our bodies decline, we lose our hair, acquire wrinkles. The person we marry at twenty-five will not be the exact same person at forty or fifty. Not even at thirty. Change touches all of us physically and emotionally. Intellect, too, undergoes transformation. Interests change; we acquire new attitudes and different values. However long you have been married, even if it is only a few years, you are basing your relationship on a shaky foundation if you expect your spouse to remain the same as he or she is now. The decrees of nature will not allow it. To be alive is to change.

You Used to Be So . . .

Neither individuals nor relationships are static. You as a couple and your love for each other are in a continual state of change and evolution. As you mature, you hope that your spouse will complement your growth. And as you age, you hope it will be hand in hand. Unfortunately, for some couples, this does not happen. One ages more quickly than the other. One acquires new interests and activities that the other does not enjoy. One becomes more conservative and serious; the other stays frivolous and carefree.

Frequently, "being out of sync" with each other is noticed in the first few years of married life. Couples who are caught unaware by this might begin to doubt the wisdom of having married. Especially in the Early Years this does come as a shock. You may have expected that much later in your lives you would change at different rates. But so soon? Yes, even in the first year or two. One partner grows psychologically or matures emotionally at a more rapid pace than the other. Usually the partner who notices the change in his or her mate expresses it with something like, "He's changed so much since we married," "He's much more serious and ambitious," "She's not as fun-loving as she used to be," "She used to be giddy and spontaneous." And these comments always end with the somber refrain, "But now . . ."

Statements such as these usually indicate that one spouse has been growing and maturing while the other is staying the same. In some cases a husband may actually fear the changes in his wife, or a wife may have no respect for the way her husband is turning out. To be healthy emotionally, we must grow and develop throughout our lives. If we can't do it together with the person we love, we begin to change— and live—separately. And separation seems the logical choice.

HARRIET AND ROB: GROWING OUT OF MARRIAGE

Shortly after little Bobbie was born, Harriet and Rob agreed that she would go back to work for the public relations firm she had worked for before they were married.

She did so, and for the first time in the seven years that they knew each other, Rob wondered if he really understood the woman he was in love with.

Because of a death at the company, Harriet was promoted rapidly to a supervisory position, which she filled efficiently and enthusiastically. As she received praise both from her boss and the people in her department, she developed an increasing sense of self-esteem and self-worth. She became more decisive and independent, characteristics that began to spill over into her homelife with Rob and the baby. Whereas before, Harriet used to ask Rob to make simple decisions and give her advice about how something should be done, now she was taking situations into her own hands, making choices and executing them, sometimes without even informing Rob, much less seeking his advice. As she became more her own woman, Rob felt that she was excluding him from her life. Actually he was letting himself be excluded. But of course, being emotionally threatened, he could not see it that way.

When Harriet talked about the camaraderie she enjoyed with her male colleagues, Rob grew jealous. He suspected that Harriet was sexually attracted to one in particular, and he even hinted that perhaps something was "going on between them." He dropped none-too-subtle hints that their lives would be better, if Harriet quit her job and devoted herself to being a full-time mother. When she refused, he jumped to the irrational conclusion that she had fallen out of love with him. From there, it was easy for him to justify having an extramarital relationship himself, since he was convinced that Harriet was having one and that she didn't care about him or Bobbie anymore.

Over the next two stormy years nothing Harriet did could persuade Rob that she still loved him and the child, but that she needed to keep her job if she were to develop and mature in ways that would tap her skills and talents. So finally Rob left her, convinced that he was in love with his secretary.

Unfortunately, when Harriet called me on "Talknet" asking for help, the only advice I could give her was that she try to find a man who was not threatened by her emotional growth and her success. Since Rob was not interested in any kind of professional help, Harriet had little choice but to move on and try to start over with someone else.

*   *   *

Outgrowing each other, as in the case of Harriet and Rob, is one way that a couple can draw apart from each other, even to the point of ending their marriage. In cases like this, neither person feels in control. The partner who is maturing and evolving into a fuller and more fulfilled human being cannot imagine stopping and remaining stagnant in a less exciting or stimulating role. The one who is changing less or not at all feels completely out of step with his or her mate and perceives the relationship as turning into something with which he or she simply cannot live. Both perceive the other's wishes as totally intolerable.

The Pygmalion Problem

In George Bernard Shaw's *Pygmalion,* and then in the musical version, *My Fair Lady,* we see what can happen when one partner decides the other is stupid, ugly, uncouth, dumb, sloppy, irresponsible, or just plain "wrong." Then the course of action is to transform the loved one into a more "acceptable" version of what he or she is. Usually it involves more than getting the other to pronounce words correctly or learning how to handle a teacup at a party. Frequently, the reformer wants to change basic personality traits in the other. While it's true that we all have rough edges that need smoothing down at times and must rely on our mates to help us in this, a total overhaul can be threatening indeed. It also suggests the often unspoken demand: "Either change your habits, or I won't love you anymore."

JUDY AND CHARLIE: IF ONLY YOU WERE ... WELL ,... PERFECT!

Charlie was not perfect. Not yet anyway. When she married him, Judy decided that he was a "diamond in the rough," and if she worked on it, someday he would be a real gem. Thus Judy set out to remake Charlie into the man of her dreams.

Charlie wasn't all that bad. After graduating from high school and with the financial backing of an elderly uncle, he opened a small sporting goods store in town. A topnotch athlete who had made a local reputation playing varsity football, Charlie quickly turned the store into a thriving enterprise. Business flourished, and at twenty-six when Judy met him, Charlie was one of the most eligible bachelors in the area.

Shortly after they were married, Judy's true feelings about Charlie's manners and personality traits came out. She had very definite ideas about how Charlie should change. His dress, his language, the way he related to people, even his continuing interest in sports and athletics of every type needed to be revamped. In spite of his being six years her senior, she was determined to "give him some class." She bought clothes for him that he didn't like; she corrected his imperfect grammar in front of their friends; she criticized his use of slang and slightly off-color terms; and she fretted and pouted if he didn't take a strong enough interest in what she wanted to do, such as go to concerts, visit art shows, or listen to classical music. No matter what he did, Judy always compared him unfavorably to someone else— her brothers, a college friend, her own father. Finally Charlie lamented, "I can't stand it any longer. No matter what I do, it's wrong."

They came to me for couple's therapy during their Settling-In Phase to try to iron out their differences, but each was adamant. For Charlie, his personality was at stake. He didn't want to change and saw no reason to, since what he was had provided him with a good life of friends, activities, career, and financial comfort. Furthermore, after almost ten years of Judy's harping on how he was not the man she would like to have married, his anger was so intense that he found it difficult to forgive her. On Judy's part, she saw no reason for not trying to make Charlie into the best of all possible husbands. She couldn't understand what was wrong with trying to get someone to be perfect. I worked with them for several months to no avail. Finally they decided that the "perfect" solution was an amicable separation and divorce with joint custody of their two children.

* * *

So the question is: Should change occur of its own accord or be under our control? Both. Change is important. We must encourage it in our spouses in a manner consistent with the ways we ourselves are changing. But we must respect the true core of our partner's personality and not destroy vital aspects of his or her character. The best tactic is to channel both your changes in a parallel direction as much as possible, always realizing that you don't have complete control over another's natural growth and development. If you yourself are not changing, but believe that your spouse is, it is time to start looking at yourself to find out what has happened to you, or what has *not* happened to you! Why are you standing still when the world around is moving forward? Why are you stagnating when your wife, husband, or children are growing into more mature human beings?

If the two of you are changing out of sync with each other, you should initiate an open and frank discussion about why this is happening. Each of you should make a list of the ways you believe the other has changed, the ways you have changed, and the ways you now differ. Use these lists to explore the changes in yourselves. Try to understand why you are changing in uncomplementary and incompatible ways. Then try to negotiate some adjustments to get yourselves more aligned. A healthy relationship not only tolerates appropriate change but thrives on it.

In Sickness and in Health

Illness and death are two topics furthest from the minds of a newly married couple. Traditionally, people marry in the prime of their youth, when the realities of taking ill, becoming disabled for life, and dying have not made an impact upon their lives. We all expect to be reasonably healthy throughout most of our lives, live to a ripe old age, and meet our inevitable deaths in some peaceful manner to which we give little thought during courtship, marriage, and the first busy years of living together as husband and wife.

The shock of marrying someone in robust health who deteriorates into a chronic or disabling illness within a few short years after marriage is truly traumatic. To be faced with the necessity of living with and caring for an invalid or semi-invalid is a test of personal character that can be utterly overwhelming. And yet it happens. When it does, the healthy partner needs to reaffirm his or her commitment to the marriage and be ready to live a life of self-sacrifice for the good of the other and their relationship. If there are children present, the sacrifice becomes even greater. Living with a disabled partner requires continuous adaptation, for it is a crisis unlike others that can be conquered and overcome. The problem is never conquered, nor does it go away. It becomes a reality you must live with and adjust to day after day. Making the initial adjustment of accepting this critical situation can be a very painful passage for both people.

When serious illness strikes, every role is turned inside out. The wife may now become a wage earner if she has not previously worked. If her job was part-time, she might now have to find full-time employment to pay for the medical bills that the illness will incur. If the mother becomes disabled, then the father will become not only the primary breadwinner, but the major child-raiser as well. Again, there will be added costs, if the husband's job necessitates day care for young children in addition to medical assistance for the wife. Everything falls upon the healthy spouse's shoulders and the responsibilities are indeed enormous. Only a marriage based on a solid foundation of love and commitment can survive the years ahead, years that will not be normal ones in comparison to friends' and families'.

*   *   *

Much can happen in the Early Years of a marriage that may cause a couple to wonder if all the happiness they had dreamed about was in vain—from meddling parents to sexual incompatibility to chronic illness. And yet happiness is as much a reality as disappointments and crises. Through all the early problems that reach crisis proportion, a man and a woman can deepen their commitment to each other and renew their pledge of love and fidelity so that they work their way through transitional times and cross the marital passages with renewed hope. True happiness is not the same as the first thrills and novelties that come when two people begin living together. Moving in with each other or tying the knot is indeed thrilling; but as you progress through the years, you find that staying together and helping each other resolve personal and marital issues create the real happiness, a happiness not based on external events that come and go, but an abiding happiness that rises from the love inside and the desire to live for the good of the other. It becomes that joyful participation in the sufferings of life that pulls you closer together and eases the passages from one period of your life to the next.

PART III

THE MIDDLE YEARS

16.

Introduction

There's no warning. One day you realize it's happened. You've entered the Middle Years of your marriage. For the majority of couples, the Middle Years begin when you suddenly notice your lives are almost totally taken up with your children's needs. This is usually after about ten years of marriage. At the start of the Child-full Phase you are still hopeful and optimistic. You enjoy the challenge of parenting. But eventually, the newness wears off; you are confronted by the financial impact of raising a family; you worry about how your family unit relates to your in-laws and relatives; you feel the impact of children on your sexual relationship, and perhaps on your careers; and you wonder about the ways the two of you will change in the midst of all this. You may struggle with mid-life issues, perhaps have a genuine mid-life crisis, or grow depressed over the impact of menopause.

During the second half of the Middle Years, after perhaps twenty years of marriage, you'll start to enter the Us-Again Phase, when the children emerge from adolescence, enter early adulthood, and leave home. Then the two of you have the chance to rediscover your relationship and once again enjoy the luxury of paying more attention to each other's needs than the needs and demands of your offspring.

The flavor of the Childless Middle Years for the couple who have either opted not to have children or who have

111

been unable to have children is, of course, quite different. For them life is busy, balancing careers, hobbies, and social responsibilities with the needs and demands of being, for each other, the primary focal point of their lives. Pressures to succeed professionally may be so great that they don't pay enough attention to each other's personal requirements. They may become snarled in tensions over dependence and independence in their relationship. I have known a number of such couples who seemed to be hit harder by their own mid-life issues than were their friends with children. Perhaps the pressure of children deflects some of our attention from personal mid-life concerns. Because most couples are often slightly out of phase chronologically as they approach mid-life, it's especially important for Childless-Phase couples to be aware of the onset of these issues and confront them together openly, honestly, and directly as a way to lessen or possibly even to avoid the likelihood of any major crisis.

Statistically, more marriages go on the rocks during the Middle Years than during any other period of marriage. Many couples who barely limped through their Early Years become overwhelmed by the pressures of the Child-full Phase. They find that all the negative passages from unsuccessfully resolved earlier issues come back to haunt them, even to destroy their marriage. The more smoothly you handled the issues of your Early Years passages, the better prepared you'll be to deal with the passages of your Middle Years. Sometimes, a mid-life crisis overwhelms one of the partners and drives him or her from the relationship because the couple hasn't learned how to support and help each other through personal problems. Ironically, the divorce often comes as a surprise, because the couple thought they were basically happy. When we explore this situation, however, we find that there had been a number of unresolved or poorly resolved issues from earlier years. While none of these alone was overwhelming, together they had the ultimate effect of building up pressure, which drove the mid-life partner out of the marriage. Obviously, the more solid the relationship, the better prepared the partners are to deal with the pressures of an individual crisis that may occur at mid-life or as one of them approaches old age at the end of the Middle Years. So again, the principle holds true: dealing successfully with each issue that confronts your relationship, no matter how large or how small, builds up a series of positive passages that provide the experience you need for the later passages in your marriage.

17.

The Passages of Family and Friends

As transitions from one relatively stable period of your marriage to another, Middle Years passages usually involve the destabilizing influence of growing children in your Child-full Phase. And how they grow! You might begin to think that there are no stable periods in a household with children and adolescents. But you'll see that everything is relative, and the issues that unsettle family life can be met and turned into successful phases that lead to the next stage of growth and development, both in the kids and in your own love for each other.

Let's look at three common boundary issues that usually occur during the Middle Years: the doting grandparents, the continuing feud of in-laws and its effects on growing children, and the problem of what can happen when your friends' children are your children's friends.

Doting Grandparents

I've come to the conclusion that most grandparents seriously believe that hidden somewhere between the lines of the U.S. Constitution is a statement guaranteeing their inalienable right to spoil their grandchildren! Thinking back on my own childhood, I now suspect that my grandmother intentionally saw to it that something wonderful was cooking in the oven every time I was brought over, so that the delicious aroma that spread through her big house would subtly lure me into the delights of "spoildom." It was fun! And grandparents are supposed to be fun. In a close family, kids learn early that these four lovable people are somehow their parents' parents (exactly how is not very clear to a small child!), and that they are special! Grandparents can give the attention, love, understanding, and pampering that children can't always get from their parents. Grandparents should be everything that we as kids wanted them to be. If the world consisted of just grandparents and grandchildren, there would probably be no problems.

But there *you* are. You are both child yourself *and* parent. You're in the middle whether you like it or not. And in spite of what your parents think is their inalienable right, you, not they, have the final word on how to raise your children. Grandparents, even with their pockets stuffed with candy, should never be allowed to undermine your own position. Whether they approve or not of your methods of discipline, their responsibility is to support you. They should never sabotage the limits set for your children by reinforcing inappropriate behavior or by becoming a third party that your children use to manipulate you.

This doesn't mean that grandma can't be frivolous at times and that grandpa can't be lavish and extravagant. But you must have a clear understanding with them that they are to acquiesce in your household rules and follow your directions in regards to what little Mikey or Susie may and may not do, have, or say. In order to gain their support, you and your spouse must present a united front to both sets of grandparents. Be unified, but also respectful. Remember, they did raise you, and probably didn't do a half bad job! Try not to get into a standoff with grandparents because this always seems to drive a wedge into your relationship as husband and wife. And this has the potential of splitting the relationships you have established between you and your children. If one of you agrees with the grandparents and the other disagrees, it is better to try and work out your differences between the two of you in private rather than in an extended family powwow with the grandparents. This avoids the potential problem of three against one, which can obviously sow seeds of discord in your marriage.

LINDA AND BERT: DOES MOTHER KNOW BEST?

Little Missy's grandmother gave her a number of expensive outfits for her entry into first grade. What seemed like a simple act of love and generosity on the part of Linda's mother was, in fact, the straw that almost broke the camel's back. Obviously, a marriage doesn't fall to pieces because of one incident, but this was simply the most recent episode in a series of problems that had been growing for several years. It was the incident that convinced Linda to call me on "Talknet."

Linda and Bert had been married twelve years, were in their early thirties, and had two children, Gary, age nine, and Missy, age six. Linda's mother lived only thirty miles away and had always been a devoted and bubbly grandmother to Gary before Missy was born. But when Missy arrived, grandmother saw her chance to "raise Linda" all over again. Linda had been an only child, and although her mother enjoyed spending time with Gary, she didn't feel she really knew how to raise a little boy. But Missy was her chance! She became almost exclusively devoted to Missy and felt compelled to give Linda unwanted advice on how to raise her.

As Gary got older, he quickly perceived that he was not his grandma's favorite since Missy received all of grandmother's attention. Naturally, this increased sibling rivalry between the kids, and Gary began picking on Missy mercilessly. To make matters worse, Bert recognized the problem and brought it up to Linda, who didn't think that her mother's favoritism was harmful. She sympathized with her mother feeling more comfortable with a granddaughter and pointed out to Bert how much Missy looked and acted as Linda did when she was a child. Linda thought it natural for her mother to favor Missy.

So when she shared their family dilemma with me, I

helped her to realize that their crisis was more than just a doting grandmother. It included sibling rivalry, tension between Linda and Bert, and the necessity of performing a "mother-ectomy." Linda wrote me a followup letter saying that she realized how her mother's actions, even though well-intentioned, were dividing her children and alienating her husband. After discussing it, she and Bert decided to set some reasonable limits on what grandmother could give and do for Missy. They also pointed out to her how she was losing the love of Gary and would continue to do so as he got older and understood even better how he played second fiddle to his younger sister.

Being a reasonable woman, Linda's mother understood that she would have to change if she wanted to maintain harmony within her family. She proceeded to make a concerted effort to abide by Linda and Bert's wishes. Within half a year, they noticed that Gary was much less aggressive and competitive with Missy, and they themselves were having fewer spats. Tension in the household had decreased a great deal simply because grandmother's good intentions were curtailed.

*   *   *

A major point to remember in dealing with grandparents is this: They have accumulated wisdom and understanding over the years and can make valuable contributions to your family whether they provide an ear for you to test ideas on, a shoulder to cry on occasionally, or companionship for your children. You should value their advice whether it seems appropriate or not. They are a rich resource for you and your children that may become invaluable as the years progress. But no matter what, you and your spouse must have the last word when it comes to decisions about raising your children, and grandparents must defer to your judgments. They will always believe that they have the right to influence your thinking (and they do to a certain extent); but once you have decided matters, it is their obligation to abide by your wishes.

And the Feud Goes On

If your in-laws are still battling as your marriage goes into the Middle Years, chances are this will go on until they die! But now you have another unsettling issue to confront and work through, namely, the role your teenage children will play in the family feud. As your children mature, they will understand more thoroughly why your two sets of parents don't see eye to eye, and the grandparents may look at this adolescent period as their last chance to "prove their point" or enlist your teenage son or daughter into their camp.

In the best of all possible families, teenagers should stay out of their grandparents' problems. In most families, they don't. Your role as parents is crucial in helping your children understand why their grandparents act so childishly. By now, you and your spouse should have come to some decision about which set of grandparents is in the wrong, emotionally disturbed, or irrationally misguided. If you have done so, draw the family boundaries to isolate them as much as possible. They have no right to disrupt your family's peace and harmony. Explain to your children the issues that make their grandparents feud, and explain to them why you and your partner believe the "disturbed" set of grandparents is wrong. Teenage children understand better than you might think. Be honest without trying to undermine their love for grandma or grandpa.

CARLA AND ROGER: PLAYING TUG-OF-WAR

Carla's parents were college graduates. Roger's had high-school diplomas. That, more than anything, was the crux of their disliking for each other. Carla and Roger had grown up in the same New Hampshire town, but Carla's family always considered Roger to be from the wrong side of town because he grew up in a working-class neighborhood. It was never concealed from Carla that her parents and relatives thought she had married beneath her. When Roger and

Carla had both sets of parents over on Thanksgiving, Christmas, and other holidays, an iciness always hung in the air regardless of the temperature in the dining room. Roger had become a successful businessman, so money and standard of living were never an issue. But Carla's parents continued to consider him "lower class" and his parents practically immigrants, even though they had been born here.

When their son Ricky was thirteen, both sets of grandparents tried to influence his decision about high school. Carla's thought Ricky should go to a private boys' school to prepare him for college. Roger's wanted him to go to the local high school where Roger and his father had graduated. Typical grandparent-type questions such as "Where do you want to go to school?" and "What do you want to be when you grow up?" led to inflammatory arguments peppered with snide comments whenever such questions came up at family gatherings. Carla and Roger could see both sides of their parents' arguments and understood the roots of their mutual disliking, but they tended to side with their respective parents, which created an impasse for them. Eventually they came to me for couple's therapy to get a fresh perspective on the matter.

In four hours of couple's crisis intervention they realized that more important than either grandparents' or their own positions on the question of Ricky's education was Ricky's position. What did *he* want to do? As time for a decision drew closer, it became obvious that Ricky wanted to go to the local high school rather than off to prep school. At this point, Roger and Carla realized that if her parents continued to pressure Ricky or bribe him into changing his mind, they would be in the wrong. Of course, Carla's parents didn't give up so easily. They continued to make life unpleasant for everyone and dropped doomsday statements about Ricky ruining his life or missing important career decisions if he didn't go to a better school. At that point Carla and Roger confronted her parents and laid down the law. They were not to bring up the subject of school or Ricky's career while he was in high school, but to support Ricky in whatever choices he made. Of course, Carla's parents didn't like it, but they knew that if they were to continue as active members of the extended family, they would have to abide by their children's decision.

Your Friends and Their Children

It seems that some neighborhoods are swarming with children and station wagons; others have none. And a curious observation is that the children—and the station wagons! —all seem to be the same age! It's great for kids to grow up in residential areas where young couples raise families at about the same time. There will be plenty of other kids to play and fight with over the years. It's a children's paradise!

But one of the most common problems in family neighborhoods of this type is what to do when your children's best friends are the children of your best friends with whom you don't share the same philosophy about raising children. Even the best of friends can disagree, and coming to terms with that and accepting it can be a trying passage, one that needs to be met if the following years are to be lived in relative harmony. For the most part, children accept the fact that different families run on different sets of rules: "David's parents let him cross the street alone, but I have to have someone help me." "Ginger's parents won't let her go past the lamppost, while I can go all the way to the corner." "Billy can stay up to watch Merv Griffin, but I have to go to bed." "Joanie can't stay out till eleven o'clock on Saturday nights, but I can."

In general, children learn that the world is not completely fair, but that it isn't completely stacked against them either. Although they don't particularly like all your decisions, respectful children usually accept them even though they grumble.

As they enter their teenage years, however, they will come to doubt the wisdom of your decisions more and more. It's natural. Adolescence is the time when they are testing their own "adult" thinking against yours, and confrontations are one way to do this. Also, the issues become more serious: "David can drive all the way out to Baldwin for a party, but I can't." "Ginger can date a guy two years older, but I can't." "Billy can go to R-rated movies, but I can't." And, "Joanie's parents don't care whether she smokes marijuana or not."

Drugs, sex, and rock 'n' roll! The issues get serious; and if your friends' children turn out to be real problem kids, you have the right to worry about their influence on your own children. When they were all younger, the problem usually centered around a child being a "spoiled brat" and teaching your son or daughter to whine and nag to get what he or she wanted. But now the problems loom larger and can even involve getting into trouble with the law. Again, as with in-laws, you are in the middle: what to say to your friends about the way their children behave, and what to say to your own children about the things you won't allow them to do? Where to draw the boundaries?

Assume from the start, if you haven't learned it already, that you are not going to change the way your friends raise their children. It's just something you'll have to live with, trying to maintain your friendship with them while at the same time maintaining your own set of values. The other side of the problem is to help your children understand that even though you are friends with their friends' parents, you don't agree on everything, nor do you always approve of what they let their children do. There is no easy way out of this dilemma, except to wait for the years to pass; but while going through them, you will have to maintain a delicate balancing act, much like walking a tightrope. Stay on as good terms as possible with your friends, and yet counteract their children's harmful influence on your own children.

MARGIE AND JIM: MARIJUANA AND CAMPING TRIPS

Margie and Jim had been friends with Liz and Reggie "Johnson" for over twenty years. They played cards once a week, went camping together, organized picnics, and let each other's kids sleep over with their own. Even though little Davey Johnson was somewhat spoiled and bratty, Margie and Jim managed to deflect his influence on their own son, Bobby, during his younger years. As the two boys were growing up together, the two couples' differing views about child-rearing never became an issue that disturbed their friendship.

But when the boys got into high school, things got worse. One night at supper Bobby mentioned that the Johnsons didn't care if Davey smoked marijuana, and that, in fact, Davey had tried it and wanted Bobby to "take a hit" too. Bobby had refused. Margie and Jim praised his action and told him that they thought he would be better off not getting involved in drugs. Several months later, Margie found a joint under Bobby's bed. When she presented it to Jim, they got into an argument over Davey's influence on their son, which led to an argument over the Johnsons' responsibilities as parents, which led to an argument over whether to confront the Johnsons with the whole matter.

Jim wanted to let things ride because the two families were planning a weekend camping trip at Easter, and it was only a few weeks away. But Margie was determined to have it out, and she called Liz to discuss it. As Jim had predicted, the two couples disagreed so vehemently over the issue that the camping trip was wrecked. Jim blamed it on Margie's not being willing to let well enough alone, and this caused a crisis in their marriage.

They discussed it with their minister, who happened to be in my consultation group. He helped them see that they were confronting a multifaceted problem. Several issues were involved, each of which might set the direction for the next few years: their friendship with the Johnsons; their disapproval of the Johnsons' parenting methods; the negative influence of Davey and other kids who were experimenting with drugs; how to present a unified front to Bobby on the issue of drugs; his relationship with his friends who used them; and last, but definitely not least, their own difficulties communicating which had been present for some time and how the tension over all these matters was placing an unbearable strain on their own relationship.

They met with the minister for several months, but because of their inability to negotiate, they could not sort out their problems. Liz and Reggie remained angry with them, and Jim remained angry with Margie. Bobby started to believe that his parents were irrational, and he gravitated toward Dave and his other "drug friends." As the tensions increased, the minister tried to refer them to me for family therapy, but Jim refused, claiming he wasn't "crazy" and didn't need "a shrink." They stopped seeing the minister, and a year later they separated.

*   *   *

As you can see from these case studies, the problems of boundaries—to what extent you will allow outsiders into your family circle—always boil down to another and more important issue: how the outsiders, family and friends alike, impinge on your own marital happiness. A strong married couple can face any serious disruption and make it through the thorniest passage. Couples in the best marriages have surmounted great obstacles and used them to strengthen their relationships. Married life will always involve problems and crises, but only a couple who refuse to let the problems disrupt their love for each other will preserve their marriage. No matter how serious or heartbreaking the passages of your marriage are, they can be weathered if you keep the lines of communication open and never stop demonstrating your love for one another.

18.

The Passages of Career and Finances

The Dual-Career Family

Consider the following statistics. Almost three-fifths of all American women between the ages of sixteen and sixty-four work or consider themselves to be in the labor force. Over half of all two-parent families have two wage earners, both husband and wife. Two-fifths of all mothers with preschoolers are working. Last, consider the enormous number of divorced mothers who work, and we see how truly revolutionary the impact of the women's movement has been on society. It becomes clear that many cultural institutions, not the least of which is the family unit itself, need some sort of restructuring to accommodate the "new" working woman.

As I have become increasingly aware of the number of working mothers from my own experience with patients and listeners who phone in their marital problems to my radio show, it has dawned on me that we also need to do some restructuring regarding the way we *think* about the working mother. In fact, I would like to ban the term "working mother" altogether, for it is a concept that can create disaster in any marriage. In my view, the so-called working mother is a full-time wife, full-time mother, and full- or part-time wage earner living in a family that hasn't noticed!

124

Yes, it's true. Husbands and children can live with the concept of the working mother and not make any adjustments to that momentous fact. It's clearly seen in the attitude that I've heard from ten-year-old kids and forty-year-old husbands who say, "It's okay for her to work, but I still want her to cook my meals, do the laundry, clean the house, and take care of me when I feel bad." Well, it's time for everyone to take notice. Including the mother. For starters, let's stop thinking of "families with working mothers" and rename them "dual-career families," considering them to be families in which the wife's job or career is given *equal attention* to that of the husband.

In a dual-career family each spouse is supportive of the professional activities of the other, and the children should feel proud about their parents' respective endeavors. Of course, such families don't just spring up over night; but I've seen enough of them over the past few years to know that they work successfully if all the members of the family, including the children, take an active part. How can you turn a family with a working mother into a dual-career family? First, each member of the family has to make numerous adjustments and trade-offs. It might mean father helping prepare meals, children doing the dishes, everyone pitching in on shopping. It might mean readjusting the usual hours of meals or family activities. It could mean teenagers running errands after school or on weekends. Perhaps dad will occasionally get laundry duty. The point is that the usual domestic chores that keep the family functioning must be shared by everyone.

Second, it should be clear to everyone (again including the wife who may have to resist feeling guilty about it) that the mother's career or job is as important as the father's. Even if she makes less money or has a less prestigious position, her career is equally important *to the family*. It doesn't matter if father is a banker and mother is a part-time secretary, everyone must value the contributions of both parents to the financial well-being of the family as a whole. They must also realize that the secretarial job can be as satisfying for mother's personal well-being and psychological health as foreclosing mortgages is for the banker father's. Both parents are total human beings with personal needs for growth and development. Never should the dual-career family foster the attitude that mother's happiness and fulfillment could be achieved if she stayed home. A woman who sincerely wants to work outside the home should not have to hide that fact by complaining about her job or telling her children that she would rather just stay home and be a mother if she really doesn't want to.

Third, family decisions should be made as democratically as possible since everyone has to shoulder the burden of holding the family intact. This means that children should have some voice in decision making because of their contributions to family chores and their cooperation with family schedules and responsibilities that may be dramatically different from their friends' families. They will expect to be treated more like adults if they assume an adultlike attitude toward familial needs. When everyone is treated as a partner in the family enterprise, family life becomes more fulfilling for everybody because it is clearly realized and accepted that the standard of living, the affluence, the happiness of living together are dependent on the joint efforts of all.

Success in establishing a dual-career family does not depend on your completely reversing traditional roles or transforming each family member into an interchangeable part, ready to fill in for anyone else in the family. Division of labor should be clear and distinct, based on who is most efficient, most capable, and has the most time for a particular task. If you are a better cook and your spouse is better at fix-it jobs, it doesn't make sense for you to take turns cooking meals and fixing leaks. The family will run more smoothly when each of you performs the jobs each has the talents for. Personal gratification is important too, although there will always be jobs that no one likes. But try as much as possible to let each one do what he or she enjoys doing or gets a kick out of. The underlying attitude should always be mutual supportiveness, regard, and respect.

In my own family, I and my three boys derive as much satisfaction out of Diane's law career as she does out of my psychiatry and our sons' school achievements. We all make efforts to support each other's pursuits whether they be winning a law case, helping a patient in therapy, or making the eighth-grade soccer team. As far as we are able, Diane and I include our children in our professional activities, taking them to career-related picnics or parties, letting them meet our colleagues and visit us in our offices so they understand where we spend so many hours of the day. All these things give them a sense of commitment to what we are doing, and hopefully they feel less shortchanged by the amount of time that we must devote to our professions.

JEAN AND TED: IT'S OKAY TO FEEL OKAY

When Jean came to see me about her marital problems, she phrased what she thought was the key issue this way, "It seems I've lost control over my life. I used to be an excellent organizer and manager. Now I'm a failure."

Her story was typical. Jean decided that she would go back to her teaching job when all of her four children were in school. So when the youngest began first grade, she began teaching part-time as a substitute. Within a year she was teaching fifth grade full-time and watching her family life fall apart. All the tasks and household responsibilities that she had executed so smoothly in raising the four children now seemed to be major hurdles. She was late, forgetful, tired, and irritable. Her children complained that none of their clothes were ironed. Ted balked whenever dinner was a half hour late. The dog ran away from home when she forgot to close the gate.

Not only was she doubting her ability to manage her life, but she was feeling guilty over what she suspected was the root cause of her failures: her full-time job. "Ted points out to me that I'm the one who wanted to go back to work. He never pushed. It's true we're using my money for family expenses, but I know I could quit if I wanted to and everything would be okay again." With that a doubt flashed across her face. "But you know, I don't think *I* would feel okay again." And she wouldn't. Jean was the type of energetic woman who needed more intellectual and social stimulation in her life than keeping house for four children who were off to school all day and for a husband who frequently worked evenings as an insurance agent. She needed the excitement and responsibility of outside work. But something had to give.

When Ted agreed to join her in couple's therapy, the task before us was to convince him that his wife could not be superwoman, holding down a job from eight to three and then coming home and completing all the household chores that she used to do when she was home all day. Ted explained that he felt justified in not helping because of his evening work, and he argued that he really didn't know how to do most of the jobs that traditionally had been Jean's responsibilities. He did, however, appreciate the extra income, particularly now that the children were reaching their teens and raising them was becoming increasingly expensive. But what to do?

The solution, of course, was to transform, slowly and painlessly, this family with a working mother into a dual-career family. Jean started to delegate simple errands that Ted could manage, such as going to the cleaner or grocery store. Most of the involvement with the children would remain Jean's, as it always had, because she was home earlier and could handle their needs more efficiently than Ted. But together the couple would gradually give the older children more responsibilities around the house until they were holding up their end of the family enterprise. Jean and Ted both agreed to hire a housekeeper a couple of days a week. The money spent on her would be well worth it, considering the pressure that would be alleviated, particularly from Jean. They also worked out a system involving everyone in the family in their various professional and educational activities so that the family as a unit grew to understand what each member was doing and how he or she could support and encourage the others. The result was a family that operated as efficiently as it had when most of the chores fell to Jean alone before she had started working, a family that understood and supported one another more lovingly and considerately. Instead of being held together by the efforts of a superwoman, the family itself became a super-family as Jean and Ted moved through their Middle Years together with a heightened sense of love and respect for each other.

Financial Competition

A cash nexus is at the heart of so many relationships in our society that it is not surprising to find the almighty dollar creeping into family life as well. In the old days children received a meager allowance and were expected to perform a certain number of chores around the house. Today, some children actually charge for doing chores! The allowance is no longer an act of largesse on the part of the parents. It becomes a rightful wage. "No dough, no mow!" And the grass doesn't get cut.

Traditionally, a woman's work was never done and also never paid for. The working woman is nothing new; she's been the backbone of most families for centuries, but it is a curious fact that her contribution to family life was never perceived as "real work" because she was not paid. Only "real work" commanded wages or a salary. But washing clothes, cooking meals, cleaning the house, and raising children were not calculable in dollars. It's even difficult to imagine what one bottle-feeding would cost!

Today, however, women bring home part of the bacon. As we've seen, a growing number of American families have wives and mothers in the work force, and their contribution to the family's well-being is now calculated in dollars and cents. Unfortunately, because of unenlightened hiring and promotion practices, most women continue to earn less than men, even those who perform the same jobs as men. The consequence of this is that in the majority of families, the father continues to play the role of primary breadwinner, with the wife merely "contributing" her smaller salary to his own. For the husband, it's a very snug situation in which he can enjoy the added income without feeling threatened by his wife's contribution.

But an increasingly common situation is occurring, and it often becomes a very difficult passage for many men and women: namely, how to get through those times when the wife is earning more than her husband or is the sole source of support for the family. This can be true especially for a couple with Childless Middle Years, where the wife devotes herself full-time to her career. In these cases, husbands can experience really difficult problems coping with the reversal. They find it demeaning to be earning less than their wives. They feel less like "real men." If they have children, they wonder if their children will continue to respect them. They are ashamed to socialize with their friends. Underlying all these issues is the old male ego. Women have never been bothered by the fact that their husbands earned more than they did, but for many men to earn less is a real threat to the traditional notion of masculinity built up over years of living in a society that teaches the superiority of men and the suppression of women.

How can that tender ego be salved?

For men who feel they are under just such an attack, the best defense is to adopt, as much as possible, the concept of the dual-career family. Take stock of *all* the work, both inside the home and outside, that contributes to the total functioning of the family. Discover ways to increase your overall contribution to the family and compensate for the smaller income. Remember that family life is *not,* nor should it ever become, a total cash nexus. Some services and jobs should always be priceless in the sense that they can never be evaluated by a dollar and cents figure, and priceless because only you can provide them with love and affection. If by joint consensus you determine the total amount of work and services that the family requires, then the fact that for a given period of time your wife is the primary breadwinner should not become an insurmountable ego problem for you. If you are in a satisfying job and feel fulfilled, and your personal contributions of work and support around the house are meaningful and appreciated by the other members of the family, the competition between you and your wife should diminish.

If you are unemployed or unhappy with your job, the situation is more difficult. Times of unemployment or intense job dissatisfaction can be extremely demoralizing periods of transition. Hopefully they will pass and more normal circumstances will return. To get through these passages you should be as active as possible in trying to better the situation. Seek other employment or find other activities in addition to your job that will be rewarding for you. Don't stay demoralized by doing nothing except stew-

ing in the juice of your own ego. Get involved in neighborhood or charitable activities, athletics, home improvement
projects, child care, or any kind of "work" that will alleviate
the pressure of being caught in an undesirable job or out of
work. If you don't do something, it is highly likely that your
marriage will suffer. You will lose self-esteem. You'll be
more likely to grow irritable with your wife and children.
Eventually your sexual relationship will go on "hold" as well.
A constellation of symptoms like low self-esteem, depression,
and anger can become a whirlwind that leaves no part of
your family untouched. The best treatment in these cases is
preventive. Block the difficulties before they make the passage totally unbearable for both of you. Be alert to the
potential danger if you are out of work, or unhappy with
your job, or your wife makes more money than you. Then
take the steps to insure that you are doing what you can to
maintain your own sense of self-worth, and most of all,
maintain an open exchange of thoughts and feelings with
your wife about all these matters.

BETH AND MIKE: YOU WIN, I QUIT

Beth was an editor for a large publisher, and Mike was
in the advertising industry. They were both so dedicated to
their professions that they had made the conscious decision
years ago not to have children. They were the types that
could easily get lost in their work and in each other, so the
absence of children in their lives posed no serious problems.
They were childless, or, as they preferred to put it, "child-
free." Neither was selfish; both were active in numerous
charitable and worthwhile organizations. They got along
well with each other, and friends thought their marriage
was one of the most stable around. Then, Beth was trans-
ferred to the marketing division of her publishing house
and received a slight raise. Within a year she was doing so
well that she received a major raise and was named director
of marketing, a position that required her to travel frequently around the country. During this time Mike was
moving steadily along in his own career, but there were no

major triumphs in his life. However, the bottom seemed to fall out for him when Beth received the major promotion. She began making more money than he did and had to travel more often and without Mike. He started feeling worse about himself, and he began to withdraw from Beth. She sensed his predicament; but when she tried to talk it over with him, he was unable to recognize what was really at the heart of his problem: a wounded ego.

Eventually Mike became sexually involved with one of the women in his office, and Beth found out. She confronted him with this, and his reply to her was that "it was no big deal." She suggested marriage counseling, but Mike refused; so she came to see me by herself. In treatment, I helped her to realize how she had inadvertently played a role in Mike's depression. At my suggestion she tried to reengage Mike in the relationship. But her efforts failed. After several months, he became even more distant and aloof. He focused most of his time and attention on his peer group, and ultimately ended up in another affair.

Beth instituted divorce proceedings and ended the relationship. She has recently become engaged to a successful attorney, and I believe that she will be able to avoid falling into the same trap a second time.

*   *   *

The sad thing about Beth and Mike is that the marriage could probably have been saved if the two of them had been able to work together to assuage Mike's ego and find reasonable ways to make him feel less competitive with Beth. Being outstripped by a wife's success need not cause the disastrous consequences we saw in this marriage. A wife's success can become a smooth marital passage for the couple if they are able to discuss the key issues, look for ways to prop up the husband's self-esteem, and minimize the competition. Unfortunately, sometimes our best efforts fail in the light of one partner's unwillingness to talk openly and honestly about the problem with the other.

Middle-Management to Mother

Most people have a genetic urge to have children. They unconsciously hope to pass on their own gene pool, blended with the genetic characteristics of the spouse they love, to the next generation. In the Middle Years, this desire can become clouded with mixed emotions for couples who have consciously postponed children in their Early Years. When a woman reaches her early thirties, she hears her "biological clock" ticking and realizes that her childbearing years are approaching their limit. Soon she and her husband will be at the point of "it's now or never."

The problem that complicates these years of decision is that usually the couple has grown accustomed to well-paying, responsible careers and affluent lifestyles. Now, if the wife gives up her job, even temporarily, to have a baby, there will be financial and psychological sacrifices. From the countless men and women I've spoken with, it seems that the sacrifices are greater—or at least *perceived* as being greater—when the first child arrives in the Middle, rather than in the Early, Years of their marriages. They have been living well on two salaries; they have come to expect the freedom of being childless. And so, a major decision needs to be made: to what extent are both partners willing to make the adjustments that children will require of them?

For the woman, reassurance is needed that she will be able to be a mother and a career woman if she chooses to keep her job. You must make a concerted effort to assure your wife that you will support her and help to raise the children so that she can eventually return to her career. If you are a woman who wants both children and a career, it is important to explore as many options as possible, learn from other women who can be role models for you, and get all the advice available about being a successful mother and career woman.

The Workaholic

BECKY AND DON: ALL WORK AND NO PLAY

"I don't understand it," Don said to me, "after all I did for her and the children. I gave them everything they wanted." A pathetic and broken man, deserted by a loving wife after twenty years of marriage, he sat in my office and wept. What had gone wrong?

When I later talked with Becky, she told me that throughout their marriage, Don always had several projects going at any one time: building a canoe, putting in a swimming pool, taking flying lessons. He never seemed to be finished. Often, he left one project to take up another. He also put in long hours as president of his construction company, hours Don was proud of, hours that brought in enough money to give Becky and the kids what they wanted: a house in the country, a new barn, horses, tennis lessons, a swimming pool.

They were long hours that accomplished many admirable goals that he, Becky, and the children shared. But they also met another goal, one that Don would never have admitted to himself. He was avoiding his family. Sure, there were generous moments when he doled out allowances or helped make expensive purchases, but he acted more like a friendly supervisor of daily chores or a kind but distant payroll clerk. And because he was working so hard all the time, nobody could criticize him, not even when the time spent with his family grew less and less.

Don worked exceptionally hard. He believed in doing a good job. He wanted only the best for his family. He took great pride in how well he was doing, how everything (apparently) was working out so perfectly. But even this attitude alienated Becky. How could she live with someone who was such a workaholic, who demanded perfection in everything he did, without herself feeling guilty if she wasn't as perfect and hardworking as he was? Even the children felt the unspoken pressure that they had better be as good as dad, or they would be failures. Eventually, Becky and the children couldn't take it any longer. They wanted to lead more relaxed, less pressurized lives.

This pattern of family life is rather typical. Don, a seemingly loving husband, gave his family everything they wanted—everything but love and attention. Finally, after twenty years, Becky gave him back just what he had given her emotionally—nothing. His tokens of love were cold and impersonal, just as were those his own parents showered on him when he was a boy. Without warm and affectionate parents of his own as role models, Don avoided any loving contact with his family because he simply could not handle it. But they needed it; and not finding it with him, they deserted him.

In therapy I was able to help Don see through these problems. He tried to reestablish a relationship with Becky and his children, but they had misgivings. They were hesitant to believe that someone they knew so well could really change. I brought Becky into the sessions to try couple's therapy. I even tried several family sessions. Gradually, it became clear that after so many years of taking a back seat, Becky no longer felt any love for Don. She cared about him and didn't want to hurt him, but she could not remain in the marriage. She relished her newfound independence and the sense that she really did count. Fortunately, I was able to help them achieve an amicable divorce with joint custody so that the trauma for the children was minimized.

*   *   *

The workaholic has an ironclad argument that other members of the family can seldom puncture. It seems foolproof. "I'm only doing this so that we can have enough money to live the way we want to live, so that we can send the kids to college, so that we can buy the big house in Fox Meadows." Whammo! How can anyone in the family object to that since it offers the good things of life to each of them? And thus the workaholic craftily seduces spouse and children to collude with him or her.

How do you know if your spouse is a workaholic?

There are clear indicators that distinguish the true workaholic from the dedicated and hardworking individual. First, the workaholic has an abnormal predilection for work, usually spotted by the exceedingly long workdays, sometimes peaking at fourteen or sixteen hours or more. Second, the workaholic seems to thrive on work, feels grumpy and restless when there is nothing to do, has a difficult time relaxing and doing nothing. Third, he or she is obsessed with work. Work can rarely be laid aside. Their minds are more frequently on their work than on anything else. They talk incessantly about their job or projects, the difficulties they're having (which of course require more hours!), and the successes (which of course prove the long hours were worth it!). Another indication, which is not always immediately noticeable to the average person, is that a workaholic is frequently not a very productive worker. Even though employers usually love them, workaholics have been shown to exhibit behavior patterns that are far less productive than those of their less obsessed co-workers. In the long run, the co-workers turn out as much work, and often work of better quality, than the workaholic. As we saw in the case of Becky and Don, the typical workaholic is frequently using his unrelenting drive to avoid more serious problems, often in his relationships with spouse or children. A workaholic can easily be a cold, unfeeling, unexpressive individual, who appears the opposite because he can bestow such wonderful gifts and rewards on the people he supposedly loves. Working becomes a convenient excuse for avoiding relationships, which inevitably suffer. At some point, you must say that you will not be able to afford a house or a car or vacation, not because you can't make the money for it, but because your family can't afford the disruption that your incessant working creates in their lives. Telling them you are working for their own good is a sham, one they will eventually see through when they need you as a human being, not as a dispenser of material goodies.

If you can't draw the line and curtail the number of hours you spend away from your spouse, or your children, if you have them, you can expect rather predictable consequences. Your children will become angry because you are not actively interested and involved in their lives, even though they will gladly take your money. Your mate will feel rejected, eventually believing that you are really married to your job or career rather than to her or him. Your spouse will probably look for warmth and affection outside your marriage. If infidelity occurs, all the negative feelings that have grown up between the two of you, all the hurt, bitterness, and resentment, will be intensified. A marital crisis complicated by workaholism and infidelity is a tough nut to crack. But it can be done.

The most successful way is to begin by finding common interests. In your Early Years, and when you were first dating, you and your mate found lots to do, talk about, be interested in. Somewhere over the years those mutually enjoyable activities slipped into the background of your marriage. At one time they were the foundation of your relationship, and they can be once again. Most likely, the crucial cornerstone of sex is one of the pleasures you have stopped enjoying. Now you must relearn how to make love with each other. Time must be found for it.

Family activities play a key role in reuniting the Child-full–Phase couple estranged by workaholism. If the children are still relatively young, this is not too difficult. Young kids are remarkably adaptable. But if the children are approaching adolescence or are already teenagers, they will probably be unresponsive. By now they have established their own substitutes for the love and attention they could not find at home. They have their school friends, their dating partners, their activities, and after-school jobs. It is their natural period of rebelliousness, anyway, and they probably don't see the point in disrupting their lives to help you out with your problems. After all, they have enough of their own.

But the effort should be made, as much as possible, to reinvolve all the children in family activities. Ultimately, the couple must get their act together and hope that as they do so, the children will come around. The important consideration here is to give the workaholic something to fill up his or her life once he or she makes the concerted effort to place work in its proper role. It is really a kind of addiction, not unsimilar to drugs or alcohol. Once the addiction is removed, there must be some equally engrossing substitute to take its place and fill up the hours and days that the former addict had spent catering to the habit.

If you've been reading along and wondering whether

you or your mate is a workaholic, the natural inclination is to think, "Yes, I must be." It's a typical reaction to read about diseases or illnesses in a book such as this and imagine you have them all! So a word of caution: Don't imagine the worst if you happen to be going through a period of accelerated work right now. In all our lives there are seasons when work piles up, deadlines need to be met, extra duties are laid on us by supervisors, and so forth. That, too, is normal—unpleasant, but normal. At such times, we have to work longer hours. We might even become obsessed with tasks and lose sleep over deadlines. We'll probably worry a lot, and the rest of the family will suffer along with us because "Dad's under a lot of pressure right now" or "Mom's got those end-of-the-year reports to do." Occasional or seasonal spurts of work do not make a workaholic. You'll know immediately that you aren't turning into one because you won't be able to wait for the task to get finished!

Another legitimate reason you might overindulge in work for a temporary period is to make extra money for a particular goal, medical bills for example, a wedding, or perhaps a special vacation next summer. These and other similar reasons are legitimate justifications for spending extra hours at work or even for taking on a part-time job. They are not the indication that you're sliding down the slippery slope into workaholism. Remember, workaholism is a symptom of other, deeper emotional problems, an avoidance technique to buffer you from interpersonal relationships. In spite of what the workaholic will say, workaholism has really little to do with work, job satisfaction, or, ironically, making money.

Too Much Money, Not Enough Love

Your children and you will go through some personal passages simultaneously, not the same passages, of course, but their own and your own. These passages will overlap, and one conjunction will occur when they step into adulthood. As we have already noted, our society does not have swift, clear puberty rites or initiation passages that let the young man or woman know beyond a shadow of a doubt that he or she is now truly a "no-questions-asked" adult. Instead, we dribble out this important rite of passage in bits and pieces: a driver's license here; social security number there; off to war now; the right to marry without parental consent; the privilege of drinking, of voting, and so on. It is hard on you, too, not to know the precise moment when you should release the parental reins and treat your child as an adult. But as they work through this rite of passage, certain changes will occur in your lives too. You have been accustomed to supporting your children with love and money, hopefully realizing that the former is more important for a child's emotional growth and stability than the latter. Now the question arises: How much and for how long do I owe my son or daughter financial support?

At some point you will have to withdraw financial support from your adult children. Doing so will be even more stressful for you—perhaps creating a crisis situation—if you are living through financially strapping times yourself. Your natural desires will be pulled in two directions: one to continue helping your children, the other to withdraw support so that you and your mate can make the best of tight finances. As good parents, you are undoubtedly concerned about your obligation to help your children. You can't simply erase years of being overly solicitous about your children's welfare. It is difficult to know the wisest time and smoothest manner for withdrawing support. At the same time you have to evaluate your own financial needs and meet them for the sake of your own marital relationship.

By being continuously overindulgent with our adult children, we do not necessarily do them a service. Generosity breeds dependence, and the passage they must move through during this period of their lives is one that should carry them into independent, self-sustaining lives of their own. To be financially independent is crucial for their emotional growth and development. The more we do for our children, the less inclined are they to do for themselves. It's a fine line to draw. What are the legitimate expenses that you as a parent should help your children pay? Tuition? Down payment on a home? Hospital bills? The first baby?

Day care? Financial assistance if your son or daughter loses a job?

Whatever you decide, it is better to couch your financial assistance in the form of loans rather than outright gifts. Gifts foster a state of indebtedness on the part of the child that can never be repaid. All the years of self-sacrificing and caring for them as young children build up a kind of debt. Adding an actual cash value to this convinces your son or daughter that he or she will always owe you whatever you ask them for. A serious problem can arise in your Mature Years when you might be in financial trouble and need to go to your children for assistance. If your earlier cash supplements to them were in the form of loans, they can now be repaid. This way, they can give freely and lovingly as far as their resources allow, without feeling resentment or ill will because they still feel psychologically and financially indebted to you.

RUTH AND ED: SWEARING THEY'LL NEVER BE HUNGRY AGAIN

In Ruth's life there were several moments similar to the climactic last scene of the first half of *Gone With the Wind*, where Scarlett O'Hara swears she'll never be hungry again. Coming from a poverty-stricken family, Ruth knew times when one small chicken was cut up into eight pieces for Sunday dinner, and her own self-sacrificing mother ate the neck. When she married, Ruth and Ed had to scrimp and save through their Early Years together while Ed worked in a tool factory. Eventually, he worked his way up to shop foreman, a position he held until he retired. Always operating on a modest income, they learned how to budget wisely and raise two daughters.

Both daughters were married in their late twenties to blue-collar workers whose own salaries barely allowed them to scrape by. Consequently, Ruth always tried to do whatever she could financially to help her daughters and their families. Throughout their marriage, Ruth and Ed got sunk in innumerable minor arguments over giving the girls this or that. Ed basically felt that since his daughters had married decent, hardworking fellows, they had no need of financial assistance except in emergencies. His attitude was basically, "We've struggled our whole lives to get what we've got, and it won't hurt them to struggle a little bit also!" Case closed.

But when Ruth and Ed became grandparents, Ruth decided that the extra expenses in her children's marriages were indeed emergencies. She began saving household money to buy them gifts. Sometimes she would revert back to her own mother's survival technique of padding the meatloaf with a little too much oatmeal, so that she could buy clothes or toys for her little grandchildren. Her daughters knew what she was up to and colluded in this with her. Finally, at one Thanksgiving dinner, the youngest grandson blurted it out, thanking Grandma for the new shoes for school. Ed hit the ceiling.

For the next week, Ed, feeling doubly cheated, refused to talk to Ruth. Not only was Ruth sneaking around behind his back, but he felt she was jeopardizing their own financial security for retirement by squandering money that should be put into their savings. Getting nowhere, they called me on "Talknet" to ask what I thought. After speaking to them, I decided that they were deadlocked, and I sent them to a local family service agency for counseling. After several sessions they called me back to tell me they had worked out a reasonable compromise. Ed discovered that his long-standing belief—that the man should control the purse strings except what he gives his wife for food and household expenses—needed to be modernized a bit. Even though he was the breadwinner, Ruth had a stake in determining how the funds should be used. Ruth, on her part, confessed to, and apologized for, deceiving him and promised she would never do so again. They even decided that she should get a part-time job so she could play the generous grandmother to her daughters' children, giving them gifts, clothes, and special treats. It meant a lot to her and helped assuage her own memories of having been trapped in financial straits as a young girl. It also satisfied her motherly concern for her own daughters' financial well-being. Under the new arrangement, no one needed to be hungry—or lie—ever again.

*   *   *

You might be thinking, "What an obvious solution! They went into marriage counseling for *that!*" Yes, even though the problem was handled with what looks like common sense—and it was—couples so closely involved with emotional issues that have been festering for years simply don't always have the ability to evaluate them objectively. Having an emotional stake in how the issue is resolved can blind one to the simplest and easiest method of handling it. Just being able to talk about it with each other is a difficulty that many couples, like Ed and Ruth, cannot manage to resolve. The process of therapy can be necessary and helpful, even when the problem is not overly complex.

19.

The Passages of Parenting

The Child-full Years

It doesn't matter whether you have two, three, or more children, each child is special, and the birth of a new child into the world is a unique family event. In the past, the other children waited at home until grandma came back from the hospital with news that they had a new baby sister or brother. Then the older children waited four or five days until mother returned with the new sibling. Today, there are greater opportunities for making the birth of a new family member truly a family passage.

Some hospitals have birthing rooms where young children can actually witness the entry of their new brother or sister into the world. The decision to have your other children present, however, should be made carefully, considering the maturity and sensibilities of each child. For some children, watching their mother in pain, or the sight of a newborn babe, might be distressing. Other children, especially if properly prepared, can participate without adverse results. On the contrary, watching the birth of a new baby could be a high point in their childhood. In peasant societies, children routinely observed births and deaths, and grew up with a more relaxed attitude toward the realities of life. In our culture we isolate children from the basic facts of life, such as sex, birth, death, and pain. Consequently,

143

they grow up with little information, and their imaginations usually concoct the worst scenarios for what it's all about.

But even if there are no birthing-room facilities available, a lying-in room for the mother and child will allow the older siblings to visit the newborn within an hour or so after birth. In my own family, my two older sons were actually holding their new little brother on the bed with their mother within an hour after he was born. For them it was *their* baby too. I personally believe that the bonding and closeness that results from making birth a family affair is unparalleled as a mutually shared experience. It will be remembered by each member of the family through the years to come and through the difficulties and crises that can pull a family apart.

How Many Children?

A stressful passage many couples navigate is deciding the number of children to have. If the two of you can't agree, a running discussion, or argument, may unsettle your lives for months, even years, as each of you tries to convince the other that your preference is better. While trying to decide on the number, you should discuss all the ramifications that an extra child would entail. Here are some crucial topics you should not overlook as you weigh the pros and cons regarding a certain number of children.

There is no ideal number of children for every family. Families are too diverse. Circumstances are too varied. You may hear that two or perhaps three, or more, children is the perfect number. There is no perfect number, and all the arguments to justify a particular number theoretically mean nothing when confronted by the actualities of your own family. Sure, it's nice to have two children so that the first child has a companion and playmate. But if a second child would create considerable economic hardships on everyone, then one child is the perfect number for you.

There are key issues involved in determining the number of children you should have: finances, lifestyle, personal health, psychological and emotional characteristics of you and your spouse. It's clear that finances play an important role in the decision. In rural societies, a large number of children was an economic advantage. It meant more hands to help with chores, and feeding them was no problem since food was raised at home. In today's urban environment, every child is an economic liability. More food to buy, more tuition money for education, even more quarters in the washer and dryer at the Laundromat.

Lifestyle also plays a crucial role. One of the things that you and your mate probably began talking about from the day you decided to get married is how and where you would live. While it's true that you may have modified some of the more idealistic dreams, the two of you continue to have hopes and plans about your lives: where you will work, how involved you will be in your career, how much leisure time you want, what you will do with it, how much room in your life for friends and family, even how young or old you would like to be when the last child leaves home. All of these should influence your decision about the number of children you want.

Don't overlook physical and psychological health and makeup. There is nothing wrong with you if you know that your temperament would not tolerate the noise and commotion of three or four kids. Nor are you old-fashioned if you want a large, sprawling family. As a couple, you need to assess your personal virtues and vices, likes and dislikes, as well as physical strengths and weaknesses. Then, while talking over the pros and cons, you can decide on the optimum number of children for you.

Remember, too, that family planning is not carved in stone. Your plans can be modified as the years go on. You may have decided on only two children originally; but then as circumstances change, as you become more prosperous, as you realize that you have a talent for raising children, you might want more than two. Similarly, never feel you have failed to live up to your dreams if after having one or two children, you decide that it would be a mistake to have any more. Many couples learn that children demand much more time and attention—and money!—than they had anticipated. Adjusting to necessities is not a sign of failure, it's a mark of wisdom. The ideal marriage and family is rated on love, not numbers.

A serious mistake in a marriage is for one mate to plan another baby against the other's wishes. The unexpected pregnancy caused by the mother going off the pill without telling her husband, or the father not wearing a condom, could be the kiss of death. If you can't decide on the number of children you want, the wise move is to talk it out and negotiate. If negotiation is not possible and the two of you remain polarized, then one partner may have to compromise and give in, or give up willingly and make the commitment to accept the additional child and love it as much as the older children. But tricking your mate by an unwanted pregnancy is never the way to settle the crisis. The issue may remain and grow as the child grows and may later come to be the ticking time bomb that blows your marriage apart.

The Oedipal Triangle: The Three-Way Free-For-All

Sophocles' original drama was filled with blood, death, and self-blinding. Fortunately, the drama that we psychiatrists see in modern families is usually free of blood and death! But self-blinding, in the figurative sense, is frequently there. In whatever combination, the three-way tension between mother, father, and child can prevent them from seeing the real issues in a critical passage of marriage—one of which could be a misplaced love for the child as in the following case of Howard and Judy.

HOWARD AND JUDY: WITH ALICIA IN THE MIDDLE

Howard married Judy when his daughter Alicia was eight years old. Judy was unable to have children due to a hysterectomy when she was twenty-six; and now at thirty, she welcomed the chance to have a stepdaughter with whom she might have a mothering relationship. Although Alicia lived with her mother Sandy, she spent weekends with Howard and Judy. Since Sandy was basically unstable and indulging herself in the role of being a "swinging single," she often left Alicia at Howard's for weeks on end. While Alicia was still shy of puberty, the relationship between her and Judy went smoothly, so much so that Howard, believing Sandy was a bad influence on Alicia, convinced the court to give him full custody of his daughter. The new living situation worked out fine until Alicia reached age thirteen.

Because of her past experiences in a contentious family and then a split family, she entered adolescence more willful and petulant than might be hoped. Confrontations between Judy and Alicia became frequent and bitter. Alicia cagily used her relationship with Sandy (who lived nearby) as a wedge to get what she wanted from Howard and Judy. Sandy, always ready to cause Howard havoc, sided with Alicia so that Alicia could bring her natural mother's support up in any argument. It bothered Howard that Alicia was drifting back to Sandy, so he occasionally began to side with his daughter against Judy in the heat of their disputes. He also grew to suspect that Judy was deliberately trying to turn his daughter away from him. For Alicia the situation became a teenager's dream! Three parents to play off against each other!

Not understanding Judy's precarious position in the mess, Howard eventually came to believe that it was all Judy's problem, that she was bitter about not being able to have children of her own. The relationship between them deteriorated steadily, until Judy, fearing that she and Howard were about to split up, came to see me. When Howard came for sessions with Judy, we looked at the way his natural affection for his daughter became her leverage with which she was not only getting what she wanted, but was also destroying his relationship with Judy. It was clear that the limitations that Judy wished to set on Alicia's behavior were not inappropriate for her age and temperament. Howard's inability to cooperate with her way of handling Alicia was widening the breach in their marriage.

Alicia also attended family sessions, and when confronted with her behavior, she refused to admit to what she was doing and dropped out of therapy. At this point Howard realized the seriousness of the situation. After asking her to return to therapy with him and Judy, and Alicia's adamant refusal to do so, he decided to agree to a request that had been simmering for several months: Alicia wanted to go back to live with Sandy. Howard agreed, hoping that with Alicia out of the picture, he and Judy would have more time—and peace and quiet—to work at strengthening their own relationship.

They were making fairly good progress when one day Judy called to tell me that a new problem was brewing: Alicia was not getting along with her mother and wanted to come home.

Judy was afraid she wouldn't be able to handle it. After making such good progress with Howard, she didn't want to see all their work go down the drain because of renewed arguments and three-way battles that would inevitably lead back to the old mess they had found themselves in. Howard, of course, was in favor of Alicia's moving back home; but being more realistic now in his approach to handling his daughter, he agreed to her return only if she would join them in family therapy once a week.

When we started meeting again, our sessions proved much more successful: Alicia could no longer intimidate her father with threats to return to Sandy. Also, Howard had come to value his renewed and strengthened relationship with Judy and did not want to jeopardize the progress they had made on that. Together he and Judy presented a united front to Alicia in their decisions about what she could and couldn't do. Even though heated arguments continued, some right in my office, Howard and Judy stood their ground and ultimately Alicia realized that she would get nowhere by her ineffectual attempts at manipulation. In about a year Judy and she developed a reasonable mother-stepdaughter relationship, and the passage that had caused so much turmoil for Howard and Judy during those months truly tested and solidified their own love for each other.

*   *   *

In the case of Howard and Judy, Howard's love for his daughter was a form of self-blinding. Wanting to please her and win her loyalty away from her natural mother, he couldn't see how the situation became intolerable for Judy. Oedipal situations often blind one parent or the other and prevent them from seeing the dynamics of the confrontations that take place.

What Freud called Oedipal situations are perfectly normal. There is always competitive tension in a family when a baby arrives, and around age four or five, a son's love for his mother places him in a position of competition with his father. Freud used the phrase Electra complex (Electra being the Greek maiden who instigated the murder of her mother to avenge her father) to describe the situation in the case of a daughter. Freud discovered that the parent-child affection is fraught with hidden motives and inadmissible yearnings. While we might never consciously think of murdering a parent or engaging in an incestuous relationship with the other, it is quite common for a young daughter, for example, when asked "Whom do you want to marry when you grow up?" to answer "Daddy," or "Someone like Daddy." Nor is it rare for a young boy to boast about stepping into his father's shoes and taking care of his mother and the family "should Dad ever die." If Oedipal or Electra triangles persist as the children grow older, and if the marital relationship is on shaky ground to begin with, chances are the child will learn how to use its love for the opposite-sexed parent as a weapon against the other. Sometimes a parent will welcome the three-way struggle because in it he or she finds the affection and loyalty that is lacking in the marriage. I've seen many parents who use the arguing and bickering that goes on as a way to get even with a spouse who is unsupportive, undemonstrative, inattentive, or uncaring. It's sad to see a family split into two distinct camps each headed by one of the parents. There is mother and "momma's boy" versus father and "daddy's little girl." Each parent aligns with the opposite-sexed child in order to earn the support, attention, and love that each doesn't receive from the respective spouse.

Teenagers often understand the underlying dynamics of this kind of marriage, and it becomes easy for them to manipulate situations to their advantage, as in the case of Howard and Judy. The stresses of dealing with teenagers can lead to marital squabbles even in the best marriages. When the fears and fantasies of an Oedipus complex permeate these years, they can literally reproduce the favorite theme of the old Greek tragedies—the downfall of a strong and noble family.

Surviving Teenage Turmoil

If your son or daughter could magically jump from age thirteen to twenty-one, you might bypass some of the potential trouble of your Child-full Middle Years. Unfortunately, neither magic nor modern technology has devised a method of accelerating the years of adolescence. Being parents of teenagers presents passages that cannot be avoided, since as they grow into adulthood you see how your own lives together are changing and going through their own inevitable transitions in relation to your kids. Whether you have well-behaved children or troublesome ones, their adolescent years will bring intense physical, psychological, and social turmoil and growth that will take them from childhood to young adulthood. At times the stress and pressure of having to live with, love, and guide a teenager through these tumultuous years can strain the best of marriages.

The basic goals of an adolescent are two: to establish one's own identity as an adult, and eventually to separate from the family in order to begin a life of one's own. Neither goal is achieved easily. Some children gradually evolve toward these goals; for others, there is progress with intermittent crises alternating with quiet periods. And there are some for whom the entire process is one long, continuous rebellion. Rebellion is not an inappropriate term. The way teenagers reach these two goals is by seizing control of their own lives. The intensity of the rebellion is partially determined by how willing you, the parents, are in giving up control over their lives. Obviously you cannot merely turn them loose. To do so would be irresponsible. Most teenagers are not sufficiently self-disciplined for complete freedom. They need to be guided into freedom while learning at the same time that there is no such thing as *complete* freedom, that even adults are constrained by certain necessities and limitations. They also need to be inspired to work toward these two goals of adolescence.

You may find it difficult to help your teenage children because it is perfectly natural for them to reject your advice and support. They have to test their own ideas and dreams, and you're the handiest foil for them. When your son or daughter makes unreasonable demands, holds unreasonable ideas, or challenges you at almost every turn, it is precisely that discovery of what is and is not reasonable that is personal and experiential. They don't want to take your word for it. They've *been* taking your word for things. Now they need to discover what others say, to compare values and attitudes, and eventually to decide for themselves what fits their personalities and what values they wish to live by. Even though their adult identities may end up looking very much like yours and your spouse's, they'll never mold those identities except by their own efforts.

Yet through all of this, you need to remain a solid role model for them to test things on. You must keep up as meaningful a dialogue as possible by being open and honest with them. For in spite of their protests and objections, they do not feel secure enough to do it entirely without you. And deep inside they know it. To be there when they need you means being secure in your own identity as parents, confident that you believe what you say you believe, and supportive of each other in your decisions regarding them. You have already defined the world for yourselves; you have defined your own relationship; and now is the time to let your children define the world for themselves, even when those definitions differ radically from your own, and even when they differ radically from one moment to another! Erratic behavior and erratic thinking are normal for teenagers. They have a lot to learn and evaluate in a few short years.

But let's face it, teenagers often are weird! They don't have the perfect balance in their lives. But do you? They want to experience everything for themselves and will on occasion decide that your experience has nothing to teach them. They think *you're* weird. Maybe you are. The best you can do is to stay as balanced and as centered as you can, be as reasonable and honest as you know how, listen to what they say and try to hear them, and be fair and open-minded. But expect the worst!

Fortunately, the worst doesn't usually happen. In the extreme, truly rebellious teenagers may end up in trouble at school, get expelled, maybe even get into trouble with the law. They might jump into sex too soon, too unprepared, and too proud to admit it. Certainly not to you. They might confide in their best friends or teachers at school, but you should try not to be jealous. They need other opinions, other role models. They may experiment with drugs and alcohol, and decide the experiment works! Some may run away from home. You might never know they have run away from home because they may come back by supper. Or they might just spend the night somewhere while they *think* about running away from home. These types usually get back by breakfast. On the other hand, they might actually run away for a lengthy period of time, during which you will worry about their safety, call around to their friends, maybe notify the police. It won't be easy waiting it out, but statistically, most runaway teenagers finally come home. And they return with experiences and adventures under their belts that weren't all that bad, adventures they may later tell your grandchildren about!

The point is that you are still home to them, "the place," as Robert Frost said, "where when you have to go there, they have to take you in." And most teenagers *want* to be taken back in. Be as nonjudgmental as possible when you take them back in from whatever escapade they have just escaped from. They do need you; and when they're really down and out, they need to know you are still there, willing to accept them back. Most of all, whatever form of discipline the two of you decide upon for a wayward teenager, it should never be withholding your love. Through all the crises, your children need and want to know that you sincerely love them.

If the two of you have a loving relationship yourselves, based on honesty, openness, and meaningful dialogue, chances are you have created a household where those values will temper the rebelliousness in your children. The more tumultuous your marriage, on the other hand, the greater the likelihood that your parenting techniques will not be able to deal appropriately with teenage children. If your children are not yet teenagers, make the effort now to confirm your own relationship. Strengthen it for the onslaught of the coming years, when the power of your love will be the force that holds the family together during the stage when your children are preparing for their separation from you.

PERRY AND HIS FAMILY: PROBLEMS

Perry didn't have a problem. He said his *parents* had the problem. In his view, they were being unreasonable in objecting to his dropping out of college after his freshman year. It was clear to him that barely squeaking by with *C*'s was proof that he wasn't cut out for college. In his mind the only sensible thing to do was to leave the state university, return home, get a job, and start living a life of his own.

From his parents' perspective, the problem was Melissa. They were convinced that all Perry was interested in was being with Melissa. Evidence seemed to corroborate it: he came home every weekend to be with her, he didn't study enough because of her, he couldn't keep his mind on his studies because he was always thinking about her. Neither of his parents could understand how an *A* student in a top-notch high school could slip to low *C*'s in the state university, unless, of course, one considered his wildly romantic love affair with Melissa.

Everyone agreed that Marie, Perry's sister, *did* have a problem. Two years younger than her brother, Marie was already drinking heavily and smoking marijuana. Marie even admitted she had a problem, but only at home, where she didn't "get along well." She got along well with her peers, she was popular, she wasn't flunking. She couldn't remember a time she hadn't objected to her parents' way of handling things. And since Perry was her mother's "favorite" anyway, why, she wondered, should she try to be any different at home?

When I met the whole family that summer when Perry

came home, I knew there were more problems than they realized.

My problem was putting all the pieces together. It's hard to say where and when convoluted family problems begin; but if I were pinned down, I'd say that this problem began with *Walt,* although Walt didn't *know* he started the problem.

Walt was Perry's father's older brother. Both brothers operated the family business; and when Walt proved more successful than his brother, Perry's mother lost respect for the man she had married. Over the years this loss of respect grew into resentment that she had married him. Numerous quarrels and arguments arose in all areas of their lives. As Perry and Marie were growing up, they sensed the lack of love. They realized early on that there was little love to go around for everyone, and consequently, they engaged in severe sibling rivalry to win it. Perry's mother used him as an object of affection to replace her husband and showered him with attention. Marie decided at an early age that she could never please her mother, so why try. It was easy for her to slip into drugs and drinking when she got to high school, and to center her life around her school friends, who appreciated her more than her family. Perry's Byronic relationship with Melissa was, he admitted, the only thing in his life that sustained him. He wasn't appreciated at home; he was lonesome at school. He needed her, he argued, even if it did mean doing poorly in his studies. She was worth living for when nothing else was.

Over the summer all these issues emerged in family therapy sessions—slowly, painfully, and tearfully. But from June to September an entire family of four relived and reawakened to past problems and difficulties that were never resolved. Perry returned to school in the fall. His parents continued in therapy alone and came to reestablish a relationship based on openness and directness in expressing their feelings about each other. They discovered that the old feeling of love was not really dead. Marie responded to this improvement. She was at an age when she could appreciate the new change in her parents, and out of curiosity, she hung around home more to see what was up. What was up was that they seemed to love her more.

When Perry came home at Thanksgiving, the entire

family spent the long weekend at their mountain cabin,
something they hadn't done together in years. Not one of
them could remember when he had had so much fun before. It was especially fun for Perry, who came home with
several laurels: he had made the sophomore track team, he
was getting B's, and he had met a wonderful girl named
Cindy.

Now, I guess, Melissa has a problem.

Helping (Sometimes Pushing) Children into Adulthood

Mark Twain said that at fourteen he thought his father
was a fool, and at twenty-one he was amazed at how much
the old man had learned in seven years. I'm sure young
girls have often thought the same thing about their mothers. Parents have a remarkable ability to mature in those
seven short years when their children go from being adolescents to young adults! If only children could do the same!
Unfortunately, some don't. For them, the bridge between
adolescence and adulthood is a long stretch over a seemingly endless chasm! I've seen many young men and women
in their middle and late twenties still struggling with the
major issues of adolescence: sex, identity, authority, independence. For them the leave-taking from the family unit is
not bloodless. Perry's situation is illustrative of this problem.
His parents were surprised when his first year at college
proved so traumatic, because until then he had had a relatively quiet, peaceful adolescence. But when it came time to
separate physically from his home, even a home in which he
didn't think he really fit, he continued to reach out for
something or someone back home who would take care
of him and make him feel wanted.

Whenever a child leaves home, whether it be for college, the armed services, a job, or a marriage, the departure
causes stress of one type or another on the parents. No
married couple watches their children leave one by one
without some pang of loss or regret. It is an unavoidable
passage, and it brings up related issues. Some couples view
it as a symbol of their own aging. The children they brought

into the world and raised are now truly the next generation *of adults*. It's time for them to move over. Some couples see their children's leaving home as the breakup of the family unit that they worked so hard to preserve over the last twenty or so years. In a sense, what they lived for is now finished. It means discovering new goals, new reasons for living. It means changes in their daily habits, their concerns, the activities that gave meaning to their lives. Then, too, some couples perceive the onset of the "empty-nest syndrome" as they watch their children leave. The loneliness, the emptiness in their lives, the sudden realization that their children no longer need them as they used to—all the bleak descriptions they have heard or read about now seem to be before them. The days ahead look grim, and in the midst of their depression, they overlook the joys and opportunities that also lie down the road.

In a healthy marriage these predictable transitions are merely another surmountable swell in the tide of human life. In a less stable marriage they can precipitate a marital crisis through which a couple must devise a successful passage. If the children find it difficult to break the family ties and leave, then the shaky marriage will suffer even more stress. Together, a couple must help, even push, their children into adulthood. And together they must survive the passage into the next phase of their married lives.

The reasons that some children resist the idea of leaving are many: emotional instability, feelings of inadequacy, drug or alcohol abuse, laziness, and many more. Whatever your child's problem in this regard, you need to attend to your own relationship first. This is not being self-centered. Far from it. Your ability to help your child through this personal passage of leaving home is directly related to your ability to stick together, to be open with each other, and to discuss your child's best interests honestly. Most of all, you must stand united in your love for them, so that your children know that your insistence on their starting lives of their own is grounded in your love for them. They need to know that you're not throwing them out of your lives, and that your care and concern for them have not ended.

ART AND GLORIA: DON'T LEAVE ANGRILY, JUST LEAVE

Art and Gloria, a couple I knew socially, had been married twenty-five years. They were in their late forties and facing the Us-Again Phase of their Middle Years when they realized a problem was developing in their relationship. It was hard for them to admit that things weren't going well because for the last three or four years they had been looking forward to being alone again after their two children left home. Their son Jim had just graduated from college and had moved to California. Their daughter Candy, however, four years older than her brother, was still living at home. She had finished an executive training program at the phone company over a year ago and had a good salary. Art and Gloria had just assumed that when the training program ended she would move out into an apartment of her own. She was twenty-four, employed, and still living in her room upstairs.

What irked Art most, however, was that Candy seemed totally disinterested in helping around the house. She got up, went to work, came home, ate supper, and watched TV. When he spoke to Gloria about it, she made excuses for Candy. After all, Gloria argued, Candy never had to help while she attended the local college because she studied hard and was tired. Now she was still in training and adjusting to an important position at the phone company; and she came home too tired to pitch in with evening dishes, meals, weekend chores. Gloria's siding with Candy infuriated Art. He wanted to give Candy an ultimatum: either help or find your own place. Gloria objected. Their arguments, however, did not go unnoticed by Candy. Realizing that she was becoming a source of contention, she offered to pay a token amount each month as rent for room and board. Gloria objected even to this. As a result, the situation had reached a stalemate.

As tension between them started to mount, they knew that if they didn't do something, they would have severe problems. So they went to the beach for the weekend, resolved to find a solution to their dilemma. As they delved into it, it became clear that in addition to Candy's refusal to leave home, another related problem going back many years was also surfacing. Gloria had harbored a feeling of inadequacy for not having worked during the marriage when finances were tight and the two children were growing up. She had had traditional views about a mother's place being in the home and thought she would be abandoning her children if she sought a job. At the same time, she knew that Art's salary was barely making ends meet. Having Candy at home and treating her like a teenager allowed Gloria to perpetuate her role as mother, a role without which she thought she wouldn't be able to live. She could not imagine her relationship with Art without one or two children around the house. Her talk about looking forward to "just the two of us" was a smokescreen hiding deep fears of her own inadequacy. In recent months Art had been encouraging her to look for a job and expand her horizons, but the thought terrified her.

The more they thought about it, they decided that Candy was terrified too. A job was not the problem. Leaving home was. She was not very attractive, and rather shy; and judging from her experiences in school, a fulfilling social life did not come easily to her. When they spoke to her about this, it became clear that she could not imagine making it on her own socially. She was convinced that she would be lonely and unable to make friends. Even though she knew she was the crux of her parents' arguments, she felt it was better to be at home than to be floundering on her own. It was the old case of a child needing attention, even negative attention, rather than being ignored.

Luckily, Gloria was able to understand how her own feelings of insecurity were causing her to take an unrealistic attitude toward her daughter. She and Art also realized that Candy was indeed scared to leave home, and that her doing so would probably need to be gradual. They started to place reasonable demands upon her at home and asked for a certain amount of money each month for room and board. Candy decided to seek individual therapy in order to help herself stand on her own two feet. After six months Candy decided to move out. She found an apartment and a roommate and moved to the other side of town.

Once Candy was gone, Gloria began feeling better about

herself too. She got a job at a neighborhood card shop and said that for the first time in years she was actually fulfilling a lifetime's ambition. The best part, as Art and Gloria told me, was that once again they had started talking with enthusiasm about the many things they wanted to do and be involved with now that they just had each other.

*   *   *

At some point the mother bird boots the baby birds out of the nest, and they do fly. In our culture there really is no clearcut moment when a child should leave home. Every family must make that decision on an individual basis, child by child. Wise parents will discern the differences in their children's ability to fly from the nest and treat them accordingly.

20.

The Passages of Sexual Fulfillment

Making Time for Sex

In the Child-full Phase of the Middle Years, marital pressures arise that will affect your sex life differently from the earlier stresses of getting to know each other, adjusting to one another, overcoming sexual hang-ups, and developing a mutually gratifying physical relationship. A new and perhaps even greater pressure now arises—that of time. When you were just married, you had only yourselves to deal with. Then your firstborn arrived and greater demands were placed on both of you as you cared for the infant and raised him through his first few years. As long as there was only one child, however, you still could devote most of your emotional resources to each other.

In your Child-full Phase, there are likely to be several children growing into adolescence with all the demands and frustrations that that turbulent period in a child's life entails. You will undoubtedly have more financial pressures as the family grows. As a mother, you may start to work part-time or even full-time, either for financial reasons or to pursue interests of your own while you're still young enough. And both of you will probably become more heavily involved in community or neighborhood activities. And through all this, the shopping must be done, the car washed and fixed, household projects attended to, children taken to their activities, and, of course, time made to eat and sleep!

So where's the time for making love? If you make a list of the fifteen or twenty things that must get done on a certain day during the week, you might find that, even though you both love each other more than ever, making love comes last or near the end of the list. Let's hope it makes it on the list somewhere! But given the responsibilities of family life, many married couples in the Child-full Phase give priority attention to all the other commitments and omit the overriding commitment that brought them together in the first place—the commitment to express their love for each other on a daily basis in a life shared to the smallest detail.

A successful marriage is one based on a continuous expression of love, even though the manner and form of that expression may change as circumstances change. Mutual physical needs must be met, not the least of which is being held, cuddled, and gently stroked by the one you love. In a conscious and determined manner, you must assure each other of the time together so that your sexual relationship keeps pace with the changing circumstances of family life.

PHIL AND SHIRLEY: SEX BY APPOINTMENT

Phil was forty-two years old and, by profession, knew it was coming—his mid-life crisis. Phil was a clinical psychologist and on the faculty of the university medical school. He also had a thriving practice and was held in great esteem by his patients for having helped them through precisely the same thing. So when he confided to me one day that he had some vague unconscious dissatisfaction with his career, he shrugged and tossed off the all-too-easy answer that so many professionals and lay people alike use to explain that worried state that hits people around forty, the "old mid-life crisis." But something was wrong. As we talked further about it, it became clear to Phil that he was really satisfied with his career, which kept him challenged and interested.

It wasn't financial trouble. Both he and Shirley made a combined salary that let them and their three children enjoy the best of lives, the perfect "American dream," as we think of it in material terms. And it wasn't Shirley. For sixteen years they had had a wonderful marriage, each being the right match for the other. They had met in graduate school: she, studying sociology; he, psychology. As they raised their children, she lectured part-time to keep up in the field and had assumed a full-time position on the faculty when their third child entered school. She had won a certain amount of professional recognition in her field. She was happy. They were both still very much in love.

There seemed to be no other explanation for his depression other than the dreaded mid-life crisis. But something inside Phil told him that wasn't it. He could not deny the fact that he was depressed. As we explored the situation further, it became obvious that something in their sex life had deteriorated over the years. When asked, Phil said that "it isn't like it used to be." But that, too, seemed to be part of the mid-life crisis package! Or was it?

As Phil confided in me about his sexual relationship with Shirley, it became clear that the quality and the quantity of their time together had suffered. What it boiled down to was that they had very little time for making love, and the time they did have together was usually late in the evening after each of them had put in a hard day's work. Phil admitted nodding off most evenings when he read the paper after dinner. By the time they went to bed, they were both so exhausted that it was just easier to kiss goodnight and drift off to sleep. Shirley, who had a less intense sexual drive than Phil, usually didn't mind. Besides, she was tired too.

Eventually, they hit upon a solution that seemed almost too simple: sitting down at the beginning of the week with their individual appointment books and scheduling time to make love. Since they had unwittingly put sex and lovemaking at the bottom of their list of important activities, the simple solution was to move it up, schedule it first, keep at least one or two evenings—maybe time on the weekend—

open for each other. And it worked. As simplistic and artificial as it may seem, all they needed to get themselves back on the track was more time together. Within weeks Phil discovered to his amazement that his mid-life crisis had been a mirage. He was no longer depressed and discontented. What he had been blaming on his mid-life crisis was in fact a marital passage, a troublesome period of sexual frustration that was easily ended by taking steps to assure that they would have more time together.

* * *

Phil and Shirley's problem was easy to solve. Many couples in their Middle Years—either the Child-full, the Us-Again, or the Childless Phases—experience sexual difficulties that can't be corrected by pencilling "love" into one's appointment calendar. But because of the multitude of distractions that occur during these marital phases, time is often one of the key culprits in preventing a loving couple from realizing their love for each other in a mutually physical way. For many people an unspontaneous solution like scheduling is frequently a necessary component in the overall solution to the sexual problem. But, it's true, the problem may be more complicated.

Sexual Dysfunctions

It may be helpful to take a quick look at the more common sexual problems that can occur during any difficult period that unstabilizes your normal sexual pattern. The passages to sexual fulfillment in your Middle Years may be easier to handle with a little clinical knowledge to help you pinpoint the problem sooner and save worry in the long run. A sexual dysfunction is any disruption of your normal sexual functioning. The causes may be either physical, psychological, or a combination of both. Sexual dysfunction is a common occurrence in marriages that are undergoing additional nonsex-related pressures, such as those in the various phases of the Middle Years.

Impotency

Impotency is a fairly widespread sexual abnormality striking men at various times in their lives, especially when under stress. It only occurs in males and is usually experienced on a temporary basis. The condition is quite disturbing emotionally, especially for younger men. Older men often take it in stride as part of growing older. Impotency is manifested in several ways: difficulty in getting an erection, in sustaining one long enough for penetration, or in the inability to experience orgasm in spite of ejaculation.

Impotency can be caused by toxic factors, such as drugs or hormones; organic factors, such as physical illness or fatigue; or neurological disorders that prevent the proper development of the erection. Stress is a major cause of impotency, as are other psychological causes such as shame, guilt, fear, anxiety, or anger. The aggravating thing about impotency is that it can become self-fulfilling. A period of impotency itself creates additional worry, stress, and shame, which intensifies the psychological state that perpetuates the problem. The total effect is to produce an emotional climate in which a man is unable to function sexually.

Premature Ejaculation

Another common sexual abnormality in men is premature ejaculation. This is ejaculating before, or immediately after, insertion into the woman. In many cases, ejaculating before the man or woman wishes it is also considered premature ejaculation. It usually results in embarrassment or humiliation for the man, and often in a lack of sexual gratification for the woman. It is particularly annoying if you are trying for simultaneous orgasm, which, although not necessary for mutual sexual gratification, nevertheless remains a goal for many couples. Fortunately, the problem is a temporary one for most men, and the causes are not physical but psychological. After all, the man does experience orgasm. In most cases, the causes are related to feelings of inadequacy or unresolved sexual conflicts. Developing insight or having counseling can usually help to overcome this problem.

Frigidity

A woman is considered frigid if she regularly experiences partial, or complete lack of, sexual enjoyment and gratification. In the past, popular lore and medical knowledge did not place much emphasis on women's desire for sexual pleasure. In fact, it was commonly believed that "good" women shouldn't enjoy sex, but should simply put up with it for the sake of men. We live in more enlightened times, thank goodness! Today, women are profoundly aware of the distress of not enjoying sexual activity to the fullest. Some studies have shown that women actually have a greater potential for enjoying sex, including more frequent and intense orgasms than men. In some cases, this has led women to indulge in unrealizable expectations. It has also put great pressure on men as sexual partners. In any case, most women today know that frigidity is not a normal condition.

Nevertheless, it still occurs. It is usually caused by psychological problems involving negative feelings about intercourse. Some studies have shown that as many as forty percent of women have some type of difficulty achieving orgasm. And there are physical side effects, such as painful intercourse and involuntary spasms of the vaginal wall, that prevent the insertion of the penis. Both of these conditions can prevent the woman from functioning sexually.

When Monogamy Becomes Monotony

Sexual boredom is not considered a classical sexual dysfunction because it doesn't involve any abnormal functioning of the genital apparatus. But it, too, is related to pressures of marriage and has the potential to cause much distress, both in bed and out. Usually people will express it to a therapist or a friend as simply a matter of sex becoming dull or routine. They're in a rut; they've lost the desire for sex. Sometimes a man or woman perceives the problem as being that of the partner rather than him- or herself, and such is often the case. However it occurs, sexual boredom is inimical to a happy and healthy marriage. Many couples attribute it to monogamy, thinking that sex with the same person must eventually become dull and routine. While it is true that certain changes occur over time, these are not necessarily the same thing as boredom. Novelty, surprise, and the unexpected can diminish, but usually they are replaced by comfort, ease, knowledge, and security. Being at ease and comfortable with someone is not boring. Knowledge and understanding of the other's needs and how the other performs in making love need not be dull. And because a couple's sexual activities vary over the years, the current state of excitement or lack of it is not going to continue forever. Remember, as I've said before, we are inherently creative people, endowed with the capacity to experiment and innovate.

A common perception of boredom or dullness comes from watching one's lover age. Often we can imagine that "the fire has gone out" of our sexual lives because the body we have made love to for so long is no longer the young, nubile woman or the tight, hard-muscled man we originally married. Loss of physical attractiveness can account for a loss of sexual interest. Poor hygiene, obesity, unkempt appearance, bad breath, balding head, sagging breasts can act as sexual turnoffs for some people. It is important for couples, particularly in the Middle Years, to take proper care of their physical appearance. It's sad; but I've seen couples, even in the Acquaintance Phase of marriage, let their personal appearance slump, thinking that now that they've "caught" their man or woman, they don't have to look their best. But how wrong they are! While it's true that we can't prevent nature's aging process, we can and should do whatever we can to keep ourselves sexually appealing.

It's not uncommon to feel like you're in a rut sexually if the frequency and intimacy of your lovemaking declines, which it can easily do during the pressured Middle Years. With less time for making love, a couple can easily experience a decrease in intimacy, a lessening of sexual closeness, and a loss of interest in sex. As in the case of Phil and Shirley, you have to explore and invent new ways to make time and make love.

Boredom also results from one partner's sex drive being much lower than the other's. In psychological terms, this means that your libido is less active, either because of emotional or physical problems, or because you are aging. The male and female libidos have never been in sync chronologically. The male sex drive peaks in young adulthood and declines gradually and steadily thereafter. (But don't worry, it doesn't have to grind to a dead halt!) The female sex drive, however, doesn't peak until around age thirty and remains relatively stable until age sixty or older. Nature may have intended this in the early periods of evolution, when monogamy was not a moral and social obligation, so that the species would not become extinct. But the differences in sex drives can be frustrating for a couple of similar age who pledge fidelity to each other for the rest of their lives. It means that the wife's desire for sex continues to be paramount at a time when the husband is less likely to want it so intensely.

One thing about sex drives, however, is that personal expectations can greatly influence them. Some people become less desirous of sex as they age because they have been taught that it is unavoidable. Aging and the lowered sex drive thus become mutually reinforcing of each other, often leading to more extremely lowered expectations than are really necessary. Some people even feel ashamed or guilty when their normal sexual urge continues unabated into middle age and beyond. But it isn't the intensity or the frequency that causes boredom. Rather, it's an unrealistic attitude and appreciation of what to expect from each other that can make you think sex is no longer fun.

Remember, also, that situational problems unrelated to sex can influence your sex life. Loss of a job, problems with teenage children, financial worries, and other interpersonal stresses can impinge on lovemaking. Any feeling of anxiety, worry, guilt, or negative emotion can directly interfere with the desire for and the appreciation of sexual activity. Again, use your sex life as a barometer for your marriage in general. If it seems that your sexual fulfillment is in crisis, check out other areas of your relationship. You may be grappling with other issues that are adversely affecting your sex life. It is these transitions, not your sexual relationship, that may constitute the passages you must negotiate successfully.

HARRIET AND BART: WONDERING WHY THE FIRE WENT OUT

Harriet and Bart had been married for twenty years and had always had a good sexual relationship. But as they moved through their Childless Middle Years, something changed. Harriet seemed to notice it first when Bart's usual "style"—which had been one of extended foreplay, much tenderness and gentle preparation—turned into what she termed an attitude of "let's get it over with quickly." After a year of "quickies," she became bored with sex. This troubled her, so she came to me wondering if it was something about her—her aging, her appearance, her own strong desire for making love—that was turning Bart off. Or, was it some problem of Bart's?

After two sessions with Harriet, I asked Bart to join the meetings. He admitted that he had trouble maintaining an erection, so he speeded up his lovemaking for fear that he would lose it. I suggested that Bart have a physical examination since he had a family history of diabetes, which can sometimes lead to impotency. A few weeks later, his doctor gave him a clean bill of health. There was no physical cause.

On further exploration, it became clear to me that the problem had begun a few years earlier when Harriet had become involved with a church choir where she developed a strong, platonic friendship with a baritone named John. The friendship meant a lot to her because John shared her artistic and musical interests, but she never entertained any sexual thoughts about him. In fact, he wasn't a turn-on for her at all. But it was during this time that Bart began to feel "less like a man," as he put it, a feeling that continued even a year after Harriet and John's relationship cooled off. Bart's sexual dysfunction was directly related to his concerns about his own sexuality and the possible threat to his relationship with his wife from her church friend. In fact, Bart was angry and hurt that she had developed a friendship with John in the first place. Coming from a strongly traditional family, Bart believed that any "extramarital involvement"—even a nonsexual one—was totally unacceptable.

Moreover, Bart had been a virgin at the time of their marriage, and his lack of sexual experience had left him feeling inadequate and unsure of himself in this area. Over the years, he knew that he could satisfy his wife, but there always lingered a doubt that perhaps he lacked some quality or technique or knowledge that women expected. When he saw Harriet getting involved in a friendship with another man, he became very threatened and feared that he would lose her to John.

The Middle Years proved to be a very difficult time for Harriet and Bart in terms of sexual fulfillment. A problem that began years earlier and that was solely Bart's, his lack of sexual confidence, had grown into a situation of jealousy, fear, impotency, and, ultimately, sexual boredom for Harriet. They worked with me in couple's therapy for six months. They improved their communication and learned techniques to overcome this sexual dysfunction. Bart learned that he still possessed the sexual prowess to satisfy Harriet, and in time, they reduced the anxiety they both had felt about their sex life. In the end, their lovemaking became an enjoyable and fulfilling experience once again.

Infidelity and Its Aftermath

Within three years of the publication of their book *Open Marriage*, Nena and George O'Neill's own marriage opened up all the way, and they were divorced. So, too, were many of the unfortunate couples who decided that open marriage was the ticket for them. Throughout the last fifteen years, popular literature, TV shows, and trendy movies have portrayed traditional marriage as stifling and confining. The old, cynical joke about marriage being a "fine" institution, but "who wants to live in an institution?" was adopted as a way of life by many young people who later came to regret it. For all its self-indulgence and glitter, the "swinging life" can become just as much an institution, and extremely stifling and confining, because psychological growth demands commitment and fidelity at some point. A life totally rootless and self-centered cannot further personal growth and maturation. The result is an individual fixated on issues and desires that should have been resolved in adolescence. While it is true that marriage should be open, in that the couple feels open with each other to express their needs and desires, it proved grossly unwise to extend that openness to the point of each partner searching out his or her own fulfillment in any way conceivable. What couples discovered was that rampant personal fulfillment can lead to the destruction of mutual fulfillment. When someone thinks that personal fulfillment cannot be achieved *within* a relationship, there is little hope for the survival of that relationship.

At the core of this problem was the issue of boundaries. A cast of characters that should have remained outside the marriage entered into the minds, hearts, and beds of the married couple. And it doesn't take the late Cecil B. DeMille to warn you that a cast of thousands becomes unwieldy! In fact, three can be a crowd! Yet many couples experiencing the trials of their Middle Years thought that infidelity was the solution to sexual dysfunction or boredom. Such is never the case. If a marriage is going through a particularly troublesome time, sexual exclusivity, and a strengthening and deepening of sexual expression, are needed. For a marriage to thrive beyond mere survival of temporary crises, a couple must be sexually faithful to each other. In fact, the absence of fidelity makes it almost impossible for partners to open up and share their vulnerability with each other.

A solid marriage is built on the trust that the other will do everything within reason to help satisfy and support the troubled, anxious partner through personal and marital passages. We must believe that we are each doing our best to express care, love, and concern. If you learn that your spouse is taking advantage of you and abusing the faith you have placed in him or her, it becomes increasingly difficult for the relationship to continue. Sexual infidelity can destabilize your union and frequently causes its ultimate dissolution.

Not every case of infidelity leads to divorce, but infidelity always changes the nature of your relationship and hence the nature of the marriage. Many couples make their marriage survive after the breach of trust is closed and the extramarital affair comes to an end, but it is very difficult to reestablish a vital, trusting partnership without professional help. In my experience, it may not be possible even with professional help.

Not only do isolated instances of infidelity on the part of one spouse lead to a weaker union, but with couples I have treated, even mutually-agreed-upon infidelity, spouse-swapping, or group sex lead to fears and anxieties that are hard to calm after the fling is flung. What may seem like an exciting and titillating way to beef up your sex life eventually becomes a depressing and demoralizing way of diluting your trust and confidence in each other. We are always apprehensive about the unknown, and there is always so much "unknown" in any extramarital experience. Even years later, nagging doubts can arise: "Did he really enjoy it more with her?" "Does she continue to fantasize about him?" "Given a choice, would she still stay with me?" "Does he think staying with me was a mistake?" Doubt is insidious. It can become the crack that eventually splits open a marriage.

RALPH AND SUE: THE DILEMMA OF INFIDELITY

Sue had met Ralph when they both worked at IBM, she as a secretary, and he as a district supervisor. When they married and began to have children, Sue quit her job to raise the kids. When the children reached school age, Sue felt the need to better herself. But the thought of being a secretary again depressed her, so she went back to college to finish her degree. She spent evenings studying, and Ralph supported her by giving her the time to do it. It seemed only fair that after she finished her studies and Ralph needed evenings to work in order to be promoted that she reciprocate and not question his nights away from the family.

But something else seemed wrong. By now they were approaching their Us-Again Phase, and something had gone out of their relationship. Ralph was more distant. They had less to talk about. Each seemed preoccupied with individual interests. They made love less often, and it became less exciting, less special. It seemed to Sue that they weren't spending any time together, and the whole situation depressed her severely.

When she overheard from one of her friends that someone had seen Ralph leaving a motel one night several months earlier with a young woman, Sue panicked. She confronted him with it, and he admitted that he and a co-worker had had an affair about a year ago. It had started off on a professional basis, but eventually Ralph had to admit that his feelings for Sheila had changed, and that she, too, was becoming more and more interested in him. When she divorced, they began seeing each other.

Even though Ralph assured Sue that the affair was over, Sue just couldn't forgive and forget. She kept thinking about the fact that Ralph and Sheila worked side by side each day at IBM. Since she couldn't get it out of her mind, she thought that perhaps a separation would help her get a better perspective on it. They were caught in a dilemma: Ralph couldn't quit his job, Sheila would continue to be a part of his life every day, and Sue couldn't forget about the affair. She called me on "Talknet" and then wrote me twice for follow-up advice.

What both of them didn't realize at the time was that each was going through a personal mid-life crisis, one that typically occurs during the Middle Years. They didn't recognize this; all they knew was that each had to explore new areas. Sue had to go back to college; Ralph was worrying about whether he was still sexually attractive to women. After Ralph's affair, Sue also began to doubt her sexual identity, since it was defined only in terms of her husband. I suggested that they had to learn how to enhance the emotional, intellectual, and sexual aspects of their relationship. They needed to feel good with each other, to take a more active interest in each other's work and pursuits, to spend more quiet evenings together and make love like they used to. They tried this for several months on their own. When Sue wrote to say that it didn't work, I wrote back suggesting couple's therapy. Four months later Sue wrote to say that Ralph refused therapy, and she had decided to leave him. She just couldn't forgive him for what he had done.

Reasons for Infidelity

As Jimmy Carter said in his much publicized *Playboy* interview, even the most God-fearing man can lust after another woman in his heart. The crisis of infidelity may be nothing more than an unfulfilled lust in your heart, or it might become a full-blown affair. Whichever, the thought or the act, some aspect of infidelity is a fairly predictable passage in most marriages. Why does it occur? Why do our thoughts stray to other sexual partners, even when we remain physically faithful to our spouses? Why do we engage in indiscretions when we have so much at stake?

The famous Kinsey report, the first major survey on sexuality in this century, stated that half of all married men and one quarter of all married women were unfaithful during the course of their married lives. More recent studies and surveys indicate that today the incidence of infidelity is even higher, perhaps sixty percent or more. About three-fourths of unfaithful spouses cite some kind of sexual frustration as the primary reason. But sexual frustration is a vague term that can cover a multitude of problems. Let's take a look at the more specific causes.

Curiosity is a major reason for an extramarital affair: specific curiosity about what it would be like to go to bed with a certain person, or general curiosity to see what it would be like just to have an affair. The novelty of another sexual partner, or the excitement of having something "illegal" going on in one's life, can entice a man or a woman who genuinely loves his or her spouse and is committed to maintaining the marriage to delve into "forbidden waters."

Revenge is also a major reason for unfaithfulness. Over the years of married life, many hurts and grievances build up inside one or both of the partners, and the desire for revenge, for getting even or getting back, becomes intense. There are many ways to get even, of course, but often the most serious way (and a way that promises pleasure as well) is to be unfaithful. Even if the partner never finds out, there is still the satisfaction of having made up for all the little hurts and inconsiderations that have accumulated through the years.

As we have seen, boredom drives many people into the arms of another. If you think your sex life is boring, however, consider the fact that a sexual relationship is the product of two distinct people. It is hardly ever the case that just one person is boring in bed. Making love requires imagination and creativity. While another warm and willing body may temporarily prove exciting to you, chances are that the reason your sex life with your spouse became boring is that something about you is boring or prone to growing bored. Most likely, your outside romance will also grow boring.

A very common cause for infidelity is the perceived need for acceptance and recognition. When you feel that you are not appreciated for what you really are, you may have a natural inclination to seek acceptance and recognition wherever it can be found. We all need to feel appreciated and loved. The sad thing about people in their Middle Years is that they really can take each other for granted, omitting the little acts of love and tenderness that say in subtle ways, "I love you." It doesn't mean that love is gone. Far from it. It might be stronger than in the Early Years; but if it is not communicated, it might not be felt. That's why I stress that the *perceived* need for love and acceptance is what is crucial. Again, we must rely upon our innate creativity and imagination to devise ways to say "I love you" over and over, so that our mate really knows how important we think he or she is.

Some people are prone to infidelity because of deeper psychological problems and personality quirks: the immature man or woman who needs constant reassurance, constant stroking, constant attention; the person still raging against a parent now projected upon the marriage partner; the manic-depressive who engages in casual, extramarital sex for a euphoric high or to lift depressed spirits; the man who still needs to prove his masculinity or deny his latent homosexuality; the woman who must be the envy of every man. These people may have unconscious motives for being unfaithful, and it may take intensive individual treatment for them to understand themselves well enough to know why they have such difficulty in remaining true to their marriage partners.

In general, infidelity is likely to occur when a marriage is going through a particularly rough period, when one or both of the partners are having psychological problems, or when lovemaking becomes routine. In times of crisis, when we doubt our commitment or wonder if we were ever really committed at all, infidelity is an easy way out. Similarly, as the marriage goes through difficult passages of adjustment, problems arise, disappointments become magnified, and unreal expectations or demands convince the married couple that each is unwilling or unable to settle their sexual differences. At such times, each may look elsewhere for sexual fulfillment.

Variety and Other Kinds of Spice

Routines. By the time you're in your Middle Years you have many routines. If not, there's something wrong! But when routines creep into the bedroom, problems may appear where there weren't any before. Routine sex can be the expression of a wonderful, undying love, but it's like an expensive gift wrapped in an old shoebox covered with newspaper. A wonderful love needs better wrapping. But how to provide it? The spontaneous passion and excitement of falling in love are gone. Making love becomes a willing but lackluster duty, and all the roles that a person must play during the Middle Years—husband, wife, father, mother, professional, neighbor, friend, and so forth—can leave you too tired to play the role you performed so easily and expertly when younger: that of ardent lover.

BILL AND MARTHA: ONLY ON SUNDAY

Bill and Martha had no deep-seated marital problems. After ten years of marriage, they loved each other even more than on the day they wed. Bill was a successful salesman who spent more evenings away from home than he would have liked, but made up for it whenever he could by spending extra time with their three small children. Martha was a patient mother, an active PTA member, and a good neighbor in the block association of which she was vice president. Their life together was busy, active, happy, and rewarding.

And they made love every Sunday morning. Like clockwork.

The strength of their relationship was evident in the fact that Bill immediately told Martha when he started having sexual fantasies about one of the secretaries in his office. This led Martha to confess that she, too, was bothered by the fact that she no longer had passionate feelings for Bill. Together, they decided that the zest had gone out of their sexual relationship. Being intelligent people, they realized that overall their lives were filled with energy and goals. They prided themselves on getting so much done every week. But something had to suffer because of their hectic schedules and activities, and the victim was their sex life. Making love was also often very brief, if they were to get to church on time.

Unlike many other couples, Bill and Martha knew what the problem was. But what to do about it? They both wanted a fresh start. They wanted some changes made. When they called me on "Talknet," I suggested they try marriage encounter. They enrolled in a marriage-encounter program through their church, which met for a weekend and then once a week for six weeks. As part of the program they were given various "assignments" that could not be carried out on Sunday mornings alone, and which they both found to be rather "sexy." After six weeks of improved communications, the old spark returned to their relationship, and they willingly adjusted their busy lives to accommodate the new variety in their lovemaking. They called back to tell me that they had solved their problem.

*   *   *

If only there were as many different varieties of sex as there are sex manuals! Browse through a few, though, and you'll see that most of them hit the high points, some sink to rather low and disgusting depths, and others tell you what you've known all along. Not all are worth the ink they're printed with. But some are very worthwhile, and the psychology section of your local bookstore probably has one or two—with sexual techniques that could add a little spice and variety to your lovemaking—that would appeal to you and your spouse.

But there is much beyond mere technique. Here is where the creative imagination can really diversify your sexual routines. For example, unlike most animals, the human variety can have sex any time of day or night, any time of the year, and almost any place. If your sexual habits have gotten stuck on a certain day and time and place, try varying them. Many couples get a special charge out of arranging to have sex in "offbeat" places and at times that are not the usual ones. If your pattern is to make love at night when you're usually tired, try mornings. If you can take a break in the afternoon, do it. You might want to get out of the house altogether. A wooded area, a deserted beach, even a cheap motel room might prove stimulating.

Variation on the themes of foreplay and loveplay can increase passion and fervor. You don't always have to undress, douse the light, pull back the covers, get in position, and begin your routine the same way each time. Touching, stroking, massaging, hugging, caressing, licking, kissing, biting, wrestling, tickling, and back to simple touching. . . . Well, there isn't an *infinite* number of combinations, but there are probably a good number you haven't explored or tested yet. Pulling surprises on each other, however, requires that you feel relaxed and secure with each other. Old habits and inhibitions aren't broken easily when one or the other of you is uptight. Good communication is necessary so that you can be honest with each other, letting the other know that the whipped cream, for example, was too cold, or that your knees get numb in the bathtub or whatever.

Frequency of lovemaking causes all types of worry. Some couples are bothered because they feel they *should* be making love all the time; others become concerned only when several weeks pass by. There is no optimal amount of lovemaking. Each couple is different, and different periods of your life will allow for different amounts of sex. There's nothing wrong with going for a period of time without making love. What's important is that you make love when you both really want to, and that it retains some of the spontaneity that it had early in your relationship.

One of the key elements of sex that, surprisingly, few lovers will admit to each other is fantasy. We all have our pet fantasies, and indulging in them mentally during sex is in no way disloyal, immoral, wrong, or abnormal. Some couples talk about their fantasies with each other and find it enhances the intimacy of their relationship. Some couples act out their fantasies. Then again, some people believe you should never try to experience fantasy because it will always fall short, lose its power, and no longer function as a fantasy. Whatever your own feelings on this are, you might find that talking or acting out your fantasies could freshen your lovemaking. But only try what is mutually acceptable to both of you, keeping in mind that one person's turn-on can be another's turnoff.

A Man and a Woman

We all play so many roles in the course of a week, a month, or even a day, that it is sometimes hard to slip from one role into another. The role we often overlook is the very basic one of being a man or a woman. Many sex lives can be reenergized when the partners reconsider their roles as men and women in their acts of intimacy. The best way to get back into these basic roles is to set aside time for each other—when the kids are away, the TV is off, the phone is disconnected, or whatever else you must do to assure your privacy together. Then talk to each other openly and intimately about what it means to be a man or a woman—how you appreciate the other's femininity or masculinity—remembering how the oppositeness of the other sex drew you together in the first place. Activities such as taking a walk together, sharing a leisurely cup of coffee, jogging together, or going on a picnic will let you relate to each other more as lovers than as husband and wife, father and mother, and all that such titles imply. Simply be a man and woman for each other, but in a way that doesn't force you into exaggerated stereotypes of masculinity or femininity. Each of you has a streak of the other sex in you. In every woman there is a masculine quality, and in every man, a feminine aspect. A well-matched couple will let each other express that oppositeness *within* them as well as that *between* them. The important point is to remember and relive what it meant for the two of you to be lovers.

21.

The Passages of Illness and Change

As a couple goes through the Middle Years, especially from their thirties into their fifties, their paths may diverge. Because so many personal passages occur during this time, such as menopause, mid-life crises, career disillusionments, and the changing relationships with our children if we have them, we may find we are pursuing what seems to be disparate paths from our spouses. If you have not been able to establish a viable relationship by this stage of your marriage, it is likely that your goals, values, and interests may become more different, and in the process the two of you become more isolated from each other. If synchronization is drastically off, one or both of you may actually decide to give up the marriage to lead your own life.

Outgrowing Each Other

When a couple realizes that they are outgrowing each other, serious steps must be taken before the marriage is hopelessly lost. Early indications that the husband and wife are marching out of step with each other are usually seen in one or both getting overly involved in jobs or careers. In the case of a mother, she may turn her attention more and more to her children so that they become her sole reason for living. On the surface, it is hard to argue with these tendencies. Who could deny a mother's love and concern for her children? How could a parent be criticized during these productive years for the hard work at his or her profession that will result in promotions, rather than being left behind by younger employees moving ahead? And how could one find fault with the major breadwinning parent wanting to do his or her best to make higher salaries now that the children are growing into the age when their requirements become more expensive? And yet it is easy to see the diverging paths as the two partners begin to exclude each other from more and more activities, including their own thoughts and the times they could be sharing together.

When such a situation arises, it is often based on a disparity of interests and expectations that has been present from the early days of the marriage but overlooked until now. Many people marry for the wrong reasons that don't become clear to them until they are older and wiser and have lived a good number of years with the "wrong" marriage partner. Unfortunately, it is in these Middle Years that a person realizes this may be the last chance to change directions, start a new life, and hope for a better marriage with someone else.

If you think you've outgrown your partner, there are no easy self-help remedies that will put you both back in step with each other. Couple's therapy may be the only recourse. It is incredibly difficult at this stage of your marriage to step back alone and take an objective look at the problem. Frequently, an outside observer, trained in the intricacies of marital problems, can really help you see what the problem is, where its roots lie, and what steps to take to rectify the situation. Individual therapy for either you or your mate may also be required. But together as a couple you must sit down, confront the fact that one or both of you are dissatisfied with the arrangement, express frankly your disappointment in the direction your relationship is going, and commit yourselves sincerely to do what is necessary to renew and strengthen your bonds.

ELLIE AND VIC: MARCHING OUT OF STEP

Ellie and Vic knew that they still loved each other after thirteen years of marriage; but now in their Childless Middle Years, they weren't sure it was the kind of love that could hold a marriage together. They both agreed that not every love should end in marriage. But should their changing love for each other end a marriage? That's what they called me on "Talknet" to find out.

Ellie was an executive secretary to one of the vice presidents of an electric utility company, and Vic was a top salesman for a wire products manufacturer. They had no children due to Vic's low sperm count, something they found out after years of trying different methods, remedies, positions, and a lot of hope. Ellie continued to be depressed over it, because she really wanted a child of her own. They decided that an adopted child would not be the same.

In recent years Vic had begun to spend more time with clients and customers in the evenings. On weekends he would get up early to go fishing or hunting. Ellie often left her office at five o'clock and diverted her attention to other matters, such as social clubs and spending several evenings a week with her aging mother who had suffered a stroke a year earlier. They both began to realize that their marriage had little substance. They were very compatible roommates, but disinterested lovers. They were not at all cohesive as husband and wife. They were literally carving out separate lives for themselves within the structure of a dissolving marriage.

Vic had suggested they try a separation to see if they might get a clearer perspective on their true feelings about each other. He wanted to move out. I advised them not to separate, that it's easier to salvage a marriage when the couple lives under the same roof rather than at opposite ends of town from each other.

Ellie called back about three months later. Vic had refused my suggestion and had moved into an apartment. After two months he announced that he wanted a divorce. Believing herself to be a reasonably attractive woman, still hoping someday to be a mother, and knowing that her childbearing years were running out, Ellie easily acquiesced to the divorce in order to begin over again and look for another husband.

*　　*　　*

It often happens this way: slowly, unobtrusively, without any major crises or disagreements. A couple gradually begins to notice that their lives are diverging; as they confront these issues, they have little investment in putting forth the efforts to negotiate them successfully. They look back over the previous months or years and realize that they have been moving through a transitional period, which rather than strengthening and deepening their commitment to each other, is in reality leading them down separate roads. And a series of such negative passages ultimately lead to divorce.

The Impact of Menopause

There are a lot of myths and misconceptions about the impact of menopause. The topic has been given a lot of press lately; many women believe it to be the major mid-life issue. The symptoms of menopause vary from woman to woman. Some women suffer hot flashes, flushing, perspiration, headaches, dizziness, palpitations, sleeplessness, depression, and weight gain. Others have only hot flashes and perspiration. How do we account for this difference of experience?

For one thing, at the cessation of menses for at least one year (the technical definition of menopause, or change of life), a woman's ovaries gradually cease to function. The result is a change in hormonal balance, which produces hot flashes and increased perspiration. Those two symptoms are standard. But what about the various other discomforts? They frequently are due to psychological factors. Many are the same problems that can strike anyone, even men who are going through unwanted biological or social changes. When a person is seriously upset, stress and worry can trigger a host of other physical and emotional symptoms.

It's understandable that women who have preexisting emotional problems will likely suffer more symptoms when they reach menopause than women who are relatively well balanced.

Since some women have very little traumatic reaction to what is indeed a major turning point in their adult lives, it's best to look at the change of life in the context of the woman's entire life. For example, if a woman has spent the majority of her adult years in the role of mother, heavily investing her emotions in her children and family, when she reaches the time in her life after which she can no longer be a mother again, she may feel the loss of a role in which she found great satisfaction. This type of woman is a likely candidate for depression and its accompanying other physical symptoms during menopause. On the other hand, if a woman never had children, or if children were not the total center of her life, and her identity as a woman was not limited solely to them, then she will probably pass through menopause with greater ease. Childless women with fulfilling careers or social lives often have very little difficulty with change of life.

It's curious that many women find reaching thirty a more troublesome passage than going through change of life, possibly because if a woman has not yet had children, or if she wants more children, she knows that time is running out. Since this situation involves hard choices and major decisions for herself and her husband, it can be a more trying passage for both of them. With menopause there is no choice, but turning thirty can be a crisis involving tough decisions about how to use those remaining fertile, childbearing years.

Mid-life Crisis and Other Excuses

There's no question about it, most of us go through a great deal of psychological turmoil in our late thirties and early forties. But none of this emotional chaos need threaten your marriage. My personal belief from the cases I have handled is that when mid-life crisis does become a stum-

bling block to a happy marriage, it is because a person uses
the crisis to mask other problems in the marriage. In both
men and women, menopause concerns a change in hormonal structure. As the reproductive system ages, it produces fewer hormones. Naturally, this will cause both physical
and psychological stress, which can be alleviated somewhat
by the love and support of the person to whom you are
married. The joy of marriage is that you do not have to go
through this change of life alone. If the marriage is not
loving and supportive, if over the years you have grown to
rely on your spouse less and less, then the lack of support
and understanding can turn a major personal passage into a
marital crisis.

Remember that as we reexamine our lives at the mid-
way point, we are bound to confront our own shortcomings.
We will have some regrets, some lost hopes, and perhaps
some guilty feelings over past events. But we should recognize the brighter side too. There have been achievements
and successes. We need to come to terms with our expectations for the second half of our lives and restate our resolve
to progress according to our plans with renewed marriage
commitments. If we have had a happy marriage, we can
look forward to continuing along the same path, nurtured
and befriended by a loving spouse. If the marriage has been
somewhat unhappy, we should resolve to work out the
problems so that we don't end up grumpy, discontented,
bickering old people. In any event, we must come to terms
with the fact that we are growing old.

It's not always easy to do. When I turned forty, I didn't
feel any older. I told everyone it was no "big deal," and, of
course, everyone thought I was bluffing. What bothered me
most was precisely that *they* thought I was getting old. And
they treated me as if I were getting old, so I did start to feel
and act old. Not old in any sense of "worse." Just older. In
other words, my place in society was changing, whether or
not I experienced any drastic changes in my mind or body.
I was becoming a more senior member of society. I was no
longer a young adult. I know I went through that period as
easily as I did because I was a reasonably happy man. Diane
helped and supported me. My children gave me great satisfaction. I was happy in my work. The same is true of

countless men and women in every walk of life. A loving spouse, a nurturing homelife, a satisfying job—and the psychological turmoil of mid-life is minimal.

Some people are not so lucky. Their marriages are unfulfilling, and their careers leave much to be desired. They reach mid-life with many regrets, a lot of bitterness, and an unhealthy amount of resentment. They have a miserable change of life and never realize that their misery is due more to the emotional problems in their marriage than to the hormonal changes in their bodies. Often these people have no severe or overt marital difficulties—only a series of minor ones—that now flair up during the mid-life crisis. In such cases, if you can't come to terms with these issues yourselves, it may take the professional insights of a psychiatrist to prevent them from becoming stumbling blocks. Sometimes the couple involved is so close to the problem that they can't see it objectively. Only when the unhappiness turns into gross misconduct, such as verbal or physical abuse, alcoholism, drugs, sexual adventurism, and other erratic behavior, do some people finally see that the problem lies much deeper than hitting forty.

The limited scope of this book prevents it from being a manual on how to handle really serious emotional problems that may plague people at mid-life. If you think you or your spouse is confronting a serious personal problem, please consult a reputable therapist and begin to explore the roots of your difficulties. All I can say here is that turning forty should not be totally disruptive to your marriage. Worrisome for you personally, yes, but never to the extent that your spouse and children should entertain serious thoughts about you as husband or father, wife or mother. It's obviously worse than measles, but in some ways it's like measles. It's a temporary disturbance that you should eventually resolve without your marriage or your family being any worse off because of it. In fact, the more successful your resolution, the more this should enhance your marriage and family relationships.

Becoming More Like Your Parents

We rarely want to be just like our parents. Or let me put it this way, there is usually something in one or both of our parents that we swear we will never repeat. But inevitably we do become somewhat like them. We can't help it. We *are* like our parents. For better or for worse, they were the chief influence on us in our formative years. Their mannerisms, traits, characteristics, temperament, values, attitudes, behaviors have been indelibly inscribed in our psyches. So, on a conscious level we say we don't want to be like them, but on an unconscious level it's all we know.

I see this in myself most often when I correct my sons in a way that I remember my father correcting me. At the moment I don't realize how much like my father I am acting. But when I reflect back on what has just happened, I have to slap the palm of my hand against my forehead for having forgotten that I promised myself I would never do that! Hopefully, we don't revert to our parents' methods of handling crises if those methods are destructive ones. Physical abuse, alcoholism, screaming, shouting, withdrawing into isolation, ignoring the needs of your spouse—these can all be behavior patterns that can eventually destroy a marriage.

JODY AND FRANK: "YOU'RE JUST LIKE YOUR MOTHER!"

To Jody those were fighting words! Frank hurled them at her frequently and with a great deal of accuracy. They hit the mark and they spoke the truth.

Frank, who was a member of a bicycle group I belonged to, had known Jody since high school; together they used to feel sorry for the way Jody's mother raised her three younger brothers. Her mother was a strict, demanding woman who would tolerate none of the ruckus and boys-will-be-boys behavior that is normal for growing youths. Jody always felt lucky that she had escaped her mother's wrath because she was a girl and rather well-behaved.

Now with their own two boys, Jody frequently slipped

into mannerisms and attitudes that she had always hated in her own mother. When Frank caught her at it, he would tell her she was just like her mother. Frank, too, was hurt by Jody's behavior because he found it unfeminine and unmotherly, and he felt that in the long run it would leave emotional scars on his sons. As in most cases like this, when someone becomes like his or her parent, it becomes a problem for the person's spouse. Resolving the difficulty is often a little understood marital passage but one that needs as much care and attention as others. Luckily, Jody recognized the problem and admitted that Frank was right. She also did not want to see their sons grow up treating her as coldly as her brothers now treated their mother.

Because she was aware of this tendency in herself, Jody resolved that she would change. She enlisted Frank's aid. Whenever he saw her start to react or behave like her mother, he would say to her, "Hi, Mom!" This would remind her of what she was doing, and she would pause and rethink her actions. Her two sons, who were seven and nine years old, eventually caught on to what was happening, and they joined in also. It became a family game. "Hi, Mom!" meant stop and think. And it had the additional, fortunate effect of causing the kids to think about their own behavior. As Jody got control of herself in this matter, Frank stopped accusing her of being like her mother. Not only did that solve the arguments between the couple, but it gave Jody much more confidence that she was raising her children in her own way—a way she could feel proud of.

A Death in the Family

No family escapes death, just as no human being escapes death. Whenever it comes, we are not really prepared for it, not even the family who watches it come to one of its members during a long, lingering illness. We think we prepare, but at the final moment, the strengths and resources we thought we could rely upon prove all too inadequate. A rug is pulled out from under our feet. We are at a loss as to which way to turn, whom to call upon for help, what to ask for or expect in our moment of grief.

A healthy family pulls together at the death of one of its members. In these families, death is a passage that unites the family and draws from each of them the love and devotion that is expressed less dramatically during normal times. The healthy family is its own primary source of strength, but it also has other resources. I've found that the emotionally stable families are networked into the larger community. They have close contacts with in-laws, cousins, grandparents, neighbors, and friends. Each of us needs support at the time of a loved one's death, and the wider the base of that support, the less isolated is our grief. We feel rooted in the mainstream of life rather than in the emptiness of death.

In general, families that find it hard to express love for one another are less able to cope with stress. Each family member feels extremely isolated at the death of a father, mother, sister, brother, or spouse. Emotional health, in one sense, is the ability to cope with stress, and nothing is more stressful than the death of someone dear. If a family's natural method of dealing with stress is to lash out at each other, start quarrels, and make accusations, then this will typify their response to a death in the family. It's sad; but at a time when you want and need your family to be there supporting and expressing their love, they sink into petty bickering, renewing old battles, reinflicting old wounds.

The way to prepare for a death in the family is to create a stable, well-functioning family unit that can cope with the multiple, stress-inducing events of life. Remember, all the passages of life and marriage have the ability to strengthen your character and your relationships. Each passage, no matter what it concerns, is preparation for the most serious passage of death. You can learn how to cope with the stress, even though you cannot ever really cope with death itself. You must survive it.

I consider a great deal of my work as a family therapist to be preventive psychiatry. Most of what I do with troubled couples and their families is to help them learn how to deal with stress—how to cope and survive—with big problems and little ones, with the major passages of life and the minor disruptions of daily living. It is all preventive. It is something we must learn as we go along: something we can train for as a warrior or an athlete trains, but which is only realized in the actual event. At the moment of death, when the love you have developed and expressed over the years for each other comes and rescues you from the natural weakness of being all too human, this enables you to go on.

The Chronically Ill Or Disabled Household

If you have a chronically ill or disabled child, the effect can be devastating upon your marriage. Even the healthiest relationship will be shaken to some degree. If the marriage had difficulties brewing before the birth of the disabled child or the discovery of the illness, it is exceedingly difficult for the couple to pull through the initial shock and readjust their lives, even with professional help. Such a child becomes a stumbling block for even a sound marriage.

Like death, there is very little you can do to prepare for the psychological upheaval you will experience on learning about your child's problem. Perhaps knowing how most couples react will at least reassure you that your own response is somewhat natural. There is a classic set of responses that you might think of as the "predictable pattern of grief." Initially, the couple will react with shock and disbelief. They refuse to believe that the life they had envisioned for themselves will now be drastically challenged, possibly even thwarted, by the burden of raising a disabled or chronically ill child. Eventually, the initial disbelief is followed by anger—anger at fate, God, themselves, life. During this period, the generalized anger may be focused on each other. One partner may blame the other. For example, a husband may accuse his wife of not having taken proper care of herself during pregnancy or for having used medications that she didn't really need. The wife may blame her husband for some genetic flaw that she perceives coming from his side of the family. Usually these recriminations are unfounded, but understandable, considering how intense is the parental pain for a couple who has given birth to a child whose life, they believe, will be filled with suffering. Blaming each other may be irrational, but the effect is often a real sense of guilt in the parent who is being blamed or who thinks he is most at fault. There is often an abiding suspicion that the illness or disability could have been prevented. "If only I had done such and such," or "if only I had not done that," the parent thinks to him- or herself.

The next phase is depression, as the parents come to realize the true impact of the situation. But most parents eventually lay aside the guilt and depression and come to accept this reality. Final acceptance is important. If one or both parents continue to harbor a secret guilt or fail to overcome the initial depression, their ability to raise the child is hampered even more seriously. What the child needs most is loving, optimistic parents, free of anger, resentment, and self-doubt. The child's own life will be a struggle to overcome anger and resentment, and it is crucial that the household doesn't breed these negative moods. The family with a disabled or chronically ill child must strive to create an environment of love, cheerfulness, and acceptance.

Expect permanent changes in the nature of your relationship with your spouse. New burdens and responsibilities must be shared, more love and support must be expressed just to get through the practical matters of trips to the doctors and hospitals, transporting the child to rehabilitation centers, buying special equipment, paying medical bills. You may both need special training in order to care for the child; and as your other children become old enough, you will be training them to care for their sister or brother. You may even have to see that one member of the family is always at home if your child needs round-the-clock attention. Furthermore, the two of you will never have the social life, perhaps not even the career opportunities, that you had hoped for. Community and recreational activities may be severely limited, and your other children may develop emotional problems because of this as well.

The picture is grim, but as a psychiatrist, I can assure you that a healthy, loving marriage can hold a family like this together. I have seen husbands and wives pull together as a team, organize other family members including the grandparents, and the results have been beautiful examples of how human beings who truly love one another can surmount the greatest obstacles. As a team you can meet these terrible situations; and should you need professional therapy to help you hold that "team" together, by all means get it.

MARK AND RACHEL: PULLING THE FAMILY TOGETHER

When Mark and Rachel were in the middle of their Child-full Phase, their third son Josh was born. They had decided this would be their last child, since Rachel wanted to become an interior designer and had planned to return to design school when Josh began first grade. But shortly after his birth, it became clear that he had numerous problems. After several months of evaluations by pediatric neurologists both as an inpatient and outpatient, he was diagnosed as suffering from cerebral palsy.

Both Rachel and Mark went through the classic pattern of shock and disbelief followed by anger and guilt. There seemed to be no good explanation for Josh's problem. They came to me for treatment, and Rachel was so upset that I treated her with antidepressant medications for several months. Together in couple's therapy, they overcame their initial grief and depression; Rachel went off medication, and they terminated therapy after nine months.

But two years later, they returned totally "burned out." As Josh grew older, he required special chairs and feeding equipment. Rachel attended instructional classes to learn physical therapy techniques to use in handling Josh. They had switched therapists and doctors several times when they had grown dissatisfied with Josh's slow progress. In addition, Rachel was having difficulty dealing with her six- and nine-year-old daughters after school and in the evenings. Mark did as much as he could in his spare time, but as director of marketing for a large company he had evening meetings and business trips with some frequency. The two had no time for any satisfying social life or recreational activities together because one would stay home with Josh while the other went out with the two older girls. Needless to say, their sexual life waned under this stress, and they were not taking adequate time to care for each other.

In therapy the second time around, I pointed out that for the family to function and for the couple's own relationship to grow, massive reorganization was needed. Weekly schedules to care for Josh were worked out. Both sets of grandparents were called in to sit with him at least once a week. Even friends and relatives took part on a regular basis to give Rachel blocks of time now and then to pursue her own interests and get out of the house. She even got a part-time job in a local furniture store, working only a few hours a week; but it was a step in her continuing career goal of interior design. Most important for their own relationship, Mark and Rachel arranged through a respite program provided by the community for families of the disabled, to have one weekend a month for short trips or visits to friends.

The new scheduling worked. Both Rachel and Mark became more relaxed, their relationship improved, and as Josh grew older, they could take him more places. Eventually they enrolled him in a daily program for disabled children. Ultimately, they developed a reasonably satisfying lifestyle for themselves and their children, as they successfully adjusted in the face of this overwhelmingly devastating situation and moved into their Mature Years.

*   *   *

As you probably know, the stress level in a household with a disabled person is extremely high. It's important to turn to others for support. Don't expect government aid to solve your problems. It is woefully inadequate. You are really on your own as far as soliciting assistance from friends, relatives, and community organizations. If you do this successfully, you'll be ahead of the game in preventing the familial burdens from becoming stumbling blocks to a successful marriage. Maintaining your relationship with each other is paramount. Inspiring your children and close relatives to participate and share the burden is also crucial. I have seen families perform incredible acts of devotion and sacrifice in this regard. When I worked with a nonprofit home health care agency, I saw a remarkable family who went to extreme lengths to allow a grandfather to die at home rather

than in a hospital. Each member of the family learned how
to insert feeding tubes into the grandfather's stomach when
he would accidentally pull them out at night. They provided a round-the-clock vigil in his last months. Held together and inspired by the love of a superb marriage, each
family member came to understand the real meaning of
family life. What other example of devotion could possibly
top that of a family who provided a warm, loving home so
that one of them could die in peace?

Institutionalizing the Disabled Child

The decision to place a child in an institution is an
agonizing one. Even when it is perfectly clear that you and
your spouse can no longer care for the child at home,
taking the actual step to place your own child in another
home is a traumatic passage. The typical reaction is to feel
guilty, to think that somehow you have failed. Perhaps you
blame yourself twice, once for having had a child so severely disabled, and second, for "giving up" when you can
no longer keep the child at home. Many couples continue to
harbor a doubt that perhaps they could have done more or
kept the child just a bit longer.

You may even feel a bit selfish, since part of your
decision to institutionalize the child is to save your own
marriage. But that motive is a perfectly legitimate one. You
must save your marriage. The divorce rate among couples
with severely disabled children is high. And a disabled child
with divorced parents is, indeed, twice handicapped. For
the good of everyone, it can be important to place the child
in a home. In going through a marital passage as traumatic
as this one, it is crucial to keep your own relationship
centered, for it is the source of strength that will radiate out
to those around you. Do not feel guilty or selfish about
providing for your own love to grow and mature. If you
don't, you could lose your child and your marriage.

FRED AND CHRISTINE: CONSUMED WITH GUILT

Fred and Christine's twenty-two-year-old daughter Gail took a drug overdose from which she never fully recovered. The couple, in their Us-Again Phase, blamed themselves for not doing enough for Gail to prevent her from resorting to drugs. To ease their guilt, they felt they should keep the girl at home, even though only a professional could have really provided the assistance she needed. The brain damage was severe. She couldn't talk or recognize anyone. She could be placed in a chair where she barely managed to feed herself finger food from a tray. Finally, after several months of attempting to cope with the situation, Fred and Christine decided that a nursing home was the only solution. The strain of caring for Gail at home was beginning to take its toll on their marriage. They became irritable, quarreled with each other, and found no time to go out or engage in the activities they had both enjoyed before Gail's accident. Life for them had come to a standstill.

After Gail was institutionalized, Christine visited her daily. But she soon came to realize that doing so was too demoralizing. The daughter never recognized her, and it was impossible to carry on a conversation. Christine's visits became weekly, then monthly. Finally, she could bring herself to visit Gail only once every two months. Throughout it all, she was overcome with guilt. When she called me on "Talknet," I told her that individual psychotherapy would be most effective in helping her deal with her guilt. A year later she wrote to tell me that therapy indeed had helped her resolve her grief and self-blame. Together she and Fred learned that in such a situation, their marriage came first, and that to maintain a healthy relationship they could not live consumed with guilt.

Alcoholism and Drug Abuse

If one member of your immediate family abuses drugs or alcohol, the entire family will suffer. If it is your spouse, you have a very serious problem on your hands. People addicted to drugs and alcohol have the potential of doing terrible things to others, even those they love. In response, the other members of the family get pulled into the whirlpool of abuse and insults, and respond in like fashion. The result is a household always teetering on the brink of destruction.

How should you handle an alcoholic or a drug abuser?

There's no easy method. It requires strong and patient effort by everyone in the household. First, it is the nature of the sickness that the abuser or alcoholic will undoubtedly deny the problem. The alcoholic will probably accuse *you* of having the problem! He'll say that he really doesn't drink that much and that you are the one who has difficulty accepting his drinking. He'll project the "problem of drinking" onto you, accusing you of being unreasonable with his use of alcohol. Also, alcoholics are great rationalizers. If they should admit that they drink a little too much, they always have good explanations for why they do. They'll say it's because of pressure at work or family tensions, perhaps even suggesting that some problem in their marital relationship is the reason they have taken to drink. If your spouse uses that line of rationalizing, then you become the "cause" of the problem!

These three behaviors—denial, projection, and rationalization—are to be expected in alcoholics and drug abusers. It's almost impossible to deal with them on a rational basis. The more you argue, the more they feel the pressure to escape through their addiction. In the end, only outside intervention will save the addict in the majority of cases. You must get your spouse or child into therapy or Alcoholics or Narcotics Anonymous, or a drug or alcohol clinic. You and the rest of the family should seek counseling through Alanon, Alateen, or other support groups, in order to learn how to minimize the effect of the disease on the rest of the family.

In a clear crisis, such as trouble with the law, drunk driving, loss of job, failure to perform adequately at work, or tardiness and absence from school, getting help is a question of immediacy. There is no longer time to wait to see if your mate will get over the problem or if your child will ease up on the drugs. Once there is a clearcut case of breaking the law or of not being able to function in one's duties, it is your responsibility to get the family member to a helping resource at once.

There is, however, no easy way to do this. One way is talk to the "experts" yourself for advice on how to handle your particular situation. Under their direction, you might have a direct confrontation with him or her. Have everyone—family, friends, supervisors at work—confront the addicted person's destructiveness. You often have no other choice because alcoholics rarely go into therapy voluntarily. They need to be pushed and confronted continually with the hell that the addiction is creating for themselves and others.

The Physically or Emotionally Ill Spouse

A few special words should be said about the problem of how to cope with serious illness when it strikes your spouse and there are children in the family. In one sense, when illness strikes a child, it creates the need—obvious to everyone—for the husband and wife to pull together. But when one of the married partners is the disturbed or disabled member, then even greater stress is generated for the healthy spouse. You are required to shoulder an increasing share of the responsibility for the marriage, the family, and the home. It all rests on you. And to make matters worse, the ill spouse may actually turn on you in anger over being disabled and may even express displeasure over the way you are running the household. It's an almost no-win situation.

If your children are old enough to understand what has happened to their father or mother, their help can be solicited. They can share the household duties and care for the impaired parent. If they are still young, you will have to seek comfort and solace from relatives or friends. In a marital relationship that had previous problems, the healthy spouse is likely to seek love and attention in an extramarital relationship. This is especially true in the case of mental illness, which is difficult for the healthy partner to cope with and understand. Physical illness elicits our pity and concern because we understand pain and suffering. Mental illness is more mysterious. I have seen emotional and mental illness fragment a family more often than physical illness. The spouse turns to a lover, the children become more withdrawn from family events and eventually find support and affection from their friends. In most cases, mental illness in an already troubled family causes members to distance themselves psychologically from each other.

Couple's therapy is extremely difficult when one of the partners is emotionally ill. But the healthy partner, who has a strong sense of duty and loyalty to his or her mate, may achieve with great difficulty and much patience some type of viable stability to hold the marriage together. About all that I or any therapist can do is to help the healthy partner understand the nature of the problems, learn to expect recurrences, and discover ways to manage the symptoms when they erupt, especially if they are violent. With much love and patience, you can learn to live with an emotionally disturbed spouse. You must also become an excellent role model for your children, as they will look to you for ways to deal with emotional outbursts from your mate. Great care must be taken to speak kindly of your wife or husband in front of the children, and equal care must be used to explain the problems and how to handle them when you are alone with the children. Most likely, family therapy will be necessary at times as your children go through the emotionally chaotic phases of their own lives, or if they are unwilling, or simply unable, to deal with the ill parent.

As in the case of any serious problem, the best survival tactic is preventive. When the crisis strikes, there must be inner strength to draw upon. The more love and understanding that exists in a family prior to illness, the easier it will be for the family to pull together and make the necessary adjustments. In some rare cases, a physically or emotionally disabled spouse may be the cause that generates love and understanding; but usually, if it is not there to begin with, it doesn't materialize out of the crisis. So my best advice, if you have been fortunate enough to be spared serious illness so far, is to prepare for it by cementing your relationship with each other now. Learn ways to cooperate and help one another under normal circumstances, so that when, or if, your marital situation takes a turn for the worse because one of you is struck with a disabling illness, you already have a family ready to meet the challenge.

Conclusion

The Middle Years are the core of most people's marriages, filled with the excitement and joys of raising children, watching them move into adulthood, and finally watching them leave home and begin lives of their own. For parents, the marital passages in these years can be stressful and overwhelming at times because they involve issues and problems that concern both them and their children. But in a solid marriage, these unsettling times of transition can truly lead a married couple into deeper love and understanding of each other. Most couples can look back on these years and never let the troubles and disappointments blot out the good times the family shared together. They emerge from the Middle Years with the satisfaction that they have played important roles in the lives of their children and for each other. Even a couple who have had no children usually consider these years as deeply rewarding times when they supported each other in their careers and their individual activities and helped each other through their own personal passages.

Fortunately, life does not grind to a standstill when the Middle Years are over, or when retirement occurs. As you move from this period in your life into the Mature Years, be ready to accept even more changes and solve other problems, for more passages await you. And they, like the ones you've already encountered, will be the challenges that keep your marriage alive and growing.

PART IV

THE MATURE YEARS

22.

Introduction

The Mature Years of a marriage, year thirty and beyond, usually begin at the time a couple starts to move into old age. For each of us, this is an important, personal life transition. Some of us worry about it excessively and become depressed. Others take it in stride. In any event, it means we must stabilize our relationship with each other and reorder priorities as a couple; so we continue to support and enhance each other's struggles for productivity and fulfillment in the face of declining strength and energy. Although old age can be a time for the joys and rewards of being grandparents, for travel or pursuing interests for which we had no time before we retired, for sharing more simple pleasures with our spouses, it can still be a very frightening period. Some of us fear age itself, a waning sex life, or the loneliness that can result from illness or the death of our partner. We may fear our own deaths. During this period, we must deal with inevitable separations as children and loved ones grow and move away, and eventually friends and family begin to die. Every couple must come to terms with these changes, pass through them, and carry on safe and secure in their love for each other.

Throughout our Mature Years we must deal with a number of social changes in order to maintain the health of our marriage. Since one or both of us will likely retire, this usually means decreased financial means and perhaps severe economic pressures for the first time in our lives. We often must give up our house and move into a more manageable but less desirable living situation, such as an apartment or a senior citizens' facility. The fact that eighty-five percent of those over the age of sixty-five have three or more chronic illnesses means that we must confront the decline in our own physical health and learn to live with less strength and stamina. The change in our position in society and its effect on our sense of self-esteem will continue to confront every couple throughout the Mature Years.

Issues relating to the themes of power, intimacy, and boundaries that we've dealt with earlier in our marriage will face us once again, but in a different form. We must turn over the reins of power to the next generation. As our bodies age, we need to create new ways to achieve physical and emotional intimacy. And if we have married children and grandchildren, we'll need to determine how much time we'll have for them and establish reasonable boundaries that satisfy our needs as well as theirs.

If you are not yet in your Mature Years, you owe it to each other to make the most of your current passages, for each is a valuable experience, preparing you for the passages of the Mature Years. In every positive passage we learn how to relate to each other and resolve successfully each issue that arises. The less "unfinished business" we bring with us into our Mature Years, the more energy we'll have to tackle the problems that are unique to this time in our lives.

If we've had less fortunate marriages, with unresolved difficulties from earlier negative passages, not only will these problems continue during the Mature Years, but they are likely to intensify as we face all the other vicissitudes of late life. On the other hand, if we have a healthy attitude about ourselves and a good dose of self-esteem, we should not find it any harder weathering the passages of old age than we did the ones in our younger days.

And when marriage comes to its natural end, the memories of all that we've lived through and the love we've shared will sustain us when we're alone. Because whatever happens, the marriage that has nurtured us over the years

is still very much a part of our lives, and the love of
our husband or wife will live with us as an unshakable
memory and a source of strength that can never be taken
away.

23.

The Passages of Family and Friends

The marital passages that many couples navigate in their Mature Years regarding family and friends involve the difficult and painful issues of what to do with a widowed parent or a disabled parent who can't live alone. Together, you and your spouse will have to face the question of filial responsibilities. In some cases, the decent thing to do is to allow the widowed parent to live with you. In other cases, a retirement center or a nursing home is the wisest choice. Either decision will inaugurate a difficult passage in which you must make the transition to the new living arrangements the decision will entail. Either may cause emotional crises that might seem overwhelming. But whatever situation you decide upon, you can use the resolution of this issue as you have in earlier passages of your marriage as a time to renew and strengthen your commitment to and support of each other.

The Widowed Parent Moves In

As people age they undergo certain personality changes. Although each person is unique, we generally tend to become more intensely what we were when younger. If we were crabby, we will get crabbier. If we were complainers, we will complain all the more. If we whined to get our way, we will try even greater whining! The same holds for the positive traits too. Tolerant people tend to get more tolerant. If we were good copers with life's difficulties, we will continue to cope well. I have seen this many times in nursing homes. I look at all the various types of people spending their last days or years. Some are cheerful, smiling, ready with a hello or a new joke. Others complain, worry, gripe, or pass the time like Ole Man River, "tired of livin' and scared of dyin'." In most cases, I could tell you what types of people they were in their prime. I would simply reduce their dominant personality trait a few degrees, and I am usually right. Their children confirm it. They remember mom and dad always tended to be "like that," only it didn't seem so noticeable back then.

So it's fairly safe to say that the relationship you had with your parents when you and they were younger will be similar to the way you will get along when the widowed one moves in with you. If, for example, your mother was always critical of your husband, she will tend to be even more critical. If your father was warm and affectionate to the girl that you married, he will continue to express that affection as he ages. Whether it is your parent or your spouse's parent who moves in with you, chances are that both of you are going to be caught in the middle at various times. When disagreements arise, it is hard for three people so intimately related for so many years not to bring up old memories. Incidents of years back will surface. You may even catch yourself in arguments that were settled decades ago. Through all of this, you will be the one in the middle. And, as at other times of crisis, your primary concern should be to support your spouse and stand united in your love for each other.

MILDRED AND PERCY: GRIEF AND GRIEVANCES

Mildred called "Talknet" one night to share her experiences with another listener who had a similar problem. When Mildred's father died, her mother went out to San

Francisco to spend some time with her other daughter and her family. Eventually she got lonesome for her friends back in Milwaukee and returned. After two months of living in the old house, the memories of her deceased husband became too much for her. She began suffering depression and asked Mildred if she could "stay for a while" with her and Percy. So she moved in, everyone assuming her stay would just be temporary. As the weeks went by, however, it seemed that mother had no intention of moving back into the old house. In fact, it seemed as if she was settling down so comfortably in the guest room at Mildred's that she might be making permanent plans to stay.

During these weeks, Percy bided his time. His mother-in-law had always been critical of his drinking, smoking, and generally sloppy ways. She continued to harp on them and even began scolding Mildred in private for not having gotten her husband "to shape up over all these years." Actually, Mildred had grown to tolerate and accept Percy, loving him for what he was, not for what she could transform him into. Mother, however, viewed things differently. Finally, Percy's patience ran out. He suggested that if mother couldn't go back home, perhaps she should start searching for a comfortable apartment. Mildred was offended, thinking that such a suggestion was insensitive. When Percy complained that he was getting fed up with mother's crankiness, Mildred defended her mother, explaining that her mother's ill mood was to be expected until she got over her grief of her late husband's death. Percy wasn't sure that her orneriness wasn't due to old grievances that went back forty years rather than to her late husband's death. Soon Mildred and Percy had a running argument about what to do with mother. Finally, Percy gave his wife an ultimatum: Either mother finds an apartment, or he'll find one for himself!

Percy's reaction was a real shock to Mildred, but it caused her to take stock. Rather than resort to splitting up after forty years of what had been a strong and happy marriage, she sat down with Percy, and they started to explore the situation. Mildred realized that her mother's basic dislike for Percy's habits was not going to go away with her grief. Also, she came to understand that her mother was forcing her into the position of defending both her

husband's way of living and her own tolerance and acceptance of it. If Percy's sloppiness and minor vices had not
been cause for separation in forty years, it was foolish to let
her mother turn them into causes for divorce when they
were both in their sixties. And indeed, it wasn't Percy or his
habits that were driving them apart: it was mother living
under their roof! This new understanding helped them to
strengthen their relationship. Together they joined forces,
made reasonable plans to ease mother out of the house at
the best time, and help her get established in her own
apartment. So a difficult problem became a successful passage to help ease Mildred and Percy through their Mature
Years.

The Nursing Home

Nothing is more painful than the decision to place a
parent in an institution. Usually the decision is based on the
parent's need for nursing care rather than callousness on
the part of children who simply do not want the bother of
caring for an aged parent. Ninety-five percent of the elderly live in the community, many with the help of family
and friends. But there is a gray zone between chronic illness
and disabling illness. When does the sick parent become too
much of a burden to care for in the children's home? It's
difficult to decide in many cases since over eighty percent of
all Americans age sixty-five or older have three or more
chronic diseases. Although these are not disabling, sometimes the discomfort they cause and the complaining that
ensues seem reason enough to get the parent into a situation where perhaps they will feel better and complain less.
Fortunately, only five percent of the elderly are in convales-
cent facilities at any time, and only about twenty percent of
people in this age group ever spend time in nursing homes.
Of these, about three-fourths eventually recover and return
home.
      Nevertheless, chronic illnesses make the elderly more
demanding, less flexible, more complaining. The children
who must care for them need to restructure their own lives

whether the aged parent lives on his own or with the children's family. Whatever the situation, caring for one's parent at this time in life is always a stressful passage of marriage. It disrupts your now well-established rhythms and routines. It takes up your time. It usually means you have less time for each other at a time in your life when you were anticipating more leisure hours together and fewer responsibilities.

Particularly disruptive is the aging parent suffering from senile brain disease. Many just pass it off as "senility," but actually the term covers a multitude of disorders from the minor to the severe. Alzheimer's disease is the most common cause of brain deterioration in the elderly, followed by Multiple Infarct Dementia, which is a condition of multiple small strokes that can slowly cause a parent to function less and less efficiently. It is simply not possible to harbor a parent with severe senile brain disease under your roof and not have it affect your marriage. You are watching your mother or father die of brain disease. This is emotionally painful and creates a difficult passage for your marriage and your life. It requires the utmost support and love of your spouse to help you through it.

If an ill or dying parent causes such strain on your marriage that you begin to wonder whether the two of you will remain together after so many years, then you know the decision to keep your mother or father at home with you has to be changed. It's better to institutionalize your parent at an earlier date and save your marriage than to be forced to institutionalize him or her after your own marriage has been destroyed. When a parent is slowly deteriorating, the outcome is inevitable. You will have to put him or her in a facility sooner or later. Better sooner than later.

SOPHIE AND HANK: JUST A MATTER OF TIME

Sophie and Hank, parents of friends of ours, were in their late sixties, well into their Mature Years and living in an exclusive retirement settlement. Hank's eighty-seven-year-old father had been living with them for ten years, and the three of them had gotten along quite well through Hank's retirement and the move out of the city. But when dad developed Alzheimer's disease, both Sophie and Hank found it more and more difficult to maintain the social life they had come to enjoy and that, in fact, was keeping them both young and active. Hank made up his mind that his father should be institutionalized, even though his mind had not deteriorated to the point that he could never be left alone or that he was an embarrassment to their friends. Sophie, on the other hand, disagreed, thinking that Hank just wanted to get back at his father for the countless "injustices and hurts" over the years. Hank tried to explain to her that it was nothing of the kind. One of his bowling friends had told him it was just a "matter of time" before a person suffering from Alzheimer's disease reached the point where he needed constant supervision. So why not now, rather than later? In fact, dad would be better able to adjust to a nursing home while he still had some of his faculties.

Hank argued his case well, pointing out to Sophie that eventually one of them would have to stay with dad all the time. They would have to give up golf, potluck suppers, visits to their five children who lived scattered across the country, and the "good life" they had worked and saved for all their lives. Sophie read up on the disease and asked her doctor about it the next time she had a checkup. She became convinced that Hank was right. Her marriage came first. They owed it to themselves to accept the inevitable regarding dad and place him immediately rather than wait. They themselves still had so much to live for, and making this decision allowed them to enjoy their Mature Years to the fullest.

24

The Passages of Career and Finances

Financial Survival after Retirement

Many of us look forward to retirement while others dread it. Granted, retirement presents the married couple with a major marital passage to weather, a passage filled with various issues that need to be addressed, many decisions to agree upon, and important changes to make in lifestyle. Probably the most pressing issue is financial survival.

When money problems complicate the emotional and social issues of retirement, a marriage can suffer severe stress. Considering the state of our economy during this decade, it is a truly fortunate couple who can move into retirement with a complete sense of financial security. What's more common is that couples must be ready to adjust their lifestyles to a fixed income and scale down the hopes and dreams that have sustained them over the years. Many of the couples retiring today grew up in an era when the wife did not work, an era that preceded pension plans, Keogh's, and IRA's. Many of them were convinced that social security alone would provide enough, when in reality social security payments barely allow you to live above the poverty level if you have no other source of income. Medicare also created a false sense of security since it covers only the

212

most acute health care needs, and, as we have seen, the average elderly person will have at least three chronic illnesses with which to deal. Medical bills pile up, medication must be bought, doctors' fees skyrocket, and the senior citizen often finds it difficult to meet these expenses with enough left over for a decent living.

Rent, food, utilities, as well as medical bills, can undermine a marriage when there is not enough money available to maintain the lifestyle that the retired couple desires. Decisions about how to spend the limited finances often lead to arguments, in which the past is frequently dragged out, with one partner accusing the other of not having heeded his or her mate's financial advice years ago.

Marital happiness is also diminished by the social isolation a retired couple faces when there is not enough money to travel, to have guests over for dinner, to eat out now and then, or to attend some cultural event. The niceties that make up the fabric of a reasonably pleasant life can be eliminated unwittingly when finances no longer can stretch to afford them. Here, too, the frustration over not being able to live and play the way you would like can lead to irritability and misunderstandings that undermine the happiness of the Mature Years.

The best advice for married people as they contemplate their years of retirement is to plan ahead. Adequate preretirement financial planning is critical. A job with a reasonable pension plan, an IRA account, even a small-paying retirement hobby or skill will bring much needed income after you retire from your primary job. Also, go into retirement with a healthy attitude about adjusting your life to the new financial situation. Don't grouse and sulk because you haven't the money you used to spend. Learn new hobbies, activities, and leisure time pursuits that will be emotionally and physically satisfying, but are less expensive than the ones you have been used to. Modify your ways of living accordingly, and you can enjoy retirement without undue hardship.

Working Together

Starting up a small business or money-making venture the two of you can share together is a worthwhile dream. In most marriages, the husband and wife, each pursuing separate and distinct careers, never enjoy this opportunity. Even when the wife doesn't work, the amount of time on weekends and evenings when the two can putter around the house or garden together is limited. But after retirement, all the days, weeks, and months can be shared fully in some small working capacity. The following couple found an ideal way to share their retirement years and make extra income.

MIKE AND CLARA: PARTNERS IN A DIFFERENT WAY

Mike and Clara wrote me at "Talknet" to tell their story. They were a Mature-Years couple in their late sixties. They had been married for thirty-seven years and had three children and seven grandchildren who all lived in different parts of the country. At first when Mike retired from his job as manager of a small clothing store, he discovered that his small pension did not allow him and Clara to travel as often as they would have liked to visit their children and their growing families. They needed supplemental income. Clara had never held an outside job in her life, but as a hobby she crafted silver jewelry and painted landscapes. In her early sixties she began displaying her wares in craft shows and even sold a modest amount of jewelry. The idea struck them that if they went into the crafts business in "a big way," they might be able to pull in the additional money they would need for plane tickets to visit their kids. Mike became her business partner and manager. He talked up her jewelry and paintings at various local stores and at art and crafts fairs, and he found a number of places that were willing to carry her line. He attended to the bookkeeping, buying materials from wholesalers, and eventually assisting Clara in the early stages of jewelry production.

Not only did they welcome the extra income, but Mike

discovered that his fear that he would be bored with retirement never materialized. In fact, he joyfully complained that the jewelry business was more time-consuming than the clothing store! He loved it, not to mention the added pleasure of finding a mutual activity in which he and Clara could both take part and exercise their respective talents and skills. They had financial security, a reinvigorated emotional relationship with each other, and as they were quick to attest, a "heck of a lot of fun."

Retired But Not Tired

Many people going into their retirement years discover a second wind, as it were, a hidden source of physical energy that had been lying dormant in the last decade or so of their working lives. This is not uncommon. Often, people just become stuck in routine jobs that no longer challenge them or demand peak performance. Consequently, they think their energy is drying up. Far from it! Turn them loose, and the new sources of energy and enthusiasm emerge from almost nowhere. As you prepare for retirement, you ought to assume that you will be one of these "born again" people. In some ways, it is a self-fulfilling prophecy. Barring any debilitating illness or physical disability, you should discover strengths and energies you never knew you had. So don't plan to retire to the rocker. There's more to life than watching for the mailman, cutting the grass every other day, and getting sucked into daytime television. As a couple, plan to make your retirement years some of the most active of your life. It will also help you live longer.

MILLIE AND PETE: HOW YOU GONNA GET 'EM OFF OF THE FARM?

Recently Diane and I lost two dear friends. No, they didn't pass away. They took up farming! Pete was a psychiatrist whom I had known for many years. Millie never had a career but was active in her children's school activities and countless neighborhood groups. They were two dynamic members of the community. Pete taught at the same institution for twenty-eight years while the children grew up. When the kids were gone, and as they headed into their Mature Years, Pete and Millie announced that they were moving to Georgia to buy a farm. Their friends couldn't believe their ears, but it was true. Both of them had grown up in rural areas, and although they had spent their entire married lives in urban environments, their hearts and souls were still firmly rooted in the soil. So with many good years of practice still ahead of him, Pete resigned, bought the farm, and began teaching part-time at a small college in the town closest to where they would be living.

The summer after they got settled, we visited them with our children. It was hard to believe! Vegetable gardens, some chickens, a herd of cows, pigs, a goat, and a dog named Schmoosl now constituted the world of two people whose earlier lives were made up of libraries, meetings, country club activities, and cocktail parties. When I asked them why they had "jumped the gun," since Pete would not need to retire for several years, they replied that they didn't want to get caught in retirement with nothing to do, no place to go. They both planned to be healthy and wanted to keep it that way. They believed that hard, physical work in a healthful environment would add years to their lives, and Pete and Millie were a loving couple who wanted as many years as possible. Getting the farm started before retirement was their way to insure that they would not enter retirement goal-less. They had something to work toward. Even now, with retirement still a few years off, the easy teaching schedule left both of them many happy hours and days of puttering in the garden, caring for their "livestock," walking through their woods, and from the gleam in their eyes, doing more in the haystack than just "putting up bales!"

25.

The Passages of Parenting

The Empty Nest Syndrome: Does It Exist?

Much of what people know about the empty nest syndrome is what they read about it. Some people hear exaggerated stories from their friends and relatives, and imagine it always has to be a traumatic passage of intense anxiety, depression, and grieving, similar to what we might expect were one of our children to die. Does the syndrome match reality? In some cases, yes. The intensity with which you suffer some form of depression when your children leave home depends a lot upon the nature of the relationship with your children and the relationship with your spouse. In my experience, a healthy, stable marriage buffers the anxiety and grieving. In some cases, it prevents it altogether. The reason for this is that by the time the last child leaves home, a well-bonded couple is usually tired of putting their children's interests before their own. There is nothing selfish or uncaring about this. It's normal.

The passages of parenting are not meant to last forever. When a couple first become parents, they cross a major milestone in their personal and marital lives. But as with all passages, they leave it behind. Every passage is a transition to greater maturity and understanding, not a permanent state of existence. While it's true that you will always be parents, it is equally true that the excitement and satisfaction of living for your children and putting their needs first lose some of their meaning as the years move on. You'll come to a point where you'll look forward to having them off on their own, so that you can resume your own life together. You'll look forward to the increased closeness and intimacy between you and your mate. You can travel together, play sports, sleep late, make love anywhere in the house at any time. The happily married couple usually anticipates the new freedom.

Getting to Know Each Other Again

On the other hand, in a marriage that has been excessively child-oriented or one that lacks true intimacy, the empty nest syndrome can fall heavily upon the "abandoned" couple. Focusing primarily on the children over twenty-odd years may have prevented a couple who have never been very close from confronting issues that should have been addressed early in the marriage. Now alone, they will face those issues and perhaps for the first time realize that they have conflicting differences and expectations, problems they have successfully avoided while they centered their energies on raising children. A history of many difficult and unfulfilling years will make getting to know each other again a rough task. Such a situation is ripe for the anxiety and depression you've heard so much about.

But even in a sound marriage, readjusting and restructuring your relationship can cause difficulties. For example, you may have to adjust to your spouse acting more independently than he or she used to. Husbands especially may watch their wives getting involved in outside activities and community organizations. One man I know complained that when the children were home, so was his wife. Now with them gone, his wife decided to take enrichment courses at the local college and was gone two nights a week. He found watching TV alone to be lonely. The reverse might happen also. You might find that spending so much extra time together is a mixed blessing. The weekends that used to be filled with the kids coming and going, getting ready for dates, washing the cars, having their friends over, are now relatively empty. It takes initiative and imagination to learn new things to fill up the time that was formerly spent with the kids, and now is time the two of you must spend together.

It's not just a matter of finding how to stay active. It's also a matter of talking. A couple alone hopefully find that they begin to express their deepest feelings to each other, sharing intimate thoughts about topics that were never seriously discussed with all the children's chatter. In a marriage that has always been open and direct, this new sharing of thoughts and feelings comes spontaneously. In a relationship that was not very open, a deadly silence may result if the couple doesn't learn how to open their minds and hearts to each other. In some marriages, the opportunity to communicate more freely can be threatening. Diane and I always experience this silence on "lazy" vacations without the boys. Since both of us are blessed with the gift of gab, the silence doesn't last long! But it takes us half a day or so to adjust to being alone together. It's not that we don't enjoy it; it's just that we're not used to it. And so the couple who has never had great lengths of time to be together and talk aimlessly or purposefully since they were first married may have to get used to the idea. And like those early years, you should get to know your spouse again slowly, caringly, and naturally. Don't rush things. You've got lots of time.

Staying Out of Your Children's Marriages

It's irresistible: getting involved in your children's marriages. There is so much you want to share, so many mistakes you want to help them avoid, so much experience that you know will make it easier for them. You've been instructing them for years, from toilet training to those sometimes not-so-subtle hints about what careers they should pursue. The urge to keep "picking up after them" continues into their new homes and families. If you're not careful, you can become hopelessly embedded in your children's marriages. If your children had difficulty leaving home or they still need your financial support, the urge to meddle in their affairs can be even more intense. In such cases, it is often you and your spouse who should initiate the separation and cut the apron strings once and for all. If you feel lonely because they've left, possibly because you've never adjusted to being alone with your spouse again, you may want to stay involved with them even more.

They will come home again. Most of them. They will bring you their problems, ask for advice, test ideas out on you. They still need you. It's important to be able to read these occasions accurately and know just how much support to give and how much to withhold. You run the risk of becoming overprotective and offering advice that may make matters worse. For instance, if your daughter calls and complains about how her husband is treating her, you've got to decide whether she's just ventilating her feelings about some incident or whether there is some ongoing problem. If you jump in, the husband may begin to resent your daughter turning to you for help when they're having a difficult time rather than working out the problem with him. Then you'll have problems in your relationship with him.

It's sometimes hard to reverse years of habit. You've been so ready to help when they reach out to you, that it can be difficult to resist and accept the fact that your children have established marital boundaries that partially exclude you. It's even harder to resist if your own marriage is unfulfilling and you were overly involved with your children as they were growing up, because you sought in them the attention and love that your spouse was not providing. Now you may need them even more, since the two of you are thrown into each other's company more often than you find comfortable. If such is the case, you've got to make the effort to open up a dialogue with your mate, both for your own sake and that of your children.

It's interesting that I've found fathers to be the ones to get bound up in their children's marriages more often than mothers. It's possible that mothers have traditionally been more involved with the children while they were growing up, and now they enjoy the new freedom. Fathers, on the other hand, were often too busy pursuing their careers. When they retire, they realize the time remaining to be close to their kids is short, and consequently they feel more pressure to intrude on the kids' marriages. Fathers must take care to honor the boundaries their children set up to protect their own families and marriages.

HARRIET AND RICHARD: THE ONLY CHIP OFF THE OLD BLOCK

Tommy didn't need money anymore. At least, not money from Dad. When he acquired his position at Exxon and moved out of the state with Sally and their little girl, however, it seemed to Richard that Tommy would need even more financial assistance. Tommy tried to convince his father that he was affluent and didn't need the handouts as he did in college, when he didn't work and lived at home. Harriet tried to convince Richard too. Neither succeeded. Richard's mind was made up that his only son would be financially insecure without his assistance.

And so in their middle sixties, after thirty-four years together, Harriet and Richard's marriage went on the rocks. Repeated arguments about sending money to Tommy ended in other accusations about incidents that had occurred years ago. Old hurts were dragged out of the past. They hurt all over again. Finally, desperately, Harriet came to me for advice to find out why their relatively happy marriage was becoming such a nightmare. Why had such a simple matter of letting Tommy lead his own life become the wedge that was splitting them apart?

During the next two months in couple's therapy I helped them discover certain things about themselves. Richard had felt personally insecure about money matters all his life. His own father had been a physician and had wanted him to go to medical school. Not interested in medicine, Richard went into retailing, and his father never forgave him for it. He considered his son's career not a career, but merely a job, and a second-rate job at that. Because of his father's innuendoes about his finances, Richard talked Harriet into working for a real estate agency. He wanted to make sure that he would never be in financial straits so that his father could say, "I told you so." At first Harriet didn't like real estate;

but as the years went by, she developed a genuine love for it. And she was good at it. Now that Richard was retired, she was the only breadwinner; and Richard felt insecure because there was only one salary coming in and he was personally dependent upon his wife. He even feared that should Harriet leave him for any reason, he would not be able to survive.

Because of this intricate web of hopes, aspirations, failures, and worries, Richard had developed an inordinate attachment to his only son, and he used it as a way of proving to himself that he could care for Tommy. He would prove to his own father (who was long since dead) that he, Richard, could be a successful father. A further complication was that Harriet had eventually grown to enjoy her colleagues so much that she began to find companionship in being with them, especially after Tommy left home. This increased Richard's need for Tommy's approval and support even more. And the way he sought that approval and attention was by convincing himself that Tommy needed money.

In therapy I helped Richard realize how this web was harming two marriages—his own and his son's. He was able to step back and give Tommy some space. His relationship with Harriet was more difficult to smooth out. His feelings about her working were quite mixed. For her part, she didn't want to refocus her life on Richard when she drew so much enjoyment from her career. Fortunately, she was to retire the following year. I suggested that they plan a round-the-world trip to celebrate her retirement, and that Richard take charge of making all the arrangements. The effect of this worked out well on several levels. Money for the trip was diverted away from his usual gifts to Tommy. Richard realized as he made the plans and checked into costs that they really did have enough money for retirement and a trip around the world. The months away from home would be an exciting transition period for their passage into living alone as a retired couple. The last I heard from them was a postcard from Hong Kong. They were "having a wonderful time."

How to Be "Great" Grandparents

Now that you're grandparents, you have doubtless discovered the privileges and pleasures of spoiling your grandkids. But restrain yourselves! First rights always go to parents, just as when you were both younger and having children. A reasonable amount of involvement with grandchildren is appropriate, necessary, and quite fulfilling. An excessive attachment to them can be disastrous. Not only can you cause problems in your children's marriages, but you end up weakening your own relationship. Remember, the question of boundaries is always a key issue in every marriage. Just as you needed boundaries to enable you to raise your children, now they need boundaries to raise their own; and you'll have to accept the harsh fact that those boundaries are meant to keep you out, but not totally, of course. You are entitled to spend time with your grandchildren, but you must accept your children's decisions about when, how often, on what occasion, and how much candy you can bring.

Once your grandchildren are old enough, they may try to put you in the middle between them and their parents to undermine their parents' authority. They may want you as allies in their teenage years. If you think you were too harsh in raising your own kids during their teenage stage, you may now want to make amends by convincing them to go easy on their own children. But what's past is past. You must be careful not to get caught in the middle, no matter how well meaning you are.

You may also become convinced that your children are raising your grandchildren wrong. Whether you're caught in the middle or not, you should defer to their wishes. Of course, you can tactfully point out to them where you think they might take a different approach, but don't be so insistent that it appears you are simply trying to move in and raise the kids yourself. Always respect the right a parent has in raising a child. Remember the case of Carla and Roger (p. 118) who had two sets of grandparents arguing over which high school their son Ricky should attend. Matters such as that are really none of your concern. You may not be happy

with the choices your children make, but like your grandchildren, you will have to live with them.

When you do feel the need to discuss how your children are handling their own families, be sure to do so
privately. Don't bring up your objections in front of the
kids. It's best not to let the younger ones know that you
disagree with the way they are being raised. They'll obviously agree with you! And the result might undermine their
parents' efforts. Similarly, if your grandson or granddaughter appeals to you on a specific issue, always defer to their
parents. Tell the child to speak to mom or dad rather than
using you as an intermediary. Let the grandchild know that
you support the parents and trust them.

Being a parent is a strange thing: natural, of course,
but strange. You will always be a parent, and yet at some
point—actually at many points over the years—you must
"stop" being a parent. The passages of parenting are not
meant to last forever. You were simple human beings before the children came, and you will end up being simple
human beings. True, you were other things too: friends,
lovers, companions, colleagues. And you'll return to being
those again, even though parenting was a magnificent inter-
mediate stage that consumed many years of your life and
changed you forever. But in your final years, you need to
become simply an adult human being again—to yourself, to
your children, and to your mate.

26.

The Passages of Sexual Fulfillment

George Burns has a snappy comeback to the question about why, at his advanced age, he's only interested in younger women. His answer: "There are no women my age!" George Burns seems to have made a second career out of being "old and available!" But how lucky you are that you don't have to begin another career in your Mature Years! The married couple who have lived long and well together can continue that relationship into their retirement years with all the joy and satisfaction it brought them when they were younger. Even sex can remain a vital source of happiness and consolation to them in their golden years.

Reaping Experience

For one thing, old age should be the time when you look back and recall the good times of bygone years and recall, too, how you each helped the other through bad times. For no marriage survives without the stresses of some marital passages that, at the time, seem overwhelming. If you have experienced what most longtime married couples experience, your sex life was often what sustained you through rough periods. You should compliment each other

225

for having survived and prevailed. You should also take heart in knowing that sex is not something that has to end with your last paycheck. Social security will never replace sexual security. Predictable crises will pop up. Together, you should be ready to meet and conquer them. As George Burns and other prominent senior citizens have confirmed by their own lives, one doesn't have to sit back and vegetate in old age. Nor does one's sex life have to be put in storage.

Your interest in sex may wane as you age. It's a common occurrence that the sex drive loses steam as one gets older. But a lowered sex drive doesn't mean that something is wrong with you or your spouse. The Mature Years should be times of quality in sex, rather than quantity, with sexual activities being special because they occur less frequently. Most of all, forget the idea that aging and a lower sex drive is an indication of illness. Too often older people attribute the natural effects of aging to illness. In fact, many people consider aging to be an illness! How wrong they are! It's perfectly natural. And while illness can accompany aging, and often does, the two should be thought of as clearly distinct conditions. You are growing old; you are not growing ill.

Another misconception about sex in the Mature Years is that it is somehow wrong. Isn't it surprising how we can carry myths and misinformation about sex all the way into our sixties, seventies, and eighties! We more or less assume that a teenager or a twenty year old will have some crazy ideas about sex, but so do octogenarians. And one of these is that sex between the elderly is "dirty." I suppose we have heard too many "dirty-old-men" jokes in our lives, and we mistakenly assume the implication of them is true, namely, that for a so-called old man to be interested in sex is "dirty." And there should be "dirty-old-women" jokes too, but I guess the stereotype that only men are filled with lust permeates our sense of humor. Recent studies, however, show quite clearly that our jokes don't match realities. Women, more often than men, retain a strong sexual drive into advanced age. It is far more likely for them to initiate sex (or secretly desire it if they aren't personally initiators!) than men. So through ignorance and a false sense of guilt, many older married couples, who should discuss sex openly and continue their sexual relationship into their Mature Years, decide either consciously or unconsciously that "all that's over with now."

It's important to keep your Mature Years in perspective, however, and realize that sexual dysfunctions typical of the Middle Years can occur or recur. But your attitude toward them should be the same as it was when you were thirty-five or forty; they are problems that can be resolved without precipitating marital crises. Sexual dysfunction did not mean giving up all hope for sex when you were younger, and it doesn't mean it in your Mature Years. Unlike Dante's inferno, there is no sign hanging over the "gates of maturity" that warns, "Abandon hope all ye who enter here!" (There used to be, but we took it down!)

A couple in their retirement years can expect to have a satisfying sex life if they are realistic and make the necessary modifications. This period, like earlier ones, will have passages. Transitions will occur as you face issues and move from one relatively stable segment of your lives to another. Crises may develop. You may experience boredom again, but then so can newlyweds! You may have psychological pressures from your personal passages of aging. Your self-concept is bound to change as your body ages. Financial strains may make you feel less sexy, as can worries about your children and their families. You'll also experience the deaths of friends and loved ones, and need to come to terms with facing your own death. The Mature Years are not easy, but they are not harbingers of sexual stagnation.

BETTY AND AL: THE BEST IS YET TO COME

Betty and Al walked up to me at a party recently, both of them beaming as if they were newlyweds. Their arms around each others' waists, they clearly had some good news to tell me. I hadn't seen either of them in several years. Immediately, though, I could tell that they were "holding up well" in their years of retirement. Betty was a petite, blond woman in her late fifties; Al was thin, muscular, distinguished looking, in his middle sixties. They both radiated health. Their eyes smiled gleefully at me.

They had heard I was writing a book on marriage and wanted to give me some "advice." When I asked them what it was, they said to be sure to say that marriage was "rough, but worth it." "But you don't look like you've been through rough times," I teased, remembering some of the problems they had shared with me once about their forty-one years of marriage to each other.

"Well, you know we've had our ups and downs, raising four kids and adapting to all the changes in society," said Betty, "but we also have a secret." When I asked them what it was, promising to pass it on to my readers, Al responded, "Our sex life!" They went on to tell me how, through all the trials and tribulations they had faced together, their sexual relationship had always been a source of joy and happiness. "Even when we weren't in bed," laughed Betty. Then I recalled some of the problems they had had in the passages you'll find in any marriage. The remarkable thing about Betty and Al, however, was that they learned how to keep saying "I love you" to each other, even in stressful times, periods of illness, and while mourning the death of their daughter. Their secret wasn't simply "sex," but knowing how to "be sexual" with each other, knowing how to express their deep love and devotion to each other physically, even when sexual intercourse was not possible.

I asked them about the years ahead, whether they thought things would be different now that they were retired and less involved in all the worries and responsibilities that had characterized their Early and Middle Years. They looked at each other to see who would answer, and then, as if they had talked about this many times before, Al confided in a somewhat lowered voice, "You know, we wonder about that ourselves. We still have so many years to go. We know that times in the future will be rough, but the best is yet to come!" I looked at Betty, and she winked. Later I realized the profound insight they had come to, and what wisdom and faith it takes to make the statement they had: the future will be rough, *but* the best is yet to come. What life had taught them so well was that every passage, marital and personal, has that peculiar blend of good times and bad times. Fortunately for Betty and Al, they knew from previous experience that they could weather any crisis. They had a lot going for them, not the least of which was their healthy enjoyment of each other sexually.

Courtship in the Golden Years

Happily married couples in their Mature Years—couples like Betty and Al—usually share a common trait. They still treat each other as if they had just met and were doing everything in their power to win each other's heart. The old rituals of dating and courting never cease. Especially when your children have left home and you are alone again with each other, you should renew the old customs that meant so much to you when you were first married. Happy couples will testify that they never take their love for each other for granted. While secure in knowing that the love and trust is there, they take pains to prove it day after day.

Some years ago a catch phrase from the movie "Love Story" seemed to take everybody by storm (it caused some storms too!)—"Love means never having to say you're sorry!" Well, I disagree. Love means saying you're sorry over and over and over again. Of course, I don't mean you have to have "sorry" on your lips twenty-four hours a day, but the attitude that you never want to hurt your loved one, or disappoint him or her, or cause offense, or create worry should keep you always on the verge of saying something to prove your love. We all want to know that we are loved, and a marriage that goes for years with love never spoken or proven by deeds can become a dry, lifeless kind of love.

"Wanting to say you're sorry" is also an attitude that suggests that you would like to apologize for all the times you *could* have said "I love you" and didn't, all the times you *could* have expressed your joy at being in love with your mate and didn't. As you enter the last stages of your lives together, you'll realize that time to say "I love you," "I need you," "I'm sorry" is limited. When we were courting, we could never say them enough. Now in the Mature Years we should readopt that attitude and take every chance we get to be romantic, spontaneous, creative, yes, even dramatic, in expressing our love. Bring back flowers, candlelight, theater tickets, candy, funny little cards, and plan "date nights" with each other again. Perhaps you have never lost this dimension in your relationship. Then good for you! Some of the strongest marriages I've seen have been built on this mutual striving to please the other as if, like Romeo and Juliet, the couple had just met and couldn't wait to see each other again. The strength and confidence that comes from such a relationship can buoy up a marriage to make it through the roughest passages.

JOHN AND LAUREL: LOSING THEIR TOUCH

After thirty-six years of marriage, John and Laurel thought they had lost their touch when it came to sex. They were both depressed. They recollected how they used to have sex almost constantly in their younger years, and now they were making love about two or three times a week. Actually, two or three times a week is probably about average or better for Mature-Years couples like John and Laurel who were in their late fifties. Nevertheless, the average wasn't good enough for them! They could remember the old days! So they came to me for help.

"We can't be over the hill yet," John grumbled in therapy. But Laurel wondered seriously if that weren't the case. She still had interest in sex, but John frequently seemed preoccupied with other things and put her off. The problem was that John couldn't accept the fact that even though he wanted sex more often, he was undergoing the normal decrease in functional ability. He couldn't have an orgasm each time he made love, and consequently he found sex embarrassing and dissatisfying. He felt useless if he couldn't perform as successfully as he had when he was a younger man.

I saw them for six visits of couple's crisis intervention treatment and helped them realize that a sexual relationship could be revitalized. John learned that Laurel could be satisfied by the romantic touches that had characterized their initial courtship. She didn't care if they both reached orgasm each time. In fact, just treating each other with the consideration and tenderness that go with falling in love was enough to make Laurel feel that her sex life. was as good as ever. John, too, discovered that being romantic and playing the part of a swain once more was as gratifying as being able to climax each time he made love. What's more, after several months of recharging the romance in their relationship, they discovered to their delight that the sexual aspect of their union was recharged as well. They learned new ways to please each other physically even on those nights when orgasm for one or both of them was not possible. And they settled down and accepted the fact that the average wasn't so bad!

*   *   *

Sex will always be part of your marriage. Even when, for whatever reasons, the two of you are not making love as often as you would like. Sex is still present, even by its absence. It can never go out of a marriage. The simple reason is that you never stop being a sexual person. To be human is to be sexual. You have seen your need for sex and your ability to give in sex shift and change as everything changes. Be realistic about sex; discard myths and misconceptions about sexuality and age. Strive to please your partner as much as possible. Being unselfish and, most of all, being creative about sexual activity can keep the solid cornerstone of sex well secured in your relationship. Even into old age, it can be the foundation upon which a truly great marriage is built.

27.

The Passages of Illness and Change

Gray hair. Wrinkles. Pudgy around the waist. Arthritis flare-ups. Baldhead. No two people age at precisely the same rate. Aches and pains hit each of us at different times and cause us different amounts of discomfort. Some take it all in stride, refrain from complaining, and continue to live their lives with a zest and enthusiasm typical of people far younger than they really are. Others slow down at the first signs of aging and live as if they can't forget that every minute of their lives is borrowed time. Just as our biological clocks govern physical changes in our body cells, our psychological clocks dictate how we handle those physical changes and let them influence our lifestyles.

The Critical Eye

It's natural to be critical of your mate. It is not, however, always wise to express that criticism. By now you should know that. Our egos cringe a bit when threatened with a new piece of criticism. In your Mature Years more than before, you may have a tendency to notice the physical changes in your spouse and want to say something about them. You may be genuinely worried that your spouse is aging far more quickly than you, becoming less attractive, vigorous, quick-witted, or interesting. You may see obvious signs of impending illness. How should you respond to these changes? What should you say or do to make them smoother passages?

When you feel the urge to express some negative perception about your partner's physical appearance or condition, first look at yourself in the mirror. Make sure you too aren't going through the same aging process. Look at yourself very critically. Check out your own emotional and psychological changes. Maybe you too are less interesting, more boring, living with less enthusiasm than formerly. It is always a human tendency to project our own deficiencies and faults upon others and then be critical of them.

Second, don't find fault with your mate until you attempt to understand what the physical or psychological changes mean. There's a world of difference between a husband whose hair is falling out and a husband who has put on thirty pounds because he's drinking two six-packs of beer every night. In other words, some changes are normal aging processes. Others might be a way of coping with aging or inappropriate ways of coping with other problems. Another reason behind the change might well be that a serious illness or disease is on the way. So you have three, not always clear-cut, situations to think over before confronting your spouse with your displeasure in the way he or she is growing old: Is it just the normal physical deterioration that happens to us all? Is your mate letting him- or herself go to pot because of some other unresolved problem? Is your husband or wife showing the early signs of what can lead to a debilitating physical or mental disease?

Don't criticize without exploring these possibilities. Then choose your words wisely. It is not inappropriate to call attention to a spouse's careless disregard for personal appearance. If the normal aging process is accentuated by slovenly looks, then it is your responsibility to tactfully make your mate aware of it. But remember that any harsh criticism of personal appearance may give your spouse the wrong message. He or she may think you value appearance more than individuality, or that your love and respect hinges on whether he or she rushes out to the wig shop or immediately checks out prices on face-lifts. As you learned from raising your children, let your love transcend your criticism. Make sure your mate hears clearly that you love him or her no matter what, and that your concern about his physical condition arises from that love. We all want to know that we are loved for what we are, not for what we look like.

JENNY AND ED: LOVE/FIFTY

Ed, who is a friend of mine, became convinced on the tennis court that he was getting old. As he approached his fiftieth birthday he was winning less and less. He got winded, found it harder to chase balls, and became more easily discouraged when he won fewer matches. Resigned that it was "just old age," he expected—and discovered!—that he fell asleep earlier on the couch, had less stamina at work during the day, and began putting on extra weight. He didn't age gracefully. In fact, he became demoralized about the whole situation and was convinced that there was nothing he could do about it. "You can't fight Mother Nature," he told his friends with a half-hearted laugh.

Jenny knew you could fight Mother Nature, perhaps not to win, but to call a truce. Putting two and two together, she realized what Ed was going through. She had been watching him complain more and feel dejected about his life. She agreed with him that he wasn't as fit as he used to be. But because they had a very close marriage, she also realized she would have to be part of the solution. She looked in the mirror and noticed that she too had gained a few pounds. So, rather than playing strenuous games of tennis, she suggested that they start jogging together. They altered their diet, joined an aerobics class, and found that they could cut out a lot of calories and still enjoy many of the same foods they liked to eat. Soon Ed started to lose weight. He began to feel better about himself. People at the office complimented him, and his sense of self-worth soared.

Within no time he stopped falling asleep immediately after dinner; and when summer rolled around, he couldn't wait for an evening set of tennis.

*   *   *

The case of Jenny and Ed is an important one. The poet who said, "Grow old with me, the best is yet to come," had people like them in mind. One of the comforts of growing old with someone is that you don't have to go to pot needlessly. The love of a good mate can keep you from aging before your time. Without therapy, expensive medical checkups, frivolous diets, or exercise plans, a sensible couple, who have each other's best interests at heart, can devise their own strategy for retaining strength, vigor, and good health long into their Mature Years. By all means, exercise your critical eye. But turn it on yourself as well, discern the underlying causes for unnecessary changes, and devise a self-improvement plan based on love and companionship.

As the World Changes

The world changes along with you, but often in unexpected ways. Remember the first time you saw a police officer who was younger than yourself? When that happens, you know it won't be long before you vote for a state governor who is your age. Then the president is younger. Before you know it, it seems like the whole world is getting younger while you are getting older. We all will go through this remarkable looking-glass experience and wake up to discover the social realities of growing old. Like Rip Van Winkle coming home, we discover the harsh reality that it's not the same place we called home. Attempting to regain or retain your sense of home can be a trying passage.

Let's think about "home" for a moment. If you continue to live out your Mature Years in the home in which you spent most of your married life, you should be prepared for the social transformations that home will go through. Your neighbors and friends will grow old and move away. Some will die. The children in the neighborhood will grow up and leave to raise children of their own. You may find that your social world is shrinking. There are fewer important people in your lives. For many people who remain in their hometowns, public transportation is inadequate, there is less money to attend cultural and social events, and the fast-paced lifestyle of the young can threaten their personal needs. In short, there is an increasing sense of isolation.

On the other hand, perhaps you have planned ahead and decided you won't be stranded in the old neighborhood in old age. You may decide to move into a retirement home, possibly in a retirement community in the southeastern or southwestern parts of the country. If so, you will be living with many people your own age, which is a mixed blessing. While it's true you will have a lot to share—feelings, attitudes, reminiscences of the eras you all have lived through—you will also be surrounded by the physical and mental problems of the elderly: chronic illnesses, petty bickerings, the loneliness of widowhood, frequent deaths in the community.

How can we handle these often uncontrollable social changes that are not always in the best interests of the older generation? There is no easy solution. But think about your past life. This is not the first era of swift social change that you have lived through. When you reminisce, you frequently take pride in the challenges and struggles you encountered in the past: ones you came through, ones that enriched your lives in the long run and made you, as they say, "older and wiser." In your Mature Years, you may have no desire to become any older, but no chronological age has yet put a ceiling on wisdom. Your past life has been an interesting and dramatic story, so, too, can the Mature Years. If you get in the habit of seeing your life as a total fabric of experience and not think of the retirement years as somehow disjointed from the rest, you'll see that the events and changes of your later years can be as challenging and exciting as the younger ones.

Consider the case of Helen and Sam, two friends of mine, whose long, event-filled life together is one of the major consolations of their later years. Upon learning that I was writing a book on marriage, Helen asked me to include their story.

HELEN AND SAM: TOGETHER WHEREVER THEY GO

Helen and Sam got married right at the beginning of the depression. They were young, just out of high school, and didn't have a thing. Neither did their families. People were losing their jobs and their homes left and right. It seemed to them like the worst time in history to be starting out. Yet that's what they did, not having the slightest idea where it would all end up. Jobs were scarce; but Sam was hired to be a mechanic's helper in an automobile agency, and Helen landed a part-time job as a salesgirl. They waited five years before having kids and then had four of them, two boys and two girls, before Helen was thirty. But Helen was glad that she had them while she was still young. "I know that sounds strange," she said, "with so many young people today not having *any* at that age. But Sam and I always knew we wanted to be parents and raise a family." Then Sam became a salesman and started to make more money; but it was only to last a few months.

The war came, and even though he was married with children, Sam had to go, or as he puts it, "wanted to go." When he returned, his boss gave him his sales job back, and they were able to share in the postwar prosperity. Eventually he became a partner in the business, and they bought a new home to raise their growing family.

Bill, their youngest, died in Vietnam, a war that Helen and Sam never really understood. But a strong faith in God's Will pulled them through their son's death, and they came to accept even more strongly that you don't always get your own way.

Their two girls were now married and lived on the West Coast, and their other son lived in Milwaukee. They all had children of their own, and Sam and Helen traveled to see them as much as possible. When Sam retired, they weren't sure whether to stay in Milwaukee where Ricky lived or move to a warmer climate. Neither wanted to live in California. It always seemed like life was "weird out there, even though our girls enjoy it and haven't turned out weird," they joked. But Helen's arthritis was worse in the northern winters, and Sam had a heart attack the first year after retiring. The doctor told him he needed to exercise more and live where things weren't such a hassle. So they moved to Arizona.

At first it was hard on them. They did not know very many people. But they were always friendly, outgoing types, and soon they had regular golf and pinochle partners. Luckily they had enough savings and pension money to visit their kids every year. It seemed to them that when they went back to see old friends in Wisconsin, there were always fewer of them. Helen's explanation was that "they didn't take care of themselves right, and they died before they needed to. Sam and I promised each other that moving to Arizona would be a new life in every sense of the word. We're not letting our aches and pains stop us."

Sam continued with his medication and exercise, and Helen did the same. They still enjoyed making love a lot, as often as they could. They both seemed pretty satisfied. I asked Helen if, when she looked back on all the problems and passages they had gone through together, there was anything she would have changed. She answered, "Well, there were good times and rough times, and I suppose it's natural to wish the hard times had never happened; but they did. And that's life. But, you know, Sam and I have always been pretty satisfied, especially with each other. In the long run, I'd have to say we've had it better than most, especially having a wonderful marriage. That made all the difference. So I really wouldn't want to have changed much of anything."

As you progress through your Mature Years—and if you too have had as good a marriage as Helen and Sam— you will look back on it, accepting your life as it has been and using it as a source of strength to support you through your future.

Releasing the Reins of Power

Our society systematically discriminates against its older members. The phenomenon of ageism turns many older and wiser Americans into second-class citizens. The media has stereotyped the older generation as fuddy-duddy, little old men and women who sit in rockers on broad front porches and drink lemonade—as if that's their primary pleasure in life! Our society values youth, beauty, and vigor, and we have not learned to appreciate people whose youth, beauty, and vigor have declined. Actually, the elderly have a beauty, vigorousness, and even a youthfulness all their own; but most of us can recognize these qualities only in razzle-dazzle young models and actors still in their twenties or thirties. Perhaps as our society ages, as it already is doing, we will evolve standards for strength and beauty that apply to older people as well as to the young. In the meantime, if you are in your Mature Years, you must be the pioneers to forge those standards and express a lifestyle that befits your age and that can be admired by those younger than you.

Because you are in a different age group, you have a different role to play in society. For those of you who have held positions of authority, the reins of power will be taken from you by younger hands. No one likes to see power, prestige, and positions of authority slip from his grasp; but as we grow older, we must make room for the next generation. We must be adaptable and willing to bend to new ideas, eager to learn new ways to cope with old problems. Some of us do this more graciously than others. As in the case of Pete and Millie whom we've already met, Pete was more than ready to give up his place at the university where he taught to assume a part-time position in a southern institution in order to begin preparations for retirement on the farm. In his new role, he was hired on a half-time basis to train the younger staff in the new psychiatry department. He could have held on to his former position as head of a department; but being flexible and willing to begin a new life for himself and Millie, he was happy to let younger people take over. His experience was not lost, however, as it was invaluable to the new department in Georgia. He said later that he never regretted the change. "When you think about it," he told me, "no one should stay in authority too long. Should anyone retain power forever?" Of course not. The problem is that many of us are not ready to give up the reins of power. We think the time is not yet ripe. We still have more we want to accomplish. But the situation is not always under our control, and often we must be flexible and adjust to our new roles.

Some men who have wielded power for many years in their professional lives find it exceptionally frustrating to give it up and retire to live at home with no one to boss but their wives. And they do! If you are relinquishing a position where you called most of the shots and made the important decisions, remember that you're not supposed to replace it at home. In a traditional sex-role marriage, your wife has probably been "boss" at home anyway. She has run the family household for years and certainly doesn't want you to usurp her own position now that you are around the house all day. Actually, the two of you need to rethink many roles and responsibilities when you are once again living alone with each other. It's possible that some jobs around the house are becoming monotonous chores for the wife, and the retiring husband should take on new responsibilities. The point is to talk over how you will divide up duties and tasks: which you will each do on your own, and which would be more fun if you shared them.

There are also new roles to play in the community at large. Senior citizens do not always have to be on the receiving end of charitable and social organizations. There are agencies that can find part-time or volunteer work for almost anyone, even the homebound. Baby sitting, crossing guard duty, easy maintenance, information services, home visiting, meals-on-wheels—there are a growing number of social obligations that are being met by volunteers just like you. If you find it difficult to give up responsibility to the generation that follows when you retire, look into your own neighborhood and community, parish or political organization, and get busy. There's a whole world that could use your experience, your concern, your love. If you stay actively involved in the larger world, you won't develop that sense of powerlessness and impotency that so many older people suffer in their Mature Years. Staying active will keep you healthy and give meaning and purpose to your life.

Supposedly Beverly Sills complained after her husband retired that she "had married him for better or for worse . . . but not for lunch." I suppose many women feel the same way. Their husbands retire, and because they do not keep active in the larger community, they are always around the house. Something about the old song that says "it's so nice to have a man around the house" makes me think it was not written by the wife of a recently retired business-man! When the newly retired husband imagines that he is now too old for active involvement outside the house and yard, the marriage could suffer from too much together-ness. If you have just retired, you may even be overcome by the boredom of having nothing to do all day.

Part of the problem is that you've lost a major chunk of your identity when you retire from your career or place of employment. What we "do" is a significant part of who we "are." It needn't be, of course. Being a bus driver, a nuclear physicist, a farmer, or an accountant doesn't automatically determine who you are. After all, you were *you* before you entered those occupations, and you'll be you after them. But for the years that we played at being a bus driver or doctor or candlestick maker, we were at least partly those characters. Now after retirement, you need to find the "basic you" again. If there's nothing for you to do but sit around the house, boss your spouse around, and grow old, you'll feel very alienated from the world, your marriage, and even yourself. Before long, your marriage will suffer, as you pick arguments with each other (maybe just to re-lieve the boredom!); and your physical condition will suffer as anxious and obsessive worrying about your bodily func-tions actually contributes to their breaking down. The mind-body relationship has been shown to be so intimate that the very stress and worry you show over your health has the power to destroy your health. Conversely, if you remain active and maintain a positive and upbeat attitude about growing old, your chances of living a healthy life are greater.

So you need to find out who you really are without the props and crutches of your former occupation. You should turn to friends, sports, hobbies, and other interests that get you out of the house and into the company of someone other than your mate. As Beverly Sills would advise, the two of you shouldn't have to eat lunch together *every* day.

LORETTA AND GEORGE: WHAT IT'S ALL ABOUT

"Putter around the house. Take care of my projects. Isn't that what it's all about?" George asked. It was clear the first time they saw me that they had different attitudes about what retirement was all about. If Loretta had her way, they would be busy visiting friends, volunteering at various civic and community groups, on the go from morning till night. Both were in good health at sixty-five, so Loretta could not understand why they were having so much trouble keeping active. And the reason was that George was tired. Just plain tired.

Although they were the same age and their health was good, George had aged physically in ways that Loretta had not. They had married late in life, at age fifty—Loretta after being widowed at forty and raising two girls, George after twenty-five years of living alone following the breakup of his first marriage. During those years before they met, Loretta learned how to build, use, and conserve energy. She had to with two teenage children and a bookkeeping job to hold down. George had been deeply hurt by his first wife and had spent the next twenty-five years living a rather solitary life, keeping pretty much to himself, not socializing much, not having many friends. When they met, they fell into a whirlwind romance and married quickly.

From age fifty to sixty-five most of their time was spent at their jobs. When they did socialize, it was with Loretta's friends whom George tolerated, but with whom he didn't feel he had much in common. Similarly, whenever they got together with Loretta's daughters and their families, George was civil, but not outgoing. He was just not a social person, and the isolation that had characterized so much of his adult life had aged him without his knowing it. Nor could Loretta see it. So they were in a standoff. Loretta was angry with George because he refused to cooperate and do the things she wanted to do. George, in turn, felt that she was always pushing him, and he didn't like that.

In therapy I helped them to realize that George was a much older person physically than Loretta, and his idea of retirement was to take it easy. He didn't care if he fell asleep early at night or slept in the next day. It didn't matter to him whether they were busy seeing their friends or just sitting at home playing cards together or watching TV. He didn't have Loretta's vitality and vigor. He couldn't keep up with her. Something had to give if they were to enjoy a reasonably happy retirement together.

Obviously, negotiation was called for. Neither could be expected to behave in ways that were physically or emotionally impossible. After a few months of working with me, they agreed to spend a certain amount of time together and a certain amount apart, and not consider this arrangement to be in any way a second-best option. For them it was the best. This way Loretta could take part in social activities and keep up with her friends, and George could putter around the house and nap in the afternoon. George agreed to use at least part of his week accompanying his wife to plays, concerts, or a dinner party (and not fall asleep at it!) in exchange. They soon came to appreciate the new pattern of their lives. Their relationship had a renewed spontaneity that even expressed itself in their making love at odd times during the morning or afternoon when George was more energetic and more interested.

So in the end they discovered what retirement was all about: it's about creatively planning and negotiating, so that each partner can enjoy one's own health and well-being alone *and* together. It's simply about working out compatible ways to continue aging together as you move through your Mature Years.

Aging Is Not a Disease

In spite of the way many Americans speak and write about it, growing old is not a disease, and aging is not an illness. Because we have such a narrowly defined concept of health, usually equated with youth and good looks, we may mistakenly assume that once a person passes into his or her golden years and loses those youthful looks, that person is no longer healthy. Such is not the case. Aging is a perfectly normal biological process, whereas illness and disease are abnormal interruptions in our biological processes. Growing old means the physical body grows weaker in various ways and slows down. But even though these conditions at times seem remarkably similar to sickness, an aging body is not necessarily ill.

What confounds the picture for many people is that along with the natural wearing down of the body comes the breakdown in the immune system, which then leaves the aging person more susceptible to illnesses. As we've seen, eighty-five percent of all Americans over sixty-five have at least three chronic illnesses. So there is a greater incidence of sickness among the elderly. Furthermore, life expectancy has increased during the last century. People are living longer than ever before. Diseases that formerly killed people in their forties and fifties can now be controlled so that individuals live longer lives, normally into their seventies. It is to be expected, therefore, that with so many people living far into the years when their physical bodies are wearing down, there will be a greater chance of acquiring some illness or another during that period in life when the immune system is not functioning as efficiently as it once did. As you approach your Mature Years together, you can expect various illnesses and sickness to accompany your aging process. But keep in mind, many problems can be controlled, even cured, if you take care of yourself and live a healthy life just as you did when you were younger.

Much can be done to insure a healthy aging process, especially with two people who have shared a long life together, who know each other very well, and who have each other's best interests at heart. It is a statistical fact that people who are "coupled up" in their declining years stand a much better chance of being healthy and living longer than single people. Marriage is good for you and your health. I would advise you to set your expectations high, but keep them realistic. Continue to stay active, play sports, travel, socialize, go dancing, but temper your activities with realism. You aren't as young as you used to be, and you'll grow tired more easily. But don't become pessimistic about it. Two loving people can continue to share a productive and joyful marriage if they pace themselves properly, get plenty of rest, eat well, and take good care of each other.

My wife's grandmother is a wonderful example of how aging need not prevent a person from leading a full and active life. Although she is in her nineties and (like the statistical person) has three chronic ailments, she routinely flies from Chicago to the East to be part of family gatherings and celebrate holidays. Her three ailments require her to wear a hearing aid, use a walker, and wear a pacemaker. She's been widowed for many years, but her indomitable spirit is not handicapped by the aging process or the physical weaknesses that accompany it. She is still an active and important participant in our family life.

Emotional Pressures and Physical Illness

You already know that psychological stress and pressure can create physical symptoms typical of various ailments, as well as major disease. Ulcers, bowel disorders, headaches, asthma, arthritis—all these and others can be related to emotional stress. As you grow older, therefore, you are caught in a double bind. Aging is stressful in itself: society changes around us, our friends die, our children move away, we retire from our careers, we contemplate our own deaths. All of these situations can cause stress. The double bind is that because you are more susceptible to illnesses in old age, and old age is stressful in itself, the chances of developing some form of physical ailment because of emotional pressures and crises are high. A snowballing effect often takes place as we overreact to our symptoms. For example, a minor headache brought on by worry over a grandchild can become intolerable. Then we may become obsessed with it until it becomes virtually impossible to get rid of. It is not uncommon for the elderly to sit around and complain about their physical discomforts. Many have little else to talk about. And since most of their companions are their age, the collective pool of illnesses and aches and pains is large, and sickness easily becomes a favorite topic of conversation. But be wary of this. It is one thing to notice a minor ache or pain, and another to become irrationally obsessed with the possibility that you will develop cancer or some other disabling and life-threatening disease.

Emotional turmoil in old age causes many elderly people to develop psychosomatic problems that can disrupt all aspects of married life. The couple's social life suffers, their sex life wanes, their interest in living declines. Attitudes such as these are like magnets that attract illness. Almost like self-fulfilling prophecies, worry over one's body produces the symptoms and the diseases about which you worry. In many cases, the only way to treat the pain is by treating the emotional turmoil. It is necessary for a couple to work together on this because it is just as upsetting for the healthy spouse to have to care for—and listen to!—the complainer drone on about real or imaginary pains. Trips to the doctors and mounting medical bills will also disrupt the financial base upon which you hope to spend a comfortable retirement. If your spouse suffers from physical ailments brought on by emotional stress, you must become an ally, a collaborator, to revitalize the marriage. Don't let your marriage suffer because your spouse suffers from what could easily be remedied by a brighter outlook and a more active and satisfying life.

LILLIAN AND WILLIAM: GETTING OLD, GETTING SICK, GETTING ATTENTION

To all appearances, Lillian's bursitis in her right shoulder had taken a turn for the worse. The usual treatments of heat, exercises, and cortisone injections had little effect. Her shoulder was becoming a frozen, immobile joint. She consulted an orthopedic surgeon who concurred with her internist that there was no apparent cause for her condition to become so severe. Her husband William still worked as a manager of a printing company and was too busy to provide the extra attention she required. Her married daughter, who lived nearby, started spending more time with her every day to help with shopping and household chores. Her son also lent a helping hand whenever he could on the weekends. In spite of the extra attention, Lillian did little

other than sit at home and cry. She gave up golf, refused to
see her friends or go to movies. She rarely felt like having
sexual relations with William. She considered herself worth-
less, hopeless, and useless.

At the urging of her doctor and family, Lillian reluc-
tantly came to my office. As we delved into her life during
the first few sessions, it became clear that at the root of the
problem was not bursitis, but her inability to accept growing
old and the resultant depression. She was upset about turning sixty, which William, three years her senior, laughed off
as "no big deal." She also worried over his retirement in a
couple of years, because her perception of retired people was
that they were like "cast-offs from society." Compounding
her obsessions, Lillian believed her children were not being
attentive enough. In other words, a cluster of emotional
issues related to aging triggered a response that helped
solve one of Lillian's problems: getting more attention from
her children. Her bursitis grew worse because of her worry
over other matters, almost as if unconsciously she knew that
a physical disability would solve some of her worries. She
was also becoming the exact image of what she thought an
older person should be: sick, helpless, and a useless member of society.

Because of the severity of her symptoms, I chose to
treat Lillian with an antidepressant medication that had the
beneficial side effect of raising her pain threshold. I also
brought William in for collateral couple's therapy. In sessions together, I helped them openly discuss their plans for
what life would be like after he retired. Lillian needed
reassurance that once he retired he would not get busy in
his own hobbies and leave her stranded. Together they
planned mutual activities and set new goals, including moving to a retirement community outside the city. In several
family sessions with her two children present, the family
aired their mutual and individual attitudes about the extent
to which they should interact with each other. It turned out
that the children believed that visiting Lillian and William
once a month or so was sufficient. They learned that to help
Lillian regain her emotional health, more frequent get-
togethers were needed.

Eventually, after six months of treatment, Lillian was

able to move her shoulder again and her depression resolved itself. She returned to playing golf, and had a more
positive attitude toward retirement. In fact, she was actually
looking forward to it. As she realized that the Mature Years
of her marriage need not be the dreary period of worrying
about illness and fearing death, her bursitis responded to
her doctor's treatment and in the last six years has never
returned. You might say that she has no need for it now!

Successful Widowhood

As I've said, you'll never be ready for the death of
someone close to you, no matter how long you've seen it
coming, no matter how carefully you've prepared for this
inevitably tragic passage in life. It always takes one by surprise. The important attitude to maintain through the days
surrounding the illness, the death, and the funeral is that
your life must go on. And it will. The quality of your life
without your wife or husband depends on you. You must
remain committed to living a healthy, emotionally well-balanced life when the mourning period comes to an end. If you
decide to mourn the rest of your life, then your mate's
death is a double disaster. If you withdraw and isolate
yourself from family and friends, you are, in effect, sen-
tencing yourself to an emotional death. In this case you are
actually "dying" along with your spouse. Two lives are gone
instead of one. Yes, there will be a natural period of grief,
which lasts for a year or two, during which we slowly get
over the loss and accept it; but mourning indefinitely is
never a healthy way of life. You must pick up and carry on.

Successful widowhood begins when you ask yourself
what would your spouse want you to do were he or she still
alive. Obviously, the answer is to reach out, stay active, get
interested in your old pursuits, and continue living and
enjoying the things you did when you were together. At
first there will be a strong sense of loss, even loneliness
when you visit the familiar spots, engage in the activities
you used to share, visit friends and family on your own. But

keep at it. Don't withdraw. Give yourself the time and the opportunity to recover.

Your living arrangements can take several turns after a spouse passes on. Some widows and widowers become burdens on their children. They give up the home they lived in and move in with their children's families. Unless there is some serious reason to live with them, such as a physical disability, it is wisest not to do so. Stay as independent as you can, leading your own life. If the day ever comes when it is absolutely necessary to move in with your children, they will be much more accepting of it if they know that you carried on independently for as long as you could.

People frequently wonder whether they will ever remarry after they are widowed. There are many variables in an issue like this—age, health, family commitments, opportunity, temperament—and each person must decide for him- or herself. Again, I would suggest that if your mate could somehow advise you on this, it would be to remarry if the chance arises. Life goes on, and if you are young and healthy enough and sufficiently flexible to adjust to living with another person, do so. Marriage is still good for you, even in your senior years.

Most of all, be committed to being a successful widow by staying healthy, independent, active, and making the best possible life for yourself without your mate. As you grow older, you realize that what is, is. There will be some regrets, but also much to be thankful for. An emotionally healthy person retains a balanced outlook, recognizing that the future will be like the past in at least one sense: there will be both good years and bad years. No matter how grim the future looks immediately after a spouse's death, remember that happier times await you. That's the way life is.

PART V

CONCLUSION

28.

Couple's Therapy

Someone once said that happiness is not a destination, but a way of traveling. From what we've been considering throughout this book, the analogy certainly applies to the experiences of married couples of every age. Just when you think you have arrived at a plateau or resting spot, something unexpected occurs to unsettle your life and move you along again. Life will not stand still. Neither the joys nor the sorrows last forever. It is the nature of marriage to reflect the lives of those who are married. In other words, marriage, like human life, goes through passages.

Although this book is not intended to be primarily about couple's therapy, I think it is important that you understand how it works, so you can apply some of the principles to your own relationship and strengthen your marriage without seeing a professional. If that doesn't work, then you should by all means seek outside help and work as hard as you can to save your relationship and turn it into the marriage you really want. I firmly believe that a couple who want to save their marriage can do so, because their mutual commitment to making the relationship work is the single most important factor for success. If a couple is unable to salvage their marriage by themselves, then the decision to go into couple's therapy is a major step in expressing that commitment to each other.

What is couple's therapy and how does it work?

Basically, couple's therapy is a process in which a married couple meets with a mental health professional, such as a psychiatrist, a psychologist, or a social worker, on a regular basis for a given period of time. Usually an hour a week is the minimum for most problems. How many weeks the couple will need therapy depends, of course, upon how serious the problem is and how difficult it is for the individual couple to analyze their relationship. They must understand how their predicament occurred and work out some acceptable solution. Some minor problems, such as devising a more relaxed schedule so that they have more time to spend with each other, can be achieved in a relatively short time, say three or four sessions. This brief treatment is called "couple's crisis intervention therapy," and often it is enough to get the couple's relationship back on firm footing.

But what goes on in couple's therapy?

In a calm atmosphere, the couple and the therapist talk over the problems that have arisen in the marriage. The therapist is a sounding board, an impartial observer and commentator, who helps the man and woman communicate with each other, a catalyst to get the couple to open up and share their true feelings. In the process, the partners discover what role each has played in creating the problem. Both express their true desires and wishes about how they would like the relationship to go, and how they would like to see the crisis resolved.

At this point the therapist leads the troubled couple down the path of compromise and negotiation, pointing out options and alternate ways to resolve the dilemma. A wise therapist does not dictate the solution, but attempts to give the couple a sense that there are other ways to relate to each other than the one that is currently causing them so much pain and turmoil, and blocking their passage. The therapist also strives to keep the level of optimism high so that the couple does not give up in despair, thinking that their marriage is wrecked when there is still hope if they would be willing to negotiate. They must see that a successful married life depends on *both* partners working for it, that a good marriage is the product of the joint effort of both husband and wife.

How often does couple's therapy work?

In my experience it is successful about fifty percent of the time. Half the couples who come to me are truly motivated to make their marriages work, and they come into therapy because they realize that they are at an impasse in their own efforts. They need a third party with professional expertise to help them analyze the problem and salvage their marriage. The other half of the time, either one or both spouses is not fully committed to saving the marriage. They enter therapy half-heartedly, usually with a grudge, just to please their mates or perhaps their families. Some sincerely try to overcome negative feelings about their spouses, but often the pain runs too deep. Even with their best efforts, they can't accept their spouses for some reason or other; or they don't believe that their relationship is really worth saving.

I think the greatest hurdle in couple's therapy is lack of trust. When troubles have been brewing for a long time (and they frequently have before a couple finally decides to seek outside help), a husband and wife have usually hurt each other so severely that one or the other simply can't forgive and begin to believe in his or her mate again. They have lost all trust and confidence. Without trust it's very difficult to commit yourself to another human being. And if trust can't be reestablished, the marriage is doomed to failure.

A good therapist will show the couple how to relate to each other in a mutually gratifying and fulfilling way that helps to rebuild trust. They need to learn about giving and sharing, respecting each other, trying to live more selflessly. For many couples, the crux of the problem is to learn how to be both dependent and independent. As I try to stress throughout this book, you are always an individual—unique unto yourself—with your own special needs and desires. In this sense, you must preserve a healthy amount of independence and not expect your spouse to satisfy your every whim. On the other hand, the reason you married was that you needed your mate and were willing to cast your lots together and share your lives. In this sense, you are dependent upon each other.

Related to all these concerns is the need to improve a couple's sexual relations. There aren't many couples experiencing emotional turmoil in their marriage or family life who continue to have a good sex life. Sex is one of the first casualties on the marital battlefield. Often, it is at the heart of the problem. So in couple's therapy, a man and woman may have to relearn how to please each other sexually and learn new techniques for rekindling the love and desire that drew them together earlier in their lives.

When should you seek couple's therapy?

It isn't always easy to decide. Obviously, not every trouble or difficult passage of marriage requires that you enter into therapy. Many problems we resolve through our own resources in due time. Others linger on but don't seem to be so serious as to get in our way or demand therapy. Your troubles come and go. You have times when there are quarrels, sexual difficulties, and hurt feelings, interspersed with positive times of making up and renewing your affection for each other. Each time you reach that period of relief, it encourages you to hang in there, hoping everything will take care of itself. Sometimes that's true, but often it isn't. The arguments and the pain become more frequent and more intense. Marital difficulties escalate, and the thought of escape occurs to one or both of you: escape into alcohol, drugs, an outside affair, or even divorce. You may actually act on this notion of escape, which most likely will only create a vicious circle of further arguments and recriminations.

There are recognizable danger signs that you need couple's therapy: fighting and not making up; tabling arguments and emotions because you have lost the ability (or desire) to negotiate; being convinced that you are correct and your mate is always wrong; holding totally opposite positions on every important issue that arises; one of you leaving for a few days or weeks, staying in a motel, or "going home to mother"; ignoring the fact that your mate is having a sexual fling with someone else until it begins to eat away at you, causing bitterness and anger. And a clear danger signal that couple's therapy is necessary is when the issue of divorce comes up in a serious way over some unresolved marital issue. Often it will come as a shock to one partner to realize that the other had been considering it. Frequently the mere mention of divorce triggers the couple to seek therapy. Most couples do not want a divorce when it is first mentioned, but the more often it is offered as a real possibility for solving relationship issues, the more serious the situation becomes. It is a good idea to begin talking about couple's therapy when you see some of the danger signs mentioned above, before you begin talking about divorce.

Where can you get couple's therapy?

It's your marriage and your life, so I recommend that you seek the best possible treatment. If you have insurance or can afford it, private treatment is preferable. Get referrals from friends who've had successful therapy or from your family doctor. Seek a psychiatrist who has some reputable standing in your community or is well known to friends whose judgment you trust. If you do not have insurance or can't afford private treatment, there are mental health centers and psychiatric clinics in medical schools and general hospitals. You can also go to a family service agency. Most important is that you know the background and professional credentials of the therapist you select or who is assigned to you. Don't think that just because a therapist is young, energetic, and fresh out of graduate school with all the latest theories and techniques he or she will be good. Psychotherapy is one of those professions in which a practitioner gets better with experience. An older, more experienced therapist, who has seen hundreds of couples, is usually a good choice.

Finally, no matter what background, age, or experience, if you don't like your therapist or you just don't feel comfortable with him or her, look for another. It's important to mention this to your therapist first, however. Chances are that he or she, too, perceives the discomfort and may be able to make adjustments so that your sessions go more smoothly. But in the final analysis, you are not stuck with someone you don't think is really helping you. Look elsewhere and find a therapist whose personality and style are more compatible with you and your spouse.

Saving your marriage: Is it worth it?

There are no easy answers to this question. Each marriage is as unique as the individuals who form the relationship. Each set of circumstances is one of a kind. My experience is that the more damage you have done to each other, the harder it is going to be to salvage your marriage. If you've been playing psychological "sledgehammer" with each other for many years (first you bang me over the head, and then I'll bang you over the head), it is going to be pretty difficult to realign your emotions and your daily habits so that you are once again a loving and devoted couple. Here are the key issues that need to be considered immediately:

How long have you been married?
How many children do you have?
Considering their individual ages and personalities, what will be the impact of a divorce on them?
How difficult will it be for you legally and socially to get a divorce?

None of these issues should be the deciding factor, but they are the background against which the divorce will take place, and careful thought must be given to them. In general, however, I would say that the amount of time and effort you have put into your marriage, the impact a divorce will have on your children, and the extent to which a divorce will disrupt your professional or social life are worthy considerations. They should put the brakes on a couple rushing into divorce too quickly.

In couple's therapy, one of the first tasks is to look back and discover how the marriage developed in the first place. What factors attracted you to each other before you got married? What basic similarities did you share? What compatible differences did you have? What were the conflicting differences? Were your expectations similar or dissimilar? How different were your previous life experiences? Why *did* you get married? Honest answers to these questions will give you and your therapist a much better sense about the viability of your marriage.

But even if the answers to these questions are somewhat negative, a marriage can still be saved if both partners are sincerely committed to working at it. This means committed to making changes. If there is anything that is crystal clear when a couple first walks through the door of my office, it's that changes need to be made. They know it, and I know it even before we begin to speak. *What* those changes should be, however, is something that may not become obvious until after several sessions. If both partners are willing to make honest efforts to inaugurate change in their lifestyles, in the way they treat each other, the way they handle the kids, the way they meet the challenges of marital issues in the future, then there is a reasonable chance for the marriage to survive, and with adequate work, to grow stronger.

When is divorce the best solution?

Couple's therapy is not a panacea for all marital problems. It is not a miracle cure. There is no magic involved. Sometimes I wish there were, especially when I see a young couple, who could make a good life with each other, reach the final impasse over which they refuse to negotiate or compromise. But then I'm not God, nor is any other therapist. Ultimately, the fate of everyone's life and every couple's marriage lies in their own hands. No matter how good the therapy, it may prove inadequate in the face of a stubborn couple or one that has suffered so much emotional damage that forgiveness will never heal the wounds. If one of the partners simply cannot bring him- or herself to forgive the other and start over again, then the only recourse is a divorce or an unhappy marriage. Even if one or both of you get individual therapy and correct your behavior, it may still be too late. Marital wounds run deep. Love can and does die. When there is no longer a sincere and special love for each other, divorce is possibly the best solution.

A good therapist will not tell the couple they *should* get divorced. The therapist's job in this instance is to help the couple realize that one or both of them is so angry or hurt or bitter, that forgiveness is out of the question. An unforgiving, unloving mate will inevitably undermine the other partner's best efforts to reestablish the bonds upon which the marriage had been based. Love, understanding, trust, friendship—none of these can be nurtured by one partner alone. It takes two. At this point a good therapist will help the couple decide upon divorce, and then work with them as they go through it, so that the divorce leaves as few scars as possible.

*   *   *

In this book, you've seen an interesting collection of married couples, each caught for a time in a particular marital passage. Some pulled through, others succumbed and gave up. You've seen married people in your own lives struggle through similar passages. Perhaps you thought they were merely having a fight, resolving differences, or just not speaking to each other. Now you know that in addition to their dealing with the typical problems of married life, they were encountering critical turning points—passages that would lead the relationship ahead into greater love and awareness, or deflect the couple away from the satisfactions of married life and alienate them from each other and, eventually, from their marriage altogether.

I know you too have experienced the same thing in your own life. There are continual challenges lying ahead, whether you are just starting out as husband and wife, or whether you have just retired from long, happy years of raising children and pursuing satisfying careers. The important point is to meet each passage as it comes, enthusiastically, confidently, with an open mind and an open heart to the one you have married. Often, I don't think we give our mates enough credit for being sensitive human beings, able to understand our problems and worries. We keep so much bottled up inside, when in reality we've got someone ready